RACIAL REALITIES

AND

POST-RACIAL DREAMS

JULIUS BAILEY

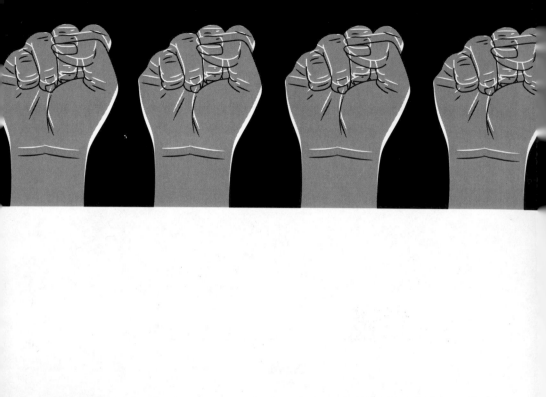
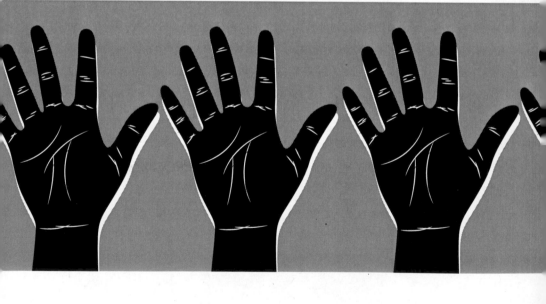

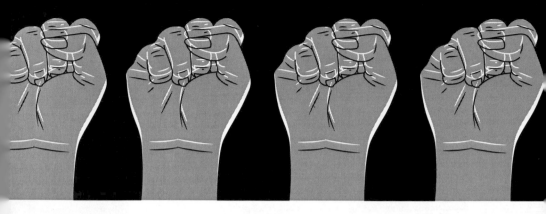

RACIAL REALITIES

AND

POST-RACIAL DREAMS

The Age *of* Obama *and* Beyond

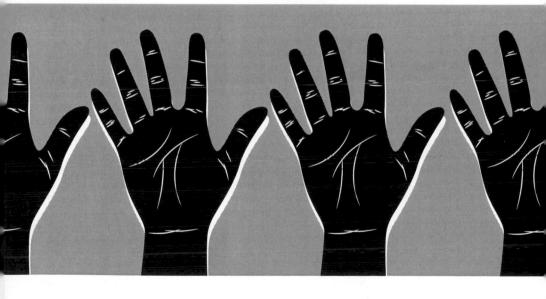

JULIUS BAILEY

broadview press

BROADVIEW PRESS— www.broadviewpress.com
Peterborough, Ontario, Canada

Founded in 1985, Broadview Press remains a wholly independent publishing house. Broadview's focus is on academic publishing; our titles are accessible to university and college students as well as scholars and general readers. With over 600 titles in print, Broadview has become a leading international publisher in the humanities, with world-wide distribution. Broadview is committed to environmentally responsible publishing and fair business practices.

The interior of this book is printed on 100% recycled paper.

Library and Archives Canada Cataloguing in Publication

Bailey, Julius, 1970–, author
    Racial realities and post-racial dreams : the age of Obama and beyond / Julius Bailey.

Includes bibliographical references.
ISBN 978-1-55481-316-2 (paperback)

    1. Racism—United States. 2. Poverty—United States. 3. Equality—United States. 4. Xenophobia—United States. 5. United States—Race relations. I. Title.

E184.A1B25 2016   305.800973   C2015-907623-4

Broadview Press handles its own distribution in North America
PO Box 1243, Peterborough, Ontario K9J 7H5, Canada
555 Riverwalk Parkway, Tonawanda, NY 14150, USA
Tel: (705) 743-8990; Fax: (705) 743-8353
email: customerservice@broadviewpress.com

Distribution is handled by Eurospan Group in the UK, Europe, Central Asia, Middle East, Africa, India, Southeast Asia, Central America, South America, and the Caribbean. Distribution is handled by Footprint Books in Australia and New Zealand.

Broadview Press acknowledges the financial support of the Government of Canada through the Canada Book Fund for our publishing activities.

Edited by Martin R. Boyne
Book design by Michel Vrana

PRINTED IN CANADA

To all Servant Leaders who labor for social justice

and

*To all the Brothers and Sisters who support me in Illinois, Indiana, and
Ohio State Correctional Facilities*

Contents

Foreword

Rev. Dr. Michael L. Pfleger
The Community of Saint Sabina, Chicago, Illinois

And your people will rebuild the ancient ruins and will raise up the age-old foundations; and you will be called The Repairer of Broken Walls, Restorer of Streets with Dwellings.
—Isaiah 58: 13

WE ARE LIVING IN A TIME IN WHICH THE STRUGGLES AND SACRIFICES of past generations seem to be unraveling before our very eyes. What is more, the prophetic American voices seem to have been compromised, bought, or simply pulled under the waves. They have gone silent at the time when we need them the most. While our restless youth boil over, the American system—the same one that has abandoned the poor, given new breath to racism, surrendered to rising violence, to unemployment, to a broken school system, to homelessness, to a militarized police force, and to a tragic love affair with guns, allowing teddy bears, balloons, and yellow police tape to become the new landmarks of urban America—is providing us with daily evidence that the "rising tide" philosophy, so long the guiding principle of American capitalism, simply doesn't work.

Dr. Bailey's project, which you hold in your hands, is deeply grounded in Christian values, values the young Julius cultivated as a high-school seminarian in Chicago under our ministry here at Saint Sabina, and values that have informed his scholarship and his tangible concern for the welfare of his brothers and sisters in this country. This is an undeniably important book for our current moment. As President Obama's term in office draws to its close, we must take this moment, as Dr. Bailey does, to unflinchingly examine the present moment and our present condition in order that we might regain our moral courage and set about our work once again. We work to make sure that America makes good on her promises—this is the absolute least we should expect of her. The great congresswoman Barbara Jordan once said, "What the people want is an America as good as she promises." In his eulogy at Mother Emmanuel (the Charleston, South Carolina church where a racist gunman took nine lives), President

Obama said, "It's time to find the best of America." So many of us hoped that Obama's landmark election to the highest office in the land represented a corner turned, a river crossed, but, instead, it has showed us just how far we still have to go. It is for us, "the caretakers of this garden," to make America accountable, to see that she makes good on her promises.

The prophet Isaiah tells us, "If we do away with the yoke of oppression and give ourselves to the need of the oppressed, we will see our cities rebuilt and watered, and the light will shine on them." The land in which we live can be fruitful, it can be healed, it can be just, but if it is to be so, we must all of us care for the oppressed and the vulnerable. We must fight to bring the best of America to the surface, and this fight must be fought on two fronts.

Let me explain what I mean by that. The fight is internal and the fight is external. The fight is within and the fight is without, because the problem is within and the problem is without. We have to confront black-on-black crime, which is within. And we have to deal with red-, white-, and blue-on-black crime, which is without. It's both, not either/or. We must have the courage to face the wickedness from without. If America is to be what she promises to be, we must face and dismantle the evil of racism. Seven black churches burnt since the killing of the Charleston Nine, and some refuse to see that the one is connected to the other. There are some who claim that lightning is behind each of these fires; if there is any truth to this, lightning must be bigoted because it seems only to strike black churches. How dare you, lightning!

We know what caused seven black churches to burn since the killing of the Charleston Nine. Racism didn't end because we lowered a flag; that flag still waves in America's heart. When four girls were murdered in Birmingham, at Sixteenth Avenue Church, Dr. King said to us, "We must indeed arrest the murderer, but we must also arrest the system, the country, the philosophy that produces the murderer." And the same is true in Charleston. We may have arrested Dylann Roof, the shooter, but the killer is still at large—the killer is the system that produced Roof, that armed him, that whetted his blade, the system that manufactures and maintains white supremacy and poverty.

So long as the (true) killer is still at large, it will continue to produce new shooters. Racism is woven into America's DNA; it is as natural and ubiquitous as the air we breathe. It's passed around living rooms and across kitchen and lunchroom tables. Eradicating it means, first of all, exposing it, wherever it raises its ugly head; it means dismantling brick by brick the system that supports it. The root of racism is, as Dr. King took pains to point out, in the heart. Until hearts are changed (indeed, until we change them), racism will continue to claim victim after victim. Changed hearts will mean that we can be more successful—successful at raising children of color who walk the lit stages of graduation, not the barred doors of incarceration.

Fighting this on both fronts means that we've got to fight that external demon, the one that tells America it's right and proper to care about the North Shore more than about the inner city. It will demand that we fight that demon that encourages us to hedge and waffle when it comes time to address the stark truth that there are two Americas: one for the haves, the other for the have nots. You can't say "One nation under God" if we're two. You can't say "indivisible" if we're divided.

We need to be outraged, and not about the small stuff. Churches and pastors want to act as if the Supreme Court's decision on gay marriage is the worst thing that's come down from the bench in living memory. They're not saying anything about the children dying in our streets, and people with no place to stay, nothing to eat, no shoulder to lean on. Where are your priorities? Where are you going to draw the line in the sand? Are you going to draw it around traditional marriage? Are you going to spew hate and tell gays and lesbians that they're going to hell, that their very existence is an abomination? That is Jesus? That is your hate and your judgment! Not mine. I'm going to side with righteousness, truth, love, God, and justice, not with judgment, meanness, hatred, bigotry, and violence. No, if you think I draw my line in the sand there, you've got the wrong person.

I will tell you where I draw the line. It's the same line they drew last night around a seven-year-old child in my city of Chicago. We should all be out in the streets in America right now demanding that our police departments be demilitarized—a change in tactics and weaponry, but also in culture and attitude toward those they are charged with protecting. We should all be out in the streets demanding that the NRA be held to account for the blood on its hands. Our twisted love affair with firearms results in 12,000 lost lives each and every year—and too many of these are our young brothers and sisters.

We need to hear the voices in our midst speaking truth to power. We need to hear the hypocrisy in our own voices when we claim that America is a beacon of freedom and democracy for the rest of the world. We're in a burning house, yet we sit inside, our eyes watering, and we swear up and down that we can't smell any smoke. We need to stop declaring war across the ocean and start declaring war here—war on poverty, on violence, on the killing of our children. We can drop drones around the world, but we can't drop jobs on America's inner cities.

We need to stop declaring loyalty to a party if that party is not working in our interests. Voting blue or red or green, it makes no difference if the person I'm voting for isn't going to do right by this community. When we put the politicians on notice, telling them that lip service isn't enough, we can determine what the issues are going to be. We can make a difference in our neighborhood. It's been seven years since 2008, and many of us are in worse shape than we were then. That's not acceptable. We have to tell them that, no matter what banner you're running under, we are not going to vote for you unless we are on your agenda.

We've got to look inward as well, to our homes and our families, both of which need to be put back together again. We've got to train our kids so that they know what's what, so that they know which way is up and which down. We need to give our kids role models—real role models that will lead by example, who will show our impressionable youth, not what success looks like (money in the bank is no kind of measuring stick), but what fortitude and rectitude look like. Parents need to be that example, but they also need to shine their light on still greater sources of light. Hang up pictures of Malcolm X and Martin Luther King Jr., of Rosa Parks and Harriet Tubman. Show them that these people matter by knowing your black history and making the home a place where this knowledge is shared and the great brothers and sisters of history are celebrated and emulated. Make the home a site of love, but also a place in which every member feels they have an intrinsic and intangible worth that will not bear debasement. I grew up in a home with a mother and a father and a sister, who long before Jesse Jackson said it, told me I was somebody. And if a child knows he or she is somebody, they don't need the world's validation. They'll wake up feeling important, feeling like somebody, feeling like they trail clouds of glory behind them as they move through and act upon the world.

If they don't feel this, if they don't know this, we are enacting a code of silence that is no different from the one outside of the home. The code of silence is the lack of caring for one another, the refusal to speak to or on behalf of the humanity in our fellows. Twenty years ago this summer, hundreds of people in Chicago died when the temperature rose to unbearable levels. Nobody died from the heat. People died from the lack of caring for each other and taking care of each other. When you knock on Ms. Maddie's door and say, "Maddie, you all right? You need anything? You got water? You need a fan? You need an air conditioner? What can I do for you?" When you say these things, when you care about your neighbor and love them like yourself, you break the code of silence. Nobody's going to die from the heat when you love each other and take care of each other. Nobody's going to be overwhelmed by the heat when we start to act like a real community—one that recognizes the intrinsic value of every life from the least to the greatest among us. A community in which every child grows up knowing that, even in the face of poverty and oppression, they are worth something, they are somebody.

If America is to be as good as she promises, we've got to stop acting like crabs in a bucket, pulling each other down rather than helping each other out. The residue of racism may be self-hatred, but it's high time that we mature, that we rise above what racism does (or tries to do) to us and remember that we are fearfully and wonderfully made, that we are beautiful and great, that we are the best God has to offer. We mature in this way when we put love back in our hearts. Love is supreme. It's time to put love back in the home, love back in the church, love back on the block, love back in the community. It's time to stop this rising tide of violence. It's time to care about life and to show that we care, to show that we value each other. This is our best, and this is the best of America, and we owe America and each other our best.

Of course, we're not Dorothy, and this isn't Oz. We can't click our ruby red heels together three times and make this country deliver on its great promises. America will give us its best when we give our best to it—when we fight for what we know is right, when we push for the kind of change that makes communities stronger, when we demand the kind of leadership that takes as its first principle the welfare of the people. It'll happen when we start not only fighting but also winning the battle, and winning it on both fronts. We've got to start tackling injustice, and that begins with a project like this one. It begins with a sincere and unflinching account-taking. It begins with an examination of the here and now, but also with an examination of how we got here. Without understanding our present and the history that has informed it, we can never hope to change our future.

Dr. Bailey understands the present moment, he understands the forces that have shaped it, and he understands its implications for the future. He knows that we cannot falter (not for a moment) in our commitment to keep our families, neighborhoods, our cities, and, indeed, our country beholden to humane values of care, concern, and personal responsibility. His words move me—as they will move you—to see that within and that without in a new light. The external is what defines the social justice issues of our moment, and a fresh perspective may compel the reader to participate in the ongoing movements that are changing our world for the better. The internal is the work of the spiritual man or woman, of the philosopher, of the one who wages the battle on two fronts—who knows that changing the external begins by changing hearts, and the first heart to master and then to change is one's own. Sisters and brothers, too many ancestors died waiting to see America bring forth her best. Too many ancestors hung like strange fruit on the poplar trees, too many were killed in backwoods and backwaters. Too many ancestors like Emmett Till, Malcolm, Martin, and Medgar, and the unknown millions died waiting to see the best of America. And we still wait. We wait while our children—Amari, Trayvon, Rekia, Michael, Freddie Gray, and Sandra—die. So, I ask you today, are we going to see more generations die waiting for America to be as she promises, or are we going to fight every day to make America live up to this promise? Are you a thermometer or are you a thermostat? Are you an indicator of the times or are you working to change them? Whether it's in your home, on your block, in your community, your city, your state or this whole country, it's time to do more than take the temperature. It's time to change it, to draw a line in the sand around something meaningful.

Acknowledgments

"You cannot Lead the people if you don't Love the people, and you cannot save the People if you don't Serve the people."
—Dr. Cornel West

I FIRST HEARD DR. WEST UTTER THESE WORDS IN THE SUMMER OF 2009, and they've been my mantra ever since. Love, service, and leadership are the reasons I teach, write, study, debate, get hot under the collar about current events, become overwhelmed with sadness by events of the past, and feel hope and tremendous optimism for the future of our great country. These words crystalize my entire life path. In light of this fact, I'd like to thank Dr. West for his continued love and support, which he has generously offered for twenty-five years.

I've never fully appreciated the number of people it takes to produce a book. From this moment forward, I'll be like that person everyone knows who works in TV or film: in the same way they can't watch a show or a movie without noticing and/or imagining what's happening just out of sight, off-screen, I'll never again look at a book without imagining the people behind the scenes.

I have a lot of people to thank.

To Father Michael Pfleger, author of the wonderful Foreword of this book, you have truly been a beacon of light in my world. I thank you for your wisdom and guidance.

To my family—Sandra, Bianca, and Heather Bailey—I love you too much; to Monica Peterson, thank you for being the mother to our child; to Letrisa, Lisa, Kervin, Mrs. Irma Jones, and family—you're in my corner at all times and I love you for that; to Janice Spearman-Williams, thank you for being a sister and my new best friend.

To Bryan Szabo and my new brother Angus Whyte, who carefully push me to be a better writer, thinker, and facilitator of ideas.

To my fine Wittenberg University family who support me always: I'm humbled by the kind words and acts of generosity and ongoing validation from our president Dr. Laurie Joyner; my colleagues, Drs. Lori Askeland, Warren Copeland, Jon Duraj, and Rick Incorvati, Raymond Jones, Sarah Jurewicz (aka Coach J), Reverends Anders and Rachel Tune, John Young, and Dr. Mary Jo Zembar; the project grant from the Faculty Development Fund Board; the many student comments and engagements both in and out of class, especially my spring 2015 African-American philosophy and African-American history courses. You endured my ranting, my frustration, and you helped me shape the ideas found in this important book. Drs. J. Robert Baker, Fredrick Tiffany, David Wishart, thank you for taking the time to work with me on various sections of this project—you pushed me till I couldn't go any more. If this book falls short in any way, it's all on me, because you did your best to get the best out of me, of that there can be no doubt. Thanks to Drs. Nancy McHugh and Don Reed, my philosophy colleagues who, along with Laura Harrison, always give me room to be me. And Dr. Carmiele Wilkerson, although you left me here and went to Alabama, I carry your love daily.

Very special thanks go to the following colleagues, students, former employers, and friends who served vital roles in this project through their words, deeds, or pure inspiration: Dr. Melina Abdullah, Mark Allen, Dr. Michael Anes, Tim Baker, Chaunta Banks, Ras Baraka, Brianna Betts, Toni Blackman, Dr. Regina Bradley, Dawn Brawley, Rev. Courtney Carson, Dr. Jelani Cobb, Dr. Tommy Curry, *Degreed Money Entertainment* (ShaDawn Battle, Dalitso Ruwe, A.D. Carson, and Adam Schueler), April Eddie, Maureen Forte', Davante Goins, Dr. Kamasi Hill, Muata Howard, Rev. Jesse Jackson Sr., Wilbert Johnson, Carly Jones, Brian LaDuca, Deborah Lee, Dr. David J. Leonard, Karlos Marshall, Jen Miller, Brandon Mitchell, Jacob Murray, Dr. Jeanelle Norman, Dr. Tricia Rose, Dr. Scott Rosenberg, Anna Maria (Teddi) Serrano, April Silver, Dr. Karin Stanford, Gina Taylor, Dr. Tom Taylor, Wade Tully, Rev. Thomas and Margaret Walker, Dr. James Walton, Rev. Dr. Daryl and Rev. Vanessa Ward, Pat West, Meghan White, and Rev. James Wills.

Last but certainly not least, a heartfelt appreciation is extended to everyone at Broadview Press, the esteemed publishing house responsible for producing this book. Thank you for believing in this project from the very beginning.

Introduction

"I, TOO, SING AMERICA"

IT WAS MY DAUGHTER'S FIRST DAY OF CLASS AS A SECOND GRADER. I stood outside her classroom door in the hall of the Montessori school, watching unobserved with Principal Anderson as her class began its day. As the students began to recite the Pledge of Allegiance, I was struck by my daughter's body language. She appeared to show no interest in the recitation. She was unfocused. As she started the pledge, her hand lay upon her chest, but it hung there limply, and it quickly began to wander between her shoulder and her navel. Then something changed: she reached the words "with liberty and justice for all" and, rather than concluding the pledge there, she continued with the appended World Pledge, which ends the recitation with, "I pledge allegiance to the world, to care for earth and sea and air, to cherish every living thing, with peace and justice everywhere."[1] She spoke these words with verve, and her eyes cleared, her back straightened, and her chin rose. It was clear that she was engaged in the moment, interested, even excited as she recited these words along with her classmates (I noticed a similar change in some of the other students as well).

My daughter had surprised me more times than I could count, but this staggered me. I could hardly believe what I was seeing. Was my daughter critically analyzing what America represented to her? Could she already hear the note of hypocrisy in the Pledge of Allegiance? Could this explain both her lack of enthusiasm during the rote act of patriotism and her increased sincerity in the expression of global solidarity?

Perhaps, I thought, she had overheard her daddy and his mentor Cornel West, talking, as we had done many times, about freedom, democracy, and America. Perhaps she had heard as we had discussed that bloody and undeniable precondition of American democracy, namely, the enslavement of African Americans and the imperial expansion across this land that trod untold millions of indigenous peoples underfoot.[2] I remembered, as well, her smiling face as she watched me from the front row of my modern philosophy course as I lectured on the same subject. She had come to visit me, and she had asked to join the class, but it had never occurred to me that here at my feet was a student like any other, lapping up information and forming opinions (perhaps even critically). I lectured that day on the notions of individual freedom (and its concomitant accountability) that are woven into both the vision and the practice of American democracy. From our earliest moments as both a dreamed-of and an actual nation, the United States has viewed itself as a standard bearer in the global march toward the freedom of mankind, a march that would see its conclusion in the perfect (or nearly perfect) democracy in which all are equally entitled to life, liberty, and the pursuit of happiness.

Could it be that she actually understood the spirit (even if not the letter) of our founding documents? In many ways the Declaration of Independence and the Constitution are both documents of aspiration. They are based on moral values that many would applaud (indeed, we continue to applaud them), but my daughter, at nearly eight years old, showed reservation, even incredulity. Despite an adherence to the bad faith of patriotism, it is undoubtedly true that the United States has, thus far at least, fallen short of the mark in terms of living up to one of the key concepts underpinning those documents—that is, "All men are created equal." In *Our Declaration: A Reading of the Declaration of Independence in Defense of Equality*, Danielle Allen cogently concludes that our current society has chosen liberty, not equality, as the paramount goal to be achieved by our political and social systems. It is, she says, a misconception to assume that such a choice—between equality and liberty—has to be made at all. Both can surely exist simultaneously. Such seems to be forgotten, though, and the prioritization of liberty has so engulfed our notions of equality that we "fail to notice the disappearance of the ideal of equality from our interpretations of the Declaration" (22). My second-grade daughter knows, however, that we can aspire to be greater, and I could see those aspirations at work as I saw her recite the World Creed. We have the tools at our disposal that will help us ensure that equality and liberty become, once again, the twin pillars of our democracy. The first of these is the ability to see ourselves as we truly are.

Even since our first, and most aspirational, moments, a wide gulf of hypocrisy—so wide, in fact, that a child of eight can see it—has separated our philosophy from practice. Even in terms of the most basic of democratic rights (i.e., the right to participate in the democratic process), America spent almost two centuries dragging its heels in extending voting rights to certain groups, including the poor, African Americans, Native Americans, women, and Jews.[3] The fact that minorities have had to scrape and claw their way to something roughly resembling equality in this country is papered over with page upon page of empty and triumphalist rhetoric; death rattles and anguished moans are drowned out by a chorus of false-noted trumpet blasts. As Americans, we seem never to tire of reminding ourselves and each other that we are a free and a good nation: our democracy and our morality are, we say, what make America the envy of and the model for the rest of the world. America's moral and democratic exceptionalism are pet subjects for our pundits, politicians, and preachers. Whether or not we are, indeed, a free and moral nation, we, as a people, clearly want to believe that we are, and our insecurities demand that we be told as much at every available opportunity. These declarations of American exceptionalism, says Stephen Walt, "rest on the belief that the United States is a uniquely virtuous nation, one that loves peace, nurtures liberty, respects human rights, and embraces the rule of law."[4] Freedom is apparently our chief export; the American patchwork is, we say, held together by its unbreakable (and unquestionable) moral fiber. Often, we say these things without even a semblance of inquiry into what they mean. The louder we say them—the more insistently we trumpet our exceptionalism—the more a close examination of that exceptionalism is necessary. After all, we tend to say those things most loudly that are least true.

If we are going to call ourselves a truly exceptional global leader, even the world's only remaining superpower, we must do so with a much greater degree of reflexivity than might have been expected of nineteenth- or twentieth-century superpowers (postmodernity demands at least this much of us). We must ask how (or even if) we have led by example. This and only this would qualify us as the global leader we claim ourselves to be. If we are truly exceptional, it is not our military might (an antiquated measuring stick for greatness) but our moral and intellectual vigor (put forth so clearly in the documents and speeches our founding fathers left to us) that makes us so. If we have steered away from the clear path set forth by the intellectuals that led us to our independence (and I believe we have), it is our duty to reacquaint and realign ourselves with a moral compass—particularly one that responds to the magnetic pull of postmodern notions of equality and human rights.

This is not something that can be accomplished in a moment, but America seems to rise to the occasion whenever a formidable adversary presents itself. Breaking the shackles of tyranny and oppression was by no means an easy accomplishment, but we deemed the condition of oppression to be intolerable, and, what is more, we had an adversary that was largely external to ourselves. Today, what tyrannizes and oppresses us is no longer something "over there." Rather, we are our own worst enemy. And we have faced this enemy before. Since we fought for and won our independence, we have, at pivotal moments in our history, gazed in the mirror and been disgusted at our own shallowness and bigotry. We have, in moments of great crisis, broken with the status quo, upturning laws and practices that held true to neither the spirit of the times nor the spirit of the Constitution. If we are to lead the way as we once did, we must first realize that we have lost our way: too many of us face discrimination; too many of us are languishing in poverty. In Chapters 5 and 6, we'll look at widespread poverty and income inequality in this country. Despite insistent claims that we are making poverty more bearable, the number of destitute Americans (featuring, as it ever has, a disproportionately high number of minorities) has changed very little in the last half-century; what has changed, though, is the divide between the poor and the wealthy, which has exploded since the business-friendly tax reforms of the 1980s. Income inequality has exasperated the issue of poverty by placing unscalable and still-growing barriers between the middle and upper classes. If we are to address these issues once and for all, we must first realize that we are deluding ourselves when we say that this country's economic and social playing field is a level one. So, in Chapter 1, I offer a visceral cry, one that harmonizes with the cries heard in Ferguson, in Baltimore, in Chicago, and in Oakland.

There is a single note at the heart of this cry: as a putatively moral nation, we are not what we would have ourselves be. Though we are surrounded by evidence to the contrary, we seem hell-bent on painting ourselves in only the most flattering of colors. Take for example the way that we discuss (or attempt not to discuss) race in this country. *Contra* conservative claims, *we do not live in a post-racial society*, and no amount of purportedly race-blind punditry will make claims to the contrary anything more than empty or duplicitous rhetoric. The election of President Obama unleashed a tidal wave of overt bigotry, much of which masquerades as partisan bickering. From the gutting of the *Voting Rights Act*, which allowed Southern states formerly subject to federal-elections oversight to disenfranchise minority voters, to the police departments in Ferguson, New York, and Baltimore and the clear danger they pose to Black community members, one thing is clear: racism is alive and well in America. In Chapter 2 we will examine Obama's presidency, particularly the Republican policy of *damnatio memoriae*,[5] which seeks to either erase or deface Obama's undeniably historic legacy. The often-racist conservative backlash against the President and his policies thoroughly undoes any attempts to paint America as a post-racial nation, as does the largely consequence-free state-sponsored violence with Black bodies as its target. In Chapter 3 we'll look at the racist violence (both physical and psychological that is enacted daily in America's inner cities, in our prisons, but also in our language. By allowing race to be discussed in our political and extra-political discourse in the way we have, we have prepared an ugly

legacy for the next generation, one that carries the baggage of prejudices we should have outlived ages ago. Once again, our apparent
determination to do anything but critically examine our notions of
exceptionalism has led us down the garden path.

The view that we are indeed exceptional, that we have a starring
role to play in not just our own destiny but that of the planet as well
might feel true to those of us who take our greatness for granted, but
such a vision of America sees but through a glass darkly. This vision
is shared by those akin to Donald Trump's 2016 U.S. Presidential
campaign mantra "make America great again." It ignores the narrow
range of values we are willing to tolerate both abroad and at home.
Chapter 4 will examine our inability to gracefully admit those whom
we identify as other into this country. Our xenophobia, like our racism
and our appalling social and economic inequalities, makes us play the
hypocrite on the global stage. We are not as exceptional as we would
have ourselves be, for our exceptionalism makes far too many excep-
tions. At the root of our corporatism, profiteering, and racism (each of
which dehumanizes those it acts upon) is a negation of humanity—of
unconditional love and respect for all. We took it as self-evident that
all men are created equal, yet we still have not given those words substance. They will ring hollow until we realize that, as a nation, a planet,
and a species, we either rise together or we will fall together.

The Moral Arc

In an article published in *The Gospel Messenger* in 1958, Dr. Martin
Luther King Jr. wrote: "Yes, 'the arc of the moral universe is long, but
it bends toward justice.'"[6] Dr. King was speaking of race and freedom, of the immorality of oppression, and of the inevitable end of
Jim Crow. As he wrote those words, Black Americans, many of them
inspired by King's words, were actively seeking a more perfect liberty,
one that no longer distinguished between white and black in the eyes
of the law. Though the movement gathered steam through the 1950s,
it seemed, at times, that progress in terms of race relations was to
be glacial at best. King assured his readers that time and persistence
would bring the outcomes that Black America sought. The universe is
so very large, the line of time so very long, that it can be easy to lose
sight of (or even to question the existence of) the moral arc, which

can only be perceived at a distance. If we are becoming better, we are doing so agonizingly slowly, and, although the bend in the line could be tangibly felt in the decade that followed King's statement, for many of us it is more difficult than it may once have been to find evidence that the line still arcs toward justice.

I have long sought evidence of this arc, and I found what I was looking for in what might seem a surprising place. Travyon Martin's death, and the justified outrage that followed in its wake, showed an America that was, despite the contentions of post-racial commentators, replete with racial strife. This tension only increased in the months and years that followed, with outrageous police violence that resulted in the deaths of Mike Brown (Ferguson, Missouri), Freddie Gray (Baltimore, Maryland), John Crawford (Beavercreek, Ohio), and Eric Garner (New York). But these young Black boys didn't monopolize the murderous activity of police officers. Rekia Boyd and LaTanya Haggerty (Chicago, Illinois), Natasha McKenna (Fairfax County, Virginia), Aura Rosser (Ann Arbor, Michigan), Yvette Smith (Bastrop County, Texas), Sandra Bland (Prairie View, Texas), Miriam Carey (Washington, D.C.), and eight others in 2014 alone felt the piercing pain of state-inflicted bullets or reckless disregard for their humanity. Their lives were prematurely snuffed out, though their names have lived on in their capacity as martyrs written in the *New Red Record*[7] of legalized, state-sponsored lynching. Young people in each of these communities flocked to the streets to vent their frustrations—sometimes, much to the chagrin of older civil-rights icons—in violent ways.

I too was dismayed by the violence, but I was also inspired in these moments to create this generation's *Race Matters*, aspiring to facilitate, just as Cornel West's 1994 seminal text by that title did, a necessary and timely conversation with America, not solely Black America, but people of conscience as well—all those who "sing America." What follows is a moral call, a harkening and quickening of the spirit, a demand for recognition for those whose voices are whispered, and a call to action for like-minded visionaries and progressives. The moral arc may bend, but it is frustratingly obtuse when we lose our drive to make things better. Hope is what fuels this drive, and I believe we have reason for hope (and lots of it). Apathy (perhaps the chief malaise of postmodernity) will only slow our collective progress.

The Bible tells us, "If one part suffers, every part suffers with it; if one part is honored, every part rejoices with it," but far too often those suffering are left unattended or under-attended and those who are honored rejoice at the expense of those suffering. This is as true here, where violence and poverty crush so many of those trapped in our inner cities, as it is abroad, where we kill and maim the guilty and the innocent alike. We'll take an honest look at the making of America and the making of our notions of exceptionalism, which make a blind spot of our hypocrisy both at home and abroad. While this blindness may not be uniquely American (in fact, it seems to be a common feature of superpowers),[8] it seems especially problematic in a century that has seen us awakening—albeit slowly—to the plight of the marginalized. While I recognize the tremendous leap forward that a Black Commander-in-Chief represents for American race relations, I will not give a free pass to the President, who has not done enough to address the ways in which America treats the marginalized both at home and abroad. In foreign countries we use drones in unprecedented ways to do our dirty work, we spy on allies and adversaries alike, and we have continued to wage wars in the Middle East—all of this with a Nobel Peace Prize winner in the Oval Office.

Our president may, in the end, provide future historians of the early twenty-first century with precious little of note in terms of revolutionizing the role America plays on the international stage. However, his skin color and his domestic policies (particularly the *Affordable Care Act*) will undoubtedly be defining features of his legacy—as will the vitriolic erasure of his "command" by those who surrounded the seat of power—but those of us who hoped for a peacekeeper in the Oval Office have had these hopes dashed. Though his role at the helm of the American Military Machine has been, for many, a disappointment, Barack Obama's presidency has been, more than any other, a springboard to largely meaningful national conversations about race. These have included a pronounced interest in the socioeconomic and cultural factors that have come to infect how we discuss race in this country. It is not a question of what race is, but, rather, what we perceive it to be that affects the real-world outcomes attached to it (i.e., economic, social, and political privilege, or the lack thereof). Racism in the United States has shifted from pitting an identity-based in-group against a constructed out-group to a much more nuanced battle, one that is part of a larger socioeconomic conflict.

There seems to be a widespread belief among conservative pundits and politicians that legal safeguards against *de jure* racism have run their course. Racism, they say, is no longer something that produces social or economic inequalities of any kind. Those clinging onto the bottom rung of the social or economic ladder have simply not applied themselves as diligently as those perched upon the top rung have. Yet racial demographics placed side by side with economic ones continue to tell us that Black Americans make up a disproportionate number of this country's poorest citizens and a minuscule portion of its wealthiest ones. In my discussions of poverty, we'll discuss how the wealthiest among us tend to attribute their success to a strong work ethic, a can-do attitude, and even a certain measure of moral fiber. This tendency to connect affluence and positive character traits recasts a two-generation-old shadow of Moynihanian[9] proportions. The 47 per cent,[10] as Mitt Romney termed them, are denigrated, made to shoulder all of the blame for the circumstances that surround them. As if this were not enough, they are painted as hucksters, scam artists who have duped the taxpayer into footing the bill for their ghetto-fabulous lifestyle. Such narratives placate the non-Black poor, distinguishing the oft-popularized hard-working Americans from the Black, urban poor. Herbert J. Gans noted in 1993 that "the poor function as a reliable and relatively permanent measuring rod for status comparisons" (266). Coded—and not very deeply—within this language is a covert racism that reframes our national discussion about race into one about economics. The Tea Party has, in the name of fiscal conservatism, been able to advocate policies that disproportionately target Black Americans while shrugging off criticism that highlights the racist nature of its insistence that social-assistance programs be steadily rolled back. Poverty is a proxy for race, and fiscal conservatism has beaten new paths for racism.

Renewed calls for a tightening of the welfare belt and push-back against Affirmative Action (to name just two) are backlashes against the perceived gains made by Black America—not only economic gains but demographic ones as well. Told that soon whites will no longer be the majority in the United States,[11] the right-wing base has openly lamented the "browning" of America and the spread of socially progressive values and political correctness. Inevitably, these conservative jeremiads come hand in hand with wistful nostalgia for pre–civil-rights America and its whitewashed vision of the nuclear family (even, in some extreme cases, for the days before the Thirteenth Amendment).

There is a firm belief among many that we are living in a unique time, one in which our democracy is under attack and being co-opted by people who don't share the interests of the "average American"— whoever that is. The Supreme Court's decision in the *Citizens United* case,[12] which essentially equated the spending of money with an act of speech, ensured that those with deeper pockets would be granted an ever-expanding role in the democratic decision-making process, making wealthy donors and corporations more politically powerful than ever before. In that ruling, the Court created a political finance system that mirrors our social strata, granting unequal influence to those who can afford it. We used to call that bribery; today we call it campaign finance, and, thanks in no small part to the *Citizens United* decision, the steady stream of cash into the political process has reached levels that are nothing short of ludicrous. The 2016 election is on pace to top the mind-boggling $10-billion mark.[13]

Perhaps we need to see just how pernicious an effect money will have in the 2016 elections to make the need for substantial reform to our campaign finance laws apparent, but limits aren't likely to be put in place by the Republicans who are currently running Congress. As with any of the other reforms I will advocate in the chapters that follow, we need an approach to legislation that is quite different from politics as usual in Washington. In order for my daughter to grow up in an America that aligns itself with her intersectional interests, a continued commitment to political positions of power and influence must swell. Danielle Allen concurs when she claims, "when we think about how to achieve political equality, we have to attend to things like voting rights and the right to hold office. We have to foster economic opportunity and understand when excessive material inequality undermines broad democratic political participation" (21). In short, we will need to elect people who actually care about this issue of equal access, the "lifting of every voice" within the demos, people who recognize that our democracy is a pliable, shared system that should give each person an equal say in what the government does and how it does it. Such a foundation is being laid with the influence of the Internet and social media, whereby coalition building and the democratic voice have both been technologized in major ways. But the challenge to a united democratic opposition to oligarchic control of our democracy lies, at least partly, in the dialogic opposition of these media. Too many people who are active in politics arrange themselves in battle array, directing all of their energies and activism in opposition to those they regard as their enemies. Cornel West states, "our national focus has become so dominated by narrow us-vs-them discourse that it has all but drowned out authentic debate over issues" (*Democracy Matters* 65). It's liberals vs. conservatives, Whites vs. Blacks, Blacks vs. Jews, Christians vs. Muslims, Republicans vs. Democrats, Libertarians vs. major party, or Tea Party members vs. anyone who doesn't think like they do.

The polarization of the political debate has wreaked havoc on politics—particularly in terms of the ability to reach bipartisan consensus. Though it is no fault of his own, the President himself seems to be at the center of this polarization. The conservative backlash against Obama has come with broad generalizations about the President, his policies, and his philosophical leanings. The left, too, has made assumptions about the President (some of them informed by the color of his skin). Being the first Black president made Obama the poster boy for the progressive agenda *in toto*. Every *cause célèbre*, every injustice, every barrier to complete equality was cited as something that Obama's presidency would resolve in a way that the left would surely find deeply satisfying. President Obama may be the first Black president and an advocate for many of the left's causes, but he is not a liberal crusader; he is no Black Jesus. When 2016 is behind us, many on the left may come to realize just how much of a centrist Obama has been. What's more, his unexpected leanings in support of the corporate agenda and a deep reluctance to embrace the more ambitious hopes of social progressives make his presidency much more of a compromise than a victory.

What we are experiencing is a series of transitions, and, like many socially progressive transitions, this one has been full of fits and starts. Slow though that march may be, progress does soldier on. It may be grim to say so, but the generation that once clung so desperately to segregation is dying out. The old guard is (albeit agonizingly slowly) being replaced by the new. West has underscored the need for this evolution in values: "A democratic public must continuously create new attitudes, new vocabularies, new outlooks, and new visions all undergirded by individual commitment to scrutiny and volition" (*Democracy Matters* 69). Today's children are growing up in an increasingly integrated world, and black, brown, white, and yellow are not the hard-and-fast divisions they once were. I welcome the inevitable changing of the guard, while at the same time I recognize that a future aligned with our highest hopes is not inevitable. Any sort of *cultural fulfillment*, to borrow a term by philosopher and theologian Victor Anderson, is to strive toward "the ends and goods which contribute most generally to human flourishing" (2). If history is any indicator, progressive reform is a product of changing times, but it is also the work of conscientious and persuasive reformers. Human societies do not change so much as they are changed, and I hope to bring about the kind of change I think this country needs—to reposition the moral arc so that it bends more steeply toward justice.

Notes

1   The "World Pledge" is attributed to the late Lillian Genser, peace activist and pioneer of human rights. She taught at Wayne State University in Detroit.

2   Any digestion of West's lectures, interviews, or a classroom visit will lend itself to this critique in some form. But for his full discussion, see his *Democracy Matters*.

3   See Keyssar.

4   Stephen M. Walt, "The Myth of American Exceptionalism," *Foreign Policy* 11 October 2011, http://foreignpolicy.com/2011/10/11/the-myth-of-american-exceptionalism/.

5   Translated as "the damnation of memory."

6   Martin Luther King Jr., "Out of the Long Night," *The Gospel Messenger* [Elgin, IL: Brethren Publishing House], 8 February 1958: 3.

7   The Red Record refers to the Ida B. Wells-Barnett publications that chronicled the deaths of Black souls lost during the lynchings of the Jim Crow South.

8   Walt, "The Myth of American Exceptionalism," writes: "Whenever American leaders refer to the 'unique' responsibilities of the United States, they are saying that it is different from other powers and that these differences require them to take on special burdens. Yet there is nothing unusual about such lofty declarations; indeed, those who make them are treading a well-worn path. Most great powers have considered themselves superior to their rivals and have believed that they were advancing some greater good when they imposed their preferences on others."

9   In 1965 the (in)famous "Moynihan Report," penned by then-senator Daniel
    Moynihan, called for legislative attention to the corrosive and disintegrated
    negro family structure. See Moynihan.

10 Mitt Romney, while a candidate for president, made the following statement in
    May 2012 while speaking at a private fundraiser: "There are 47 percent of the
    people who will vote for the president no matter what. All right, there are 47
    percent who are with him, who are dependent upon government, who believe
    that they are victims, who believe that government has a responsibility to care
    for them, who believe that they are entitled to health care, to food, to housing,
    to you name it. That that's an entitlement. And the government should give it
    to them. And they will vote for this president no matter what. And I mean, the
    president starts off with 48, 49, 48—he starts off with a huge number. These are
    people who pay no income tax. Forty-seven percent of Americans pay no income
    tax. So our message of low taxes doesn't connect. And he'll be out there talking
    about tax cuts for the rich. I mean that's what they sell every four years. And so
    my job is not to worry about those people—I'll never convince them that they
    should take personal responsibility and care for their lives."

11 I make this case here not to enter into a discussion about the efficacy of, or
    problems with, this racial forecast. The research on this is heavy, though I tend to
    fall into the camp of sociologist George Yancey, who argues that this prediction
    is false based on definitional grounds. The shift in who is white in America (or,
    more so, who is *not* black or brown) will likely skew this hypothesis. See Yancey.

12 558 U.S. 310 (2010).

13 Albert R. Hunt, "How Record Spending Will Affect 2016 Election," *Bloomberg
    View* 26 April 2015, http://www.bloombergview.com/articles/2015-04-26/
    how-record-spending-will-affect-2016-election.

Chapter One

"I CAN'T BREATHE!"[1]
"SO WHAT!
F*** YOUR BREATH"[2]

The brutal atrocities of white supremacy in the American past and present speak volumes about the harsh limits of our democracy over against our professed democratic ideals…. Race is the crucial intersecting point where democratic energies clash with American imperial realities in the very making of the grand American experiment of democracy.[3]

ON SEPTEMBER 24, 2014, A GREENE COUNTY, OHIO, SPECIAL GRAND Jury, after hearing from 18 witnesses and considering both audio and video evidence, failed to indict Sean Williams for the fatal shooting of 22-year-old John Crawford III, gunned down in a Walmart. Because Crawford was carrying an (unloaded) air rifle, which he'd picked up off the shelf a short time earlier, the jurors ruled that the officer who fired the two shots that killed Crawford followed active shooter protocols to the letter and was therefore justified in doing what he did.[4] But Crawford was neither active nor a shooter. He was merely a young, Black shopper, talking on his cellphone to the mother of his children, menacing no one, yet still frightening enough to be met with deadly force from a highly trained officer. Sadly, this kind of story has become increasingly familiar in recent months; similar tragedies in Ferguson, New York, Milwaukee, Charleston, and Baltimore have sparked national discussions about racial politics in America.

While there is widespread agreement about America's racist roots, we seem unable to come to any consensus on racism in the twenty-first-century United States.

For Black America, the outcomes of the justice system undeniably leave much to be desired. The absence of guilty verdicts—indeed, the absence of trials—rubs coarse salt in the still-fresh wounds of the families, the loved ones, and the communities affected by these tragedies. Rather than seeing these parents offered a pittance of consolation for their loss, we watch as they grapple with yet another travesty of justice.

For Black America, such travesties are, if not old news, at least familiar stories. In 1989, five New York City African-American teenagers, "The Central Park Five," were interrogated without legal representation and forced to confess to raping a white woman and other crimes they did not commit. In the racially tense and crime-ridden New York of this period, all of the young men were convicted, even without any airtight evidence placing them at the scene. Each of the young men spent at least four years in prison; thanks to a new confession and a re-examination of the prosecution's evidence, all of these convictions were vacated in 2002, but, by this time, their sentences had been served.[5]

In 1991, Rodney King was beaten to within an inch of his life by white police officers in Los Angeles. In 1994, a Black New York City police officer was mistaken for a criminal and shot by a white officer (a story repeated in 2009). In 2012, Trayvon Martin was chased and killed by George Zimmerman (an over-zealous neighborhood-watch vigilante who assumed that Martin was behind a spate of recent break-ins). Zimmerman, thanks to Florida's Stand Your Ground law, was acquitted. Conservative and even centrist media outlets focused on Martin's baggy clothes, his discipline issues at school, and his love of hip-hop; the pull of racial undercurrents was palpable. Speculations that painted Martin as a criminal or a neighborhood menace implied (and sometimes explicitly stated outright) that Zimmerman's actions were legally (and morally) justifiable. Zimmerman was protecting his community; Martin was a thug. Zimmerman may not have been a police officer, but he acted—and was justified as such an actor in the ensuing discussions—as a figure of authority, as a preserver of civic order. His behavior may not have been explicitly sponsored or endorsed by the state (the lack of culpability does not an endorsement make), but his act of aggression with a young Black man as its target was excused. The act and its vindication continued the practice—supposedly long ago criminalized—of the extra-judicial killing of young Black men.

Whether these various aggressions were initiated by the state or not, it's difficult to see them as anything but state-sanctioned lynchings—or perhaps it's more accurate to call them *culturally permissible sacrifices* and label their victims as collateral damage. When citizens are not held accountable for killing young people of color, police officers escape conviction for inappropriate use of deadly force, and the media rationalize racial violence as an excusable inconvenience, necessary to keep the public order, the stage is set: it's open season on Black bodies. What happens next is that Sandra Bland blows smoke from her cigarette during a traffic stop in Waller County, Texas—and this turns out to be one of her last autonomous acts. She dares express frustration and confusion at being pulled over on a technicality, and this is determined to be "threatening" action by trooper Brian Encinia, who responds, "I will light you up." Seventy-two hours later, she's dead in her cell. Then, an eight-year-old Native American girl is tased and slammed against a wall in Pierre, South Dakota for holding a paring knife; a Native Lives Matter activist, Allen Locke, a Lakota (Native American) tribe member, is killed by officer Anthony Meirose on December 19, 2014, for being "threatening" (like Sandra Bland); finally, to add insult to injury, a young girl in a bathing suit is pinned to the ground by a grown man outside a neighborhood pool party in McKinney, Texas, in July 2015. What we see, what we learn, what we must come to understand is that we live in a society that has become accustomed to monthly, weekly, and sometimes even daily acts of domestic terrorism, exacted upon young citizens of color by white citizens with badges. We seek reasons to blame the victims; we grasp at any available excuse to rationalize the behavior of the perpetrators of these violent acts. We hold them in reverence, these officers of the law, but rarely hold them culpable.

Similar narratives—with identical implications about justifiable violence perpetrated on purportedly terrifying Black bodies—have emerged with appalling regularity since the Zimmerman case made a hot-button issue of state-sponsored (or state-vindicated) violence

Millions March, Oakland: Rally against police brutality and failure to prosecute the officers who commit these crimes. https://flic.kr/p/q8D1no. Credit: Amir Aziz, 13 December 2014.

against young Black men. With the coverage surrounding the deaths of Michael Brown, Eric Garner, Freddie Gray, and other unarmed Black citizens in recent years, the pattern is no less clear, especially when an almost certainly culpable officer walks free after taking the life of a young Black man or woman. Take the case of Officer Michael Brelo, who was found not guilty of voluntary manslaughter: he shot 49 of the 137 shots that killed Timothy Russell and Malissa Williams in Cleveland, Ohio, standing on the hood of a car as if he was playing a Call of Duty video game—but with unarmed Black lives as his targets. The pertinent questions seem to revolve around the stature of the victim and, in the case of Brown, his actions in the hours before the shooting. The amnesic, mainstream public and the equally forgetful justice system—including even the District Attorney's Office—gives the officers the benefit of the doubt, forgetting that such racist and even predatory behavior is not an anomaly in Missouri, New York, or Baltimore; rather, it is the continuation of a palpable pattern of violence targeting Black bodies. It is part of a broader history of justified violence that stretches back to the establishment of the first colonies and the transatlantic slave trade upon those "generally dishonored persons."[6]

Although these patterns and their punctuations are deeply saddening, and although they highlight a continuing issue with race in this country, the attention they receive is limited (often focusing on the occasionally violent demonstrations that, with their images of broken windows, looted shop fronts, and burning cars, make for extraordinarily good copy). When the fires subside, the 24-hour news cycle changes the topic.

This is not to say that our country has not made vast improvements in dealing with race. To say so would be to ignore the seismic shift in race relations ushered in by the Civil Rights Movement. Many of those changes were monumental: forbidding violence and other forms of mistreatment against Blacks and, at long last, outlining legal protections for all races. Following the conclusion of the third phase of the Civil Rights Movement,[7] and especially with the implementation of policies aimed at correcting socioeconomic injustices by offering unprecedented assistance to minorities, it was almost as if there was a collective sigh. It felt as though America had turned a corner, as though maybe, just maybe, progress had been and was being made. Things were looking up. We took these first steps as a nation without really knowing where we were headed; while we started the journey together, the path became harder to follow as the distance in time between the Civil Rights Movement and the present grew larger. While we are still making progress, we have lost the path (and especially the togetherness that characterized our first steps on it), and we have become more and more lost, unsure of the future.

We still grapple with ubiquitous racism, and yet it is not our mother's or our father's racism. Rather, it is more subtle, more covert, and arguably more insidious for being so. Subtle though they may be, many of the racial stereotypes and racist practices (covert and overt) that non-white Americans have long struggled against remain dishearteningly prevalent today. They are still deeply rooted in our culture and institutions; this is why our country has been unable to take the giant culture-wide leap forward it so desperately needs to become the place we imagined it could be half a century ago.

By leaving the deeper issues unaddressed, we have allowed superficial progress to stand in for the real thing. Prashad, Blackman, and Kelley find that our eagerness to pivot on a dime from self-recrimination to self-congratulation has made it virtually impossible to discuss (let alone address) deep-seated racial issues in any significant way in this country: "[T]he problem of the twenty first century ... is the problem of the color-blind. This problem is simple: it believes that to redress racism, we need to *not* consider race in social practice.... The state, we are told, must be *above* race" (21). In other words, we have attempted to leap in a single bound the deep chasm that separates White and Black America. This hasty rush to a post-racial never-never land paints racial unrest on one side and overt/covert racism on the other as little more than deeply entrenched and manifestly false positions that Americans can discard so long as they are willing to do so. Perhaps most worrying is the clear evidence that some among us believe not only that we can do so, but that we have done so—that American racism is a problem that's been solved, and, but for a few stalwart holdouts (racial agitators), we are ready to hold hands and march forward together singing "Kumbaya" in chorus. We may be talking about equality, but this conversation is no stand-in for the real thing. We find ourselves now—as then—in a place of false progress, perhaps even false hope.

Being above race is a lofty goal, but it is a premature one, ignoring as it does behind-closed-doors racism and the continued existence of the racial hierarchies that inform the daily injustices and humiliations suffered by Black Americans. We may talk about race openly and relatively even-handedly in the twenty-first century, but such conversations are largely superficial—mainly because our obsession with sound bites and gaffes has made all but the most prejudiced pundits and quote generators afraid to misspeak. There is, without doubt, a taboo surrounding overt racism which has birthed a new generation of race deniers, each of whom wears identical lenses that blur or erase distinctions between the races. C.R. Lawrence recognized this almost 20 years ago, seeing in the way that race was being discussed in America a growing "color-blindness." The primary mechanism by which "color-blindness" sustains itself is denial. And further sustaining this denial is a societal taboo against honest talk about what we see, feel, and know about racism.[8] In lieu of this difficult but honest conversation, "straight shooters" feed us the "straight dope," which paints Black America as somehow a victim of its own success; the powerful race card or victim card (these two are interchangeable) has apparently been overplayed, which has resulted in a culture of entitled freeloaders and ne'er-do-wells who lack the motivation or the work ethic that they need to succeed in America. When Abigail Fisher is able to take her University of Texas reverse-discrimination case all the way to the Supreme Court, and when the political Right uses the election of Barack Obama as our nation's conversation moment away from racism into color-blindedness, those of us who don't see race-neutrality are mistakenly living in the past, obsessed with a problem that has been solved. Progress was apparently made while our backs were turned.

Minorities in this country can all speak to the disingenuousness of these claims, but it seems that the Supreme Court finds them entirely convincing. In 2003, the Court ruled in the favor of two white Michigan residents, Jennifer Gratz and Patrick Hamacher, who leveled claims of reverse racism at the University of Michigan over its affirmative-action admissions policy.[9] In 2013, the University of Michigan was again the subject of a Supreme Court case, when the Court overturned a 2012 Sixth Circuit Court of Appeals decision, ruling that the state's ban on affirmative action was, in fact, constitutional.[10] That same year, the Supreme Court gutted sections of the *Voting Rights Act* that protected minorities from discriminatory voting restrictions in historically racist states. All of these decisions were justified with reference to the tremendous leaps and bounds made since the Civil Rights Movement. So far have we come that there is little to no difference between the black experience of America and the white one—or so we are told.

The fact that such patently false characterizations of Black America are given any truck in our media means that, as a society, we have let ourselves off the hook. We have allowed a false assumption to guide us, namely, that by addressing the legal, economic, political, and educational effects of *de jure* segregation, we had also taken the necessary steps to address the sociological and psychological effects of 300 years of *de facto* segregation. It is true that white men can no longer legally chain and maim Black bodies or hang them from trees; no man or woman in this country can be refused goods or services based on the color of their skin. Our country, it is true, has changed. Our president is regularly invoked as example of this, and, indeed, he does exemplify a more inclusive America, but the continued miscarriages of justice, the constant reminders that we are not, as yet, an equal society, the persistent structures of inequality and institutionalized racism—these are all albatrosses that we can't seem to rid from around our necks in the present. This current social climate, especially the persistent stigma surrounding blackness, is, as Imani Perry argues, "a derivative, but distinct, zeitgeist" (2). We have yet to address in any significant way how this cloud of racism that hangs over our nation makes us feel—as Blacks, Whites, as Americans of all colors—and that has muddied our conception of what a truly post-racial society might look like. Though we are frequently told otherwise, we do not live in a post-racial America—not if we are collectively unwilling to articulate how we can address our past and present in remotely satisfactory ways. Doing so means—at the very least—engaging in the nitty-gritty dialog between Whites and Blacks that will compel us all to understand what generations upon generations of institutionalized racism have heaped not just upon Blacks but upon us all, as a people and as a nation. There's no doubt that this dialog will be difficult, and a discomfort is sure to loom in its shadow, but the future of our culture and our society hangs in the balance.

In order to have this conversation (and, more importantly, to make it a meaningful one), there must be some sense of agreement with respect to the nature of the problem. A good place to start would be the fact that race means different things to different people in different contexts. Rather than a racial monolith, there are competing "frames"—systems for understanding and presenting the problems suffered by African Americans.[11] The conservative framing of the race issue imagines that American democracy, business, and social life are, at least in essence, equal—that the playing field is a level one for all participants. Anything outside of that frame—be it police violence, income inequality, or social marginalization—is explained with reference to the frame: as criminality, laziness, a culture that is incompatible with the mainstream. The frames themselves are morally neutral; in practice, however, they have the power to produce detrimental and racist effects. Racially insensitive conservatives frame the African-American experience in a way that denies their lived experiences, burdening those who experience racism daily with responsibility for its continuation. This frame acknowledges that America had a problem with race in the past, but improvements since then have made its continued discussion an exercise in futility. With a Black man in the Oval Office, race is posited as a ready-at-hand excuse for what actually boils down to a lazy fatalism. Blame shifting and the overplaying of the race card are the real problems—not systemic discrimination, not the racial and economic tiering of American life. Crucially, pointing this out is an act, not of racism, but of charity. Those who frame race in this way paint themselves as racial pioneers, as prophets of a new post-racial age. Ask them what needs to be done to address the issue of race in this country, and their answer is as predictable as it is inane: "We have already done too much."

Such beliefs, and the arguments that sustain them, are blinded by privilege. With America's cornucopia at their feet, the privileged find it preposterous that anybody could not travel the same road to success that they have walked. The pernicious social structures, the institutional interference, the quotidian discrimination—such are illusory, for those either born into or easily awarded privilege never experienced any of it. It seems a common human quality to ascribe one's success to character traits—honesty, perseverance, and intelligence—that seem to be the exclusive property of those atop the social ladder. Those they look down upon (and especially the dark faces that protest from below) are a mere negative image of success.

This is due to what prominent social psychologist Lee Ross called the "fundamental attribution error" or "correspondence bias." It explains why, if we are cut off in traffic, we're less likely to assume that the other driver is in the midst of some kind of emergency or made an understandable error in not checking his blind spot. Instead, we assume the worst: either that he is a reckless driver or that he is insensitive to the needs of other drivers. So if a conservative is asked to explain high levels of underemployment or unemployment among African Americans, the fundamental attribution error leads him to believe that all things are equal and that those who languish in poverty lack the motivation to reach out and grasp the low-hanging fruit that is available (they say) to all Americans. Institutional racism doesn't so much as enter into the frame. The solutions they propose reveal a laughably myopic understanding of the effects of systemic racism. Don Lemon's "pull your pants up" solution, for instance, rejects out of hand the effects of poor schooling, inadequate health-care provision, and policies that effectively shift resources out of minority neighborhoods. The real problem, according to Lemon, is trends in Black male fashion.[12]

White privilege blinds those who would claim that Black America is its own worst enemy. They say that Black-coded culture (hip-hop in particular) uses racist language so much as to make it practically meaningless. Whites are merely echoing this language when they use it—even if the tone and context clearly indicate that the meaning they intend is more insidious (and much older) than the one contained in hip-hop lyrics. It is this view that allowed Joe Scarborough to dismiss the University of Oklahoma's Sigma Alpha Epsilon chapter's racist chant with a wave of his hand, claiming that the transparently racist chants were merely echoing contemporary hip-hop lyrics.[13] Never mind the fact that this excuse was never so much as mentioned by anybody connected to the incident; never mind the fact that hip-hop music has not (at least not to my knowledge as a hip-hop educator) ever made light of lynching—especially not in a way that would lead any reasonable listener to think that the taboo surrounding the subject had been lifted. The Scarboroughs of this world, though, seem eager to throw Black America under the bus whenever racist whites are caught on hot mics or hidden cameras. Furthermore, he, and in this case his co-host Mika Brzezinski, think that they have license (or at least an excuse) to re-appropriate language within hip-hop's vocabulary, all while knowing little to nothing of that vocabulary's explicit or implied meaning.

Any Black person who has ever been in a classroom or a town-hall meeting in which black and white mix or collide can tell you about the prevalent assumption that Blacks are somehow responsible for educating Whites on how racism is prevalent in society. I see this frequently in predominantly white classrooms in which I teach. White students—in an attempt to understand racial issues that must be at least partially commended—ask minority students to speak about the Black or Hispanic experience *in toto*, as though every minority were a deputy spokesperson of sorts for their race or even for all non-white races. In a relatively benign example of the mindset that informs this behavior, Starbucks recently debuted (and almost immediately canceled) a Race Together campaign that asked servers to write "race together" on their white and green cups in order to start a conversation about race with customers.[14] Rather than showing a commitment to advancing the national discussion on race through scholarship, in-house workshopping, or other self-focused activities, Starbucks' marketing and management teams preferred to cast their organization in the role of the facilitator. They didn't have anything palpable to add to the dialog, but, by encouraging it, they felt, they were doing enough. In this fantasy, Starbucks cafés could be the locus for heartfelt and inclusive dialogs between White and Black Americans—with the latter educating the former (or occasionally vice versa). This was an attempt on the part of an American brand so white as to be almost translucent to manage its image at a time when racial tensions were running high, and the immediate backlash made it clear that Black America and its sincere sympathizers were not amused.

This privileged mindset—grounded as it is in an often-sincere desire to understand racial issues in America—is frequently defended vigorously by the well-intentioned sympathizers who are blind to the privilege that informs the questions they ask or the tone in which they ask them. This aspect of privilege is, therefore, resistant to change in ways that more blatantly racist attitudes are not. Take the word "mulatto," for instance: informing somebody that the term, with etymological roots in the Spanish word for mule, is highly offensive is often met with some surprise on the part of the speaker (so long as he or she isn't using the term in a purposefully offensive way). Since generations of Americans used the word without thinking, a surprising number of people still think the term is an appropriate one to use when describing those of mixed race. Inform them that the term is no longer acceptable and the speaker will usually promise to strike the word from their conversation altogether and apologize for any offense caused. The problem is that disavowing racism (or, at the very least, particular manifestations of racism) in this way allows many white Americans to feel that they can wash their hands of systemic racism, in terms of both the benefits they enjoy from it and the pernicious effects it has in Black communities. It leaves privilege unaddressed.

Tell somebody that their privilege is blinding them to the position they take in conversation about race with minorities and you'll get a host of defensive responses. Challenge them further and it becomes clear that they feel that their actions have been uncharitably misinterpreted and that they are doing their part to combat racism by seeking to better understand American experience through the eyes of the country's minorities. Jay Smooth, one of America's pre-eminent hiphop deejays and commentators, has found that the best way to avoid this kind of defensive reaction is to point out that no claims are being made about whether the person is or is not a racist; what is being claimed is that the *action* or the *words* are racist.[15] Tell somebody that they're the problem and the response you'll get will be predictable (either dismissive or hostile); tell that same person that something they're doing or saying is problematic and you might just get them to see their privilege for what it is—even if only for a moment. To see white privilege operating in oneself is to want to resist it and eventually to overcome it; as this resistance moves from inward to outward, one can actually begin to make claims about actively fighting racism. It is then that claims to be free of racial prejudice can ring true.

So the challenge for those who want to have an honest discussion about racism in America is to set both the inward and the outward frames properly, which starts with an understanding that, even if overt racists are a dying breed, the *effects* of racism remain. White privilege is becoming ever better at hiding or excusing itself (conservative media outlets are providing its would-be defenders with plenty of ammunition), so even recognizing these effects for what they are is not necessarily a straightforward process. Hence the difficulty, even for African Americans, to see the true contours of the American landscape. As tempting as the post-racial vision of America may seem, it comes with a cost: it neuters blackness, rendering it powerless to assert itself; it lulls blackness to sleep, leaving a hollow and silent shell.

The combination of this lulling effect and the veil that white privilege places between fantasy and reality allows conservative commentary to frame racial solidarity and resistance that dares to raise its voice above a murmur as irrational, emotional, and over-reactive. Part of this is a residual of older prejudices that see Black bodies as savage or primitive things positively brimming with violent and sexual energy. Consider, for instance, the NFL commentator who called the Seattle Seahawks' Richard Sherman a "thug" for expressing excitement— next to a white woman, no less!—after a victory on the field. Another part of placing verbalized discontent inside a frame of uncontainable violence, though, is strategic: it is representing White America as attempting to transcend its past, to move past all the unpleasantness and to have a civilized conversation with Black America. No matter how conciliatory our tone, though, that conversation seems never to happen. That conversation, between Black America and the powers that be, is the carrot tied to the stick and dangled just beyond our reach. African Americans are told to sublimate their often-justifiable anger, to bear their burdens as though they were entirely of their own making and as though White America had done everything it can and will do to atone for its transgressions (again, the assumption being that these transgressions are entirely in the past). David Ikard and Martell Teasley echo this point in their study, *Nation of Cowards: Black Activism in Barack Obama's Post-Racial America*: "What this rhetorical erasure of white culpability in oppressing Blacks communicates to Americans in general and African-Americans in particular is that Black America has somehow arrived at this point of socio-economic crisis due, in large part, to their failure to see past systemic white oppression" (29). Conservative commentators such as Bill O'Reilly and Laura Ingraham are saying, in essence, *Get over it. Racism will end when you join White America in the assumption that it has done so.*

The fact of the matter is that the election of a Black president does not signify that racism is over. It means we've come a long way since slavery, yes. It means we've made progress since the Civil Rights Movement, certainly. But it does not mean that we live in a society that is free of racial tension, free of the systematic and structural oppression of Black people, and free of racist thought in action. Until an essential humanness replaces the hierarchized core of our racial discourse, we will continue to dehumanize the dark-skinned in both word and deed. Until the roots of structural racism are uprooted and an egalitarian worldview is planted in its place, the financial poverty of America's inner cities will remain a reflection of the moral poverty of our nation. Until the assumptions that underlie our racial discourse—that is, the concept of race as something that distinguishes one of us from the other—are eradicated, these discussions will continue ad nauseam, and our debates will be circumlocutory by definition. The hopeful seeds we cast on the earth will fall on barren soil.

Contrary to what some conservative pundits on the right or wide-eyed optimists on the left might believe, Obama's presidency has not improved racial relations in this country. We cannot sit back and feel good about ourselves because his election underscores a utopian ethos, a nascent dream-nation where democracy does, in fact, speak for and through people of all races, creeds, and colors within the country. Quite the contrary, it has torn the veneer off of our quasi-civilized national racial discourse. For those who are not willfully blind to the signs, it has shown America (White and Black alike) just how far we are from the post-racial ideal. Our Black president has flushed the vestigial vultures from the bushes, and they circle overhead once again, their broad wings darkening the land. Obama the bridge builder, Obama the peacemaker, and Obama the hope harbinger walks amid these shadows, but his hope keeps his gaze trained on the distant horizon. Hope as we might that Obama will face his racist detractors and throw some shade of his own, we all know why he'll never do so. The dignity of his office won't allow him to be a Dick Gregory, an Angela Davis, or an H. Rap Brown (towering examples of existentially free Black brothers and sisters unafraid to speak truth to power), won't allow him to call a cracker a cracker, even though his opponents might call a spade a spade.[16]

So long as White America refuses to recognize the vivid contours of its racially stratified country, so long as it remains blind to the fact that Black brothers and sisters fear (and justifiably so) those who are supposed to protect them, the Black bridge builder must continue to step wise, to talk in code to his radical brothers and sisters and let them know that he is there, working every day to push the country forward (sometimes against its will). In the face of this ongoing denial on the part of White America, the struggle must continue. We cannot allow the past to be whitewashed or to allow complacency or parochial successes to weaken our resolve. We cannot allow our justifiable outrage at the continuing legacy of white supremacy to be soothed by the lullaby of ersatz progress. It must be said, however, that progress *has* been made these last decades. Obama spoke of this change in generational terms during a 2013 press conference in the wake of the Zimmerman verdict:

> I don't want us to lose sight [of the fact] that things are getting better. Each successive generation seems to be making progress in changing attitudes when it comes to race. It doesn't mean we're in a post-racial society. It doesn't mean racism is eliminated. But when I talk to Malia and Sasha and I listen to their friends and I see them interact, they're better than we are—they're better than we were—on these issues.[17]

What kind of role models do we want to be for this generation? Do we want to pass down to the next generation the same structures of inequality and injustice that inspired the hip-hop generation to use the microphone as a weapon against the powers that be, or do we want the next generation to inherit a world that is changed for the better—one in which the near-perfect multi-racial democracy is more than a bad-time story? Malia and Sasha's generation sees race with eyes unclouded, but the blush of hope could very well be off the rose if they enter adult society with the structures of injustice and inequality virtually unchanged. We need to find the tipping point where the next generation can change the world, not be changed by it.

This means we need to accelerate our progress exponentially. Our society, which is enamored with comfort, convenience, easy answers and self-congratulation, must face the present with unclouded eyes. As the Black Liberation Movement has always done, we must ask in a clear voice whether we are serious about our democratic ideals, or—as we do with notions of freedom, equality, and justice—whether we are merely paying lip service to a hollow idol, one we only pay homage to in the abstract, never the concrete.[18] Our need to be safe and secure in our own homes and in our own land must not make us afraid of that which should be protecting us. The arbitrary and disproportionate use of power (physical power, political power, economic power, social power) as a means of keeping the poor, the dispossessed, and the dis- affected at arm's length from the spiritual and physical comforts of the satisfied life is what feeds upon our complacency. This compla- cency means that we hedge until we have reached a crisis, and we then claim to be powerless as we watch that crisis become a catastrophe. Engaging in the process early on, adding our voices to the movement, and changing minds mean that we are active agents in our moment of crisis. This keeps us from being passive observers of our catastrophe. Time and again we've seen the turmoil that precipitates meaningful change, and, now, in this moment, we stand poised on the threshold of a new dawn. If we are to leave a legacy for the next generation that is substantively different from the one we inherited, we must resist the magnetism of the status quo; we must stake our claim on this land and demand as loudly as is necessary the equal democracy and justice that America promises.

The task for mainstream Black leaders is monumental. Sadly, in order to effect institutional change, they must behave as if we lived in a post-racial society, while understanding full well that we don't. Their job is to serve as the vanguard for the Black radical. They must act as spies in the house of love, as it were, while the Black radical works the streets with fiery rhetoric. The radical must make noise. He must make a nuisance of himself, expecting the fire hose and the Taser from those he challenges. He must shout at the top of his lungs from the mountaintop and the rooftop, never allowing the American public to be lulled back into complacency by post-racial lullabies. Institutional change is glacially slow, ever tending toward inertia. Men like President Obama have a Sisyphean task. Over and over they push the boulder up the hill, but time and again it rolls back down. They are up against structures that will not change in one year, four years, or eight years. Their job is the work of generations; their job is to sit across from the racists and smile, to take what is possible, and to recognize when (even if only for a moment) to stop pushing and allow the boulder to roll down the hill once more.

Though our leaders must act with urgency, they must recognize that it will take several generations more before we live in anything resembling a truly post-racial society. The radical of today will become the bridge builder of tomorrow; tomorrow's bridge builder will look like a sellout to tomorrow's radical—such is the nature of these things. At the same time, there must exist an unspoken, horizontal integration of the mission: the radical must understand that the job of those who work within the system is to compromise, and those who work within the system must recognize that the job of the radical is to push, push, and push again against the boundaries of what is, seeking always for what must be. They must work separately, but toward the same mission, each understanding the role of the other. Though they may never join hands in the light of the public eye, the radical and the bridge builder are united in purpose and vision. Though they must work independently, neither should allow his role to blind him to the affinity and necessity of the other.

To be clear, I am not suggesting that we need a constant tension between conciliation and dissent. When the levee breaks (as it has recently done in Baltimore and Ferguson), conciliation is not an act of bridge building but of pacification. To quote my dear brother Eddie S. Glaude Jr., "One of the most efficient (and insidious) ways to discipline dissent is the appeal to civility."[19] This appeal to civility is undeniably seductive. Its demand for calm and a return to civilized discourse presupposes that civility and indoor voices are remotely effective or even appropriate in the circumstances. The lure of this appeal has caught a number of (mostly affluent) Black figures. On *The Daily Show*, Common exemplified this "good boy" approach: "We're not saying, 'you did us wrong!' It's more like, 'Hey, I'm extending my hand in love. Let's forget about the past as much as we can and let's move from where we are now.'"[20] Pharrell has offered a similarly conciliatory approach: "The New Black doesn't blame other races for our issues."[21] The fact that prominent Black voices are urging the Black community to blame only itself for the conditions against which it struggles daily and to forget the past (even if only partially) is completely blind and deaf to reality. The evidence is everywhere. "Black folk are dying, Doc," as my mentee Dalitso Ruwe often reminds me, and when the justified outrage that emerges in the wake of these killings spills into the streets, we play along with the media as they paint protests as senseless rage, protesters as thugs, widespread issues as isolated incidents. We ought not to be ashamed of our anger or its momentary expression. Only a recognition of our outrage as justified will force a new approach to the issue, one that deals with the systemic issues at its root, one that acknowledges that Black America's suffering is something that is not (at least not entirely) self-inflicted, one that recognizes that the violence, the poverty, and the misery can no longer be ignored.

Neither can they be apologized for: "Even if their apologies are sincere," says Gus T. Renegade, "the historic, ongoing, international context of collective white hostility toward Black people renders even the authentically ashamed white an impotent anomaly."[22] Renegade goes on to note how Jewish people have never been remotely expected to absolve the Germans for their role in the Holocaust, but that is precisely what Black America is being asked to do; after centuries of slavery, and a century of *de jure* segregation, "the Black petition for reparations is ignored and ridiculed as whining for welfare." And we allow this to happen, telling each other and ourselves that moving on is the only possible course because we have internalized the attitudes of our oppressors. The only way we will convince White America that we deserve better is for us to stop convincing ourselves that we do not.

Black lives matter—such is the latest rallying cry of the subaltern[23] at protests against police violence around the country—bespeaks the guttural groan of voiceless and generally dishonored Black souls in these United States. William Jelani Cobb puts it this way: "it's [Black Lives Matter] a statement that these forms of violence reinforce each other in a vicious cycle of human devaluation." In essence, it does exactly what Spivak called for, which was voice for the oppressed that challenges the hegemonic, the universal affirmative.[24] Admittedly the statement is not inclusive enough for those seeking refuge and unification under the aegis of an intersectional (Black women's lives matter), a feminist (women's lives matter), or a general postmodern democratic (all lives matter) discourse. A reformulation is needed, one that demands that the speaker say something of substance, something that challenges the hearer to examine his or her internalization of America's age-old racial hierarchies. In which case it may not be enough to say solely that Black lives matter, but rather to reinforce the issue that Black lives (indeed, all lives) matter equally. But that is the beauty of mass protest and democratic engagement, for we all can march and scream for the subaltern position we find ourselves in. For me as an overweight man, about Eric Garner's weight and age, watching his death looped on CNN was, in fact, my clarion call: "I can't breathe," he said, "I can't breathe." I lost my breath watching it. The chorus of Black Lives Matter is complicated by the dissonance of "f*** your breath," consequently resulting in the deafness of multiracial democratic energies; from fat lives, the underemployed lives, to F*** the breath of gay lives, F*** the breath of women's lives, but most specifically and far too concurrently, F*** the breath of Black (mostly male) lives. Even a cursory examination of race in America makes it quite clear that we have not come to this most basic of democratic realizations as a country. To paraphrase Cornel West, the handling of race is the litmus test for mature democracies.[25] Put to this test, America has proved itself over and over again to be but a bawling infant. It is time that we recognize we are much, much too old for the pacifier of false progress. It is time for us to use our words, to have a meaningful and, yes, at times angry conversation about how we are to begin to address racial inequality and injustice in this country.

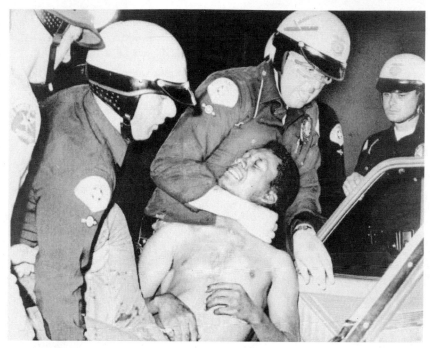

A black body choked-out by the hands of law enforcement in Watts, California, 1965. https://commons.wikimedia.org/wiki/File:Wattsriots-policearrest-loc.jpg. Credit: New York World Telegram, 12 August 1965; Wikimedia Commons.

Daily News *and* New York Post *covers depicting the choking of Eric Garner and the acquittal of the police officer involved. https://flic.kr/p/q1Z6QF. Credit: Mike Mozart, 5 December 2014.*

Notes

1   The last words of Eric Garner, the Staten Island, New York, man killed by an illegal chokehold administered by an NYPD officer who accused him of selling loose cigarettes (no cigarettes were found on his person).

2   The invidious words of Tulsa, Oklahoma, police officer Joseph Byars, spoken to a dying Eric Harris, who was complaining about not being able to breathe.

3   West, Democracy Matters 14.

4   Mark Piepmeier, the Special Prosecutor assigned to the Grand Jury's presentation of the case against Williams, responded to questions about Williams's conduct by noting that officers had recently been trained by their Ohio state police officers' academy "to be aggressive" when responding to active shooters.

5   Edward Conlon, "The Myth of the Central Park Five," The Daily Beast 19 October 2014, http://www.thedailybeast.com/articles/2014/10/19/decoding-the-crime-of-the-century-the-real-story-of-the-central-park-five.html.

6   The quotation is from the end of historian Orlando Patterson's definition of slavery, where he describes the system as "the permanent, violent domination of natally alienated and *generally dishonored persons*" (13; my emphasis).

7   I would identify three separate phases. Phase one (1857–1954), during which the struggle for equal protection under the law became recognizable as a movement, included individual African Americans but also a number of fledgling African-American organizations. During phase two (1955–59), efforts to desegregate public transportation and education began. Added to these efforts were attempts to guarantee voting rights for African Americans. Black activists openly organized and conducted mass confrontations that directly challenged the white power structure. Phase three (1960–69) saw the rise of the SNCC (Student Nonviolent Coordinating Committee), which sought to achieve its ends through acts of civil disobedience. At the same time, the third phase also saw a nascent Black Power Movement, which was decidedly less peaceful. Its members used militant, sometimes violent actions that emphasized racial pride and the creation of separate Black political and cultural institutions.

8   From Lawrence 4. See also West, "Race Matters," YouTube, https://www.youtube.com/watch?v=cRZcfEToN-A, arguing that race is a taboo subject in America. And see generally Crenshaw, who discusses how the taboo surrounding race affects legal education.

9   Pete Wiliams, "Gratz v. Michigan: Undergraduate Affirmative Action Program Struck Down," NBC News, 9 June 2003, http://www.nbcnews.com/id/3071007/t/gratz-v-michigan/#.VTVDbFwpS68.

10 Supreme Court of the United States, *Schuette v. COALITION TO DEFEND AFFIRMATIVE*, 134 S. Ct. 1623, 572 U.S., 188 L. Ed. 2d 613 (2014).

11 See Goffman.

12 See http://www.bing.com/videos/search?q=youtube.com+don+lemon+ sagging+pants+and+littering&FORM=HDRSC3#view=detail&mid= A491AC427BB0DF392459A491AC427BB0DF392459. See also Christina Coleman, "Sagging Pants and Littering Contribute to Downfall of Black Communities? Why CNN's Don Lemon Is Wrong," Global Grind, 29 July 2013, http://globalgrind.com/2013/07/29/cnns-don-lemon-reasons-the-black-community-is-failing-video/.

13 Joe Scarborough, "Morial: OU President Took a Strong Stand," *Morning Joe*, MSNBC, 11 March 2015, http://www.msnbc.com/morning-joe/watch/ morial--ou-president-took-a-strong-stand-411553347638.

14 Starbucks Newsroom, "What 'Race Together' Means for Starbucks Partners and Customers," 16 March 2015, http://news.starbucks.com/news/ what-race-together-means-for-starbucks-partners-and-customers.

15 Jay Smooth, "How to Tell People They Sound Racist," Ill Doctrine, 21 July 2008, http://www.illdoctrine.com/2008/07/how_to_tell_people_they_sound.html.

16 During the 1960s and 1970s, the term *cracker* was used pejoratively by some who sought to respond to white oppression. The term, however, has eighteenth-century Anglo roots and refers to poor whites of Maryland, Virginia (primarily), and even as far as Florida and Georgia. Over the course of two centuries it has loosely been used to represent a person of low class or even a criminal.

17 "Obama Trayvon Martin Speech Transcript: President Comments on George Zimmerman Verdict," The Huffington Post, 19 July 2013, http:// www.huffingtonpost.com/2013/07/19/obama-trayvon-martin-speech-transcript_n_3624884.html.

18 West, "Race Matters."

19 Eddie S. Glaude Jr., "One of the most efficient (and insidious) ways to discipline dissent is the appeal to civility," 27 April 2015, 8:23 a.m., tweet.

20 See Brennan Williams, "Common Says Showing Love to White People Is the Cure to Racism," The Huffington Post, 24 March 2015, http:// www.huffingtonpost.com/2015/03/18/common-white-people-cure-to-racism_n_6895864.html.

21 Stereo Williams, "Common, Pharrell, and 'The New Black': An Ignorant Mentality That Undermines the Black Experience," The Daily Beast 19 March 2015, http:// www.thedailybeast.com/articles/2015/03/19/common-pharrell-and-the-new-black-an-ignorant-mentality-that-undermines-the-black-experience.html.

22 Gus T. Renegade, "Are Black People Too Eager to Forgive Racist Behaviors?" Atlanta Blackstar 6 May 2015, http://atlantablackstar.com/2015/05/06/are-black-people-too-eager-to-forgive-racist-behaviors.

23 The use of the term "subaltern" comes from Gayatri Spivak's essay "Can the Subaltern Speak?", which is a foundational piece of work in postcolonial and postmodern studies. She coins the use of subaltern from her work on Antonio Gramsci's Marxist critique of cultural hegemony.

24 In Formal Logic terms, using the Traditional Square of Opposition that helps us determine inferences that can be made from propositions, the subaltern position is known as the I proposition, also known as the particular affirmative (PA) and is directly under the A proposition, or the universal affirmative (UA). The I then is a subalternate of the A and thus it is assumed that all characteristics of the (PA) are subsumed under the (UA). But in power relationships, of which Spivak speaks clearly within a postcolonial discourse, the universal is oppressive and hegemonic and restricts the voice and energies of the particular.

25 In the preface to the 2001 edition of Cornel West's book *Race Matters*, he prophetically exclaims, "The fundamental litmus test for American democracy—its economy, government, criminal justice system, education, mass media, and culture—remains: how broad and intense are the arbitrary powers used and deployed against black people. In this sense, the problem of the twenty-first century remains the problem of the color line" (vii).

Chapter Two

OBAMA AND THE MYTH OF A POST-RACIAL AMERICA

ON NOVEMBER 4, 2008, BARACK OBAMA WAS ELECTED THE 44TH President of the United States, becoming the first person of color elected to the highest office in the land. For a nation possessed of a history littered with the enslavement and disenfranchisement of peoples of color, electing a man of color to the White House marked a watershed moment. America, as it did during those chest-bolstering moments in its history such as Reconstruction and the New Deal, took massive strides toward being a more inclusive society. The massive wave of optimism that accompanied Obama's election was premised on the belief that something had finally changed, that America had rounded a corner and was, at long last, putting its checkered racial past to bed. The moment was felt to hold national (even global) significance: this was the long-awaited rebirth of America as a post-racial society.[1]

In no time, though, the bloom was off the rose. The early attempt during Obama's presidency to paint his victory as both symbolic and transformative quickly gave way to partisan bickering, with Obama's adversaries and allies quickly ranging themselves into separate camps. As quickly as it had arrived, the optimism faded. The realities of race in the United States proved far too complex to be swept away by a political election (or even two of them). The President's individual success is undoubtedly symbolic of a massive shift in social values in the last half-century, but the political and social response to that election has made it clearer than many would like to admit that a post-racial America is still a distant prospect. Considering the events of the last few years, seeing even that faint glimmer of hope on the horizon takes the gaze of a naïve optimist. The reality is that systemic racism is no less prevalent than it was before Obama's election. Meaningful though Obama's election may have been, it was not magical.

Still, some held that it was so, and these were not the same as those who wept tears of joy during Obama's inauguration. Make no mistake, a great many Americans were—and evidently still are—eager to see race, undoubtedly America's most divisive issue, finally placed on the back burner. They hoped that the election of a Black president could have something of an upside in that it could serve to end, or at least disrupt, the ongoing conversation about systemic racism in the United States. Unilaterally, without reparations or an Oprah intervention, a Black president seemed, as if by magic, to allow America collectively to say, *we truly are the land of equal opportunity*; a Black man in the White House meant that the race card could be torn up and discarded once and for all. This assumed that Obama's successful election(s) represented a culmination in the struggle for equality, one that would ultimately result in a representative in the halls of power who would act on behalf of Black America. In reality, it was a political victory that changed things as much as any other—negligibly. Despite all the feel-good social ceremony and commentary that followed Obama's election, the President's blackness has been little more than a distraction from the ongoing systemic issues surrounding our government's failure to respond in remotely effective ways to the still-rising social and economic inequalities that disproportionately affect people of color.

Where Did (President) Barack H. Obama come from?

Before 2004, it was widely believed, among people of all races, that the prospect of electing a Black man as president of the United States was not very good. To many, it even seemed impossible. Then came "the speech." At the 2004 Democratic Convention, a little-known African-American state senator from Illinois, who was in the midst of a campaign to become the junior U.S. Senator from that state—a man with the unusual name of Barack Obama—gave a speech that not only electrified the crowd; here before them was a viable candidate, a strong Black man, a powerful speaker, a unifier who seemed—already as he stood at that podium—presidential.[2]

The speech itself featured some of the most inclusive language in the history of convention speeches. The speech had everyone talking for weeks after, especially this section, in which he discussed the idea of inclusion:

> Now even as we speak, there are those who are preparing to divide us, the spin masters and negative ad peddlers who embrace the politics of anything goes. Well, I say to them tonight, there's not a liberal America and a conservative America; there's the United States of America. There's not a Black America and White America and Latino America and Asian America; there's the United States of America. The pundits, the pundits like to slice and dice our country into red states and blue states: red states for Republicans, blue states for Democrats. But I've got news for them, too. We worship an awesome God in the blue states, and we don't like federal agents poking around our libraries in the red states. We coach little league in the blue states and, yes, we've got some gay friends in the red states. There are patriots who opposed the war in Iraq, and there are patriots who supported the war in Iraq. We are one people, all of us pledging allegiance to the stars and stripes, all of us defending the United States of America.[3]

That message was extremely positive and resonated with a great number of people. He easily won the Senate race in 2004, in part because of the positive message that scholar Bonilla-Silva says "was a moment of real leadership ... people saw a president ... out of the ashes he rose as the candidate," but also because his ultimate opponent in the race was last minute carpetbagger Republican replacement, Alan Keyes.[4] Keyes was widely seen as a little on the crazy side, cynically chosen by the GOP leadership because he, too, was African American and would set the stage for an ad hominem attack without the charge of racism.[5]

Obama was considered a bright spot in the Senate, and he began making waves almost immediately. His name was bandied about constantly by some Democrats as a possible presidential candidate,[6] although most saw him as a "candidate of the future." In the short term, Hillary Clinton was largely seen as a shoo-in for the Democratic nomination in 2008, and that four to eight years of seasoning would be needed before he would be "ready to run." Therefore, it surprised many people when he announced his candidacy for president on May 2, 2007.[7] At first, most considered it a move designed simply to shake up the race that was looking to be rather bland. The move was likened to Ronald Reagan's 1976 presidential run, in that it was believed that Obama merely sought to challenge the party's status quo for a while, and that the more serious run would come in 2012 or 2016.

Unfortunately for the Clinton campaign, however, two things happened. First, Clinton had seriously underestimated the undercurrent against her, and how many Democrats at least wanted to see her challenged seriously. But, more importantly, Obama's strongly inclusive populist campaign caught on around the country, especially in the primary states. He was collecting small donations at a record pace, and his message was catching on as a viable alternative to politics as usual. The agenda he was promoting was effective because it was something that everyone could get behind. His overall theme was "Hope and Change," which was enormously upbeat—far more so than American politics had seen in quite some time. His campaign's specific proposals were a refreshing change from what the country was experiencing under the Bush administration, and people took to them, even though he never mentioned the Bush administration while talking about them. Though his initial platform did not include anything like the *Patient Protection and Affordable Care Act*—that came later—he did propose a National Health Coverage exchange early on, and recommended creating a comprehensive database of electronic health records. He also suggested requiring that all children be covered.[8]

His campaign was overwhelmingly positive, as was the result. A lot of things were beginning to happen during the process of running for the presidency in 2008, not the least of which was the implosion of the economy. In 2008, the economy lost more than $10.2 trillion in household wealth by the time of the election.[9] While many give those circumstances credit for Obama's victory, his campaign was winning long before then, because what he wanted to do appealed to most people, and they trusted him to carry it all out to the best of his ability. They trusted him more than they trusted Hillary Clinton, and far more than they trusted war hero and former Vietnam prisoner of war John McCain: Obama seemed competent and even-handed, while the more experienced McCain seemed more prone to anger and panic and came off as much less competent.

At the same time, the Republican Party was already demonstrating its strategy for countering the upstart senator, mostly through personal attacks thinly disguised as questions about his qualifications. While they were disguised to look like the same sort of attacks as had been perpetrated by the "Swift Boat" attacks on John Kerry just four years earlier, in reality they were far more race-based than the attacks on Kerry.

When Republicans realized that Obama was not only a viable candidate but an electable one as well, they took immediate aim at the broad side of the barn. Obama's blackness, and the threat it posed to the established white power structure, became the target of critiques on media outlets. Things that would be considered out of bounds for white candidates were fair game as soon as the Democrats fielded a Black candidate. Take, for instance, the discussion that sprang up surrounding Obama's church, Southside Chicago's Trinity United Church of Christ. Given the way in which conservatives focused on the church's pastor, the Reverend Jeremiah Wright,[10] it would be quite easy to assume that it was not Obama but Wright that was running for office. The media whipped itself into a frenzy, pitting parishioners against each other and turning the church into a circus of media attention.[11] Conservative pundits found in Wright a veritable goldmine, a fiery preacher who had delivered from the pulpit a number of sermons that, in no uncertain terms, highlighted America's bloody-handed hypocrisy and lambasted the country for decades of wrong-headed policies that had left deep wounds in so many of the families of his Black parishioners.[12] Pundits made a show of biting their fingernails and sweating bullets, wondering what would happen to the America they loved if one who shared Wright's views were to hold the highest office in the land. Two sermons in particular were played (often on a loop), while talking heads tried to outdo each other with their doomsday predictions of an Obama presidency. The first was delivered the Sunday following the World Trade Center attacks:

> We bombed Hiroshima, we bombed Nagasaki, and we nuked far more than the thousands in New York and the Pentagon and we never batted an eye. ... We have supported state terrorism against the Palestinians and South Africa and now we are indignant? Because the stuff we have done overseas is brought back into our own front yard. America's chickens are coming home, to roost. Violence begets violence. Hatred begets hatred, and terrorism begets terrorism.[13]

The second contained a sound bite that media outlets, no matter what their affiliation, could not resist:

> The government gives [Black Americans] the drugs, builds bigger prisons, passes a three-strike law, and then wants us to sing "God Bless America." No, no, no. Not "God Bless America"; God Damn America! ... God Damn America for treating her citizens as less than human. God Damn America as long as she keeps trying to act like she is God and she is supreme! The United States government has failed the vast majority of her citizens of African descent.[14]

Statements like these (but these in particular) were scrutinized, as though within them was the key to unlocking Obama's vision for America's future. Obama had indeed attended Wright's church off and on for 20 years; he was married there, and his daughters were baptized in its font.[15]

But in the midst of his campaign for the Democratic nomination, Obama disowned Wright and his views, trying to place as much distance between himself and the firebrand as possible. Wright had made a number of media appearances, during which he made remarks that were considered anti-Semitic and even repeated the oft-cited claim that the United States government had manufactured the AIDS virus as a weapon to use against Black America.[16] Obama said that the Reverend's comments were "appalling" and made it clear that, though he had suggested one month earlier that the church and its Reverend still played an important role in his spiritual life, Wright's comments had effectively severed any remaining bond between the two men. As historian William Jelani Cobb has said, "the issue between Wright and Obama was not two different worldviews—it was two different worlds. Obama knew something about race that neither Wright nor virtually anyone else knew in 2007, that the country was prepared to elect an African-American to the highest of the Land.... Obama stated that Wright's error was in holding on to a view of the country that was aged and expired. The world has changed.... He had to be right because otherwise he could not be the leading contender for the Democratic presidential nomination" (32). Here we have it: the familial breakup of two men, Rev. Wright staying at home doing the ministerial work of his Father, and Obama, the prodigal son, venturing off to pursue his Melvillian whale of national politics in an attempt to hold the greatest seat in the world—the presidency of the free world. For the callings of both these men, both standing their ground against each other, while beholding their truth among their constituencies, Shakespeare's line rang true—"Uneasy lies the head that wears a crown."[17]

The Wright controversy continued to dog Obama well into his presidency. Wright had claimed that Obama's distancing of himself from his former preacher was a transparent attempt to whitewash his past, and although Obama repudiated this notion, conservative commentators have continued to make hay with it well into Obama's second term. When it surfaced that House Majority Whip Steve Scalise (R-LA) had spoken at an event hosted by a notorious white supremacist, former House speaker Newt Gingrich attempted to excuse Scalise by suggesting that Obama was guilty of an identical infraction: "The fact is," he said, "you have a president who for years went to a church whose pastor said stunningly hateful things about Americans. ... And we all gave him a pass."[18] This free pass apparently didn't extend to Gingrich—or to any of the other pundits (Limbaugh, Beck, et al.) who seem still to struggle to utter Obama's name without mentioning his former pastor.

While some scrutiny of Obama's past associates might have been merited, there was a clear double standard in how this scrutiny was applied by the media. Take, for instance, his opponent in the election, John McCain. The coverage of Obama and his opponent was wildly asymmetrical. While there was some talk about McCain's religiosity, the fact that he was a churchgoer seemed to be as deep as the media felt scrutiny needed to go. McCain had ties with two controversial pastors, John Hagee and Rod Parsley, both of whom he distanced himself from when their own controversial sermons came to light: Hagee had suggested that Hitler was sent by God to help Jews reach the promised land, and Parsley's critiques of Islam had frequently crossed the line into outright bigotry.[19] Like Obama, McCain sternly and publicly repudiated those who had recently been his support-ers, but unlike the media's scrutiny of Obama, there were no follow-up questions for the senator from Arizona, no implications that the views of the two men that McCain publicly distanced himself from were one and the same with his own.

The same formula was applied when the media turned their atten-tion to Obama's ancestry. The birther movement, which had its roots in attempts by Hillary Clinton's supporters during the waning days of her campaign to cast doubts on Obama's eligibility for office, led to a presidential candidate who was all but forced to release his birth cer-tificate to the public in order to quell the rumors (which, of course, it didn't). Much of the nonsense that followed in the wake of this debate (including a number of lawsuits, the last of which was thrown out on March 31, 2015[20]) was an attempt on the part of the right-wing fringe to paint the President as someone who was as un-American in deed as he was in birth. To all intents and purposes, this attempt was entirely successful. In 2011, a CNN poll found that a quarter of Americans had doubts about Obama's place of birth; among GOP primary voters, that number was more than double.[21]

Once again, the asymmetry of media coverage made the game utterly transparent. McCain was born to a naval officer and his wife in the Panama Canal Zone, which was then under U.S. control,[22] but it was clear that McCain was as American as they come—though he didn't prove as electable as his opponent. Like the coverage/silence surrounding each of the men's controversial preachers, a clear dou-ble standard was in place. The man who so little resembled the men whose portraits line the walls of the White House was the one who was painted as an outsider, whose love of country was called into doubt, whose very eligibility for the office was a matter of seemingly legitimate public debate.

From the moment that Obama became a household name in this country, the Republican Party began blowing its dog whistles. Whether it was the accusation, leveled by Republican running mate Sarah Palin, that Obama had spent his youth "pallin' around with terrorists," an accusation premised on the most tentative of connections to William Ayers,[23] or the unfounded claims that Obama has allowed the Muslim Brotherhood to infiltrate his administration as part of a secret plot to transform the United States into a Islamic theocracy,[24] the underlying message remains the same: Obama may be the President, but he is not *our* President. Days before his election, his optimistic (too optimistic, perhaps) suggestion that progressive voters were days away from "fundamentally transforming the United States of America," which would have been dismissed as political rhetoric were the speaker not, in his very personhood, seen as a threat to American (i.e., white) values, was as terrifying to those on the right as a third Bush term would have been to those on the left. What they failed to understand was that the country desperately needed a reform, a change in vision and direction. Obama promised to give this country what it needed, but what it really needs is a long hard look at itself in the mirror, and that is something that conservative patriotism won't allow. Obama's suggestion that we could be better than we were was twisted into a savage hatred of all things American. Republican commitment to this image of Obama as a usurper, a tyrant, and a Black radical made any cooperation with him anathema. It made effective governance (which is built upon compromise) look—at least to the committed ideologues—like treason.

How Low Can You Go?

Partisan snipes and gripes are nothing new in American politics. Especially during presidential campaigns, Democrats and Republicans alike have long seen the efficacy in mud-slinging—after all, a negative campaign focusing on one's opponent's perceived or actual shortcomings (the veracity of information in these ads being, at best, an afterthought) is as effective or even more effective than a campaign with a tight focus on the qualities that make this candidate or that one more qualified for the job. As Shapiro notes, when the campaign ends, though, this animosity toward political rivals tends to dissipate somewhat—the hearty roil of campaign attacks settling down to the light simmer of partisan politics as usual.

After Obama's first general election, however, Republican attacks continued without even a momentary lull. Voters had been clear: Obama, if not the perfect candidate, was more likable and electable than any of the candidates that the Republicans could field. For many Americans, Obama represented the promise of anti-establishment thinking and politics, and during his first 100 days in office, the tangible whiff of optimism surrounding the new president lingered in the air. Obama enjoyed approval ratings as high as 69 per cent in these heady days,[25] but already conservative media outlets had begun to characterize him as an America-hating socialist dictator. On Fox News alone, probably the best barometer for middle-of-the-road conservative sentiment, the first 100 days of White House coverage included uncountable references to Obama's socialist agenda, his fascist (even jihadist) approach to power, and his hatred of all things American; contributors and anchors implicitly or explicitly compared him to dictators like Josef Stalin ("minus the bloodshed"), appeasers like Neville Chamberlain, and even the Manchurian Candidate.[26] What's more, a number of on-air personalities actively promoted Tea Party protests around the country—promotion that almost certainly contributed to the turnout at the events, which they then covered as though they were entirely spontaneous demonstrations of America's seething anger with Obama's socialist financial policies.[27] At least for the right-wing pundits, Obama's honeymoon was over before the groom had even lifted the veil.

As if this coverage were in any way an adequate representation of widespread American sentiment concerning the President's performance—and not the weeping and moaning of a political class that suddenly found itself on the sidelines—Republican politicians pandered to the Fox News demographic, becoming with each passing day more vitriolic in their condemnation of Obama, his socialist policies, and his erosion of the foundation of America. Very early on, these critiques began to take on a racist tone, and though the left could be counted upon to cry foul at almost anything said by right-wing media outlets, the right seemed completely uninterested in correcting racist contributors or even anchors; in fact, pundits were handed something of a gift with the election of a Black president. Valid critiques of racist overtones or undertones in conservative discussions of race were shrugged off thanks to America's chimerical transcendence of race represented by a Black face in the White House. Subtly or blatantly racist critiques of Obama or those who voted for him (apparently one and the same with those who were characterized as being dependent on state benefits) were tacitly condoned, and any backlash was dismissed with a wave of the hand as race baiting or, even more frequently, as whining or refusal to accept hard truths about the *real* causes of poverty and socioeconomic inequality in the United States—usually a lack of can-do spirit or work ethic.[28] Bill O'Reilly, after a cursory examination of the economic inequality along racial lines, found its source in a vaguely defined concept of "culture." To shore up his point, he played a recording of Ben Stein (whose short 15 minutes of fame somehow made him an authority on race relations in America) saying that "the real problem with race in America is a very beaten down, static, self-defeating Black underclass."[29]

There was also the legend of the "Obama Phone," which was a meme that started with a YouTube Video of a Black woman who said to a reporter, "Keep Obama in president, you know! He gave us a phone, he's gonna do more."[30] The insinuation of the meme was that, somehow, Obama was giving poor Blacks on welfare free phones to go with their welfare checks. As usual, this was untrue. It refers to a program to bring telephone service to poor people that was developed in the 1980s, expanded in 1996, and expanded again to include cellphones in 2008, before Obama was elected president. But it fed the notion that Obama was giving away "free stuff," paid for almost exclusively by right-wing taxpayers, apparently. This meme became prevalent when he announced his presidential candidacy, and it continues seven years after his first inauguration. After his 2015 State of the Union speech, during which he recommended a program whereby college students could get two years of community college by working for it, several media outlets repeated it again.[31] As an African American, the President is implicated through these out-and-out attacks on Black America. He is either caricatured or described outright as an enabler of this Black underclass or even occasionally—with references to his love of basketball, his multi-part handshakes, or his on-again-off-again use of Black speech patterns[32]—as somehow a covert member of it.

How conservatives understood the conversation about Obama's race, begun during the campaign and intensified after the President's election, became quite clear when demonstrators at Tea Party events proudly displayed caricatures of Obama as a monkey, a lawn jockey, or an African witch doctor complete with a bone through his nose. Signs brazenly waved aloft featured racist slogans like "Hope for the Rope," and bumper stickers warned America not to "Re-Nig in 2012."[33] It's quite easy to suggest (and it has been frequently suggested) that these instances of blatant racism are simply the work of a radical and racist fringe of the conservative movement, but they are entirely consistent with conservative critiques of Obama's policies. Unashamed racists are merely making explicit what pundits and politicians conceal beneath the thinnest of veils. For instance, early in Obama's presidency, Glenn Beck blew the following outlandish dog whistle: "Barack Obama is setting up universal healthcare, universal college, green jobs as stealth reparations."[34] Perennial GOP presidential nominee candidate Newt Gingrich joined the fray when he referred to Obama as "the most successful Food Stamp president in our history,"[35] and again when he asked, in apparent earnestness, "What if [Obama] is so outside our comprehension that only if you understand Kenyan, anticolonial behavior can you begin to piece together his actions?"[36] The racial tropes are impossible to miss here, and conservative Obama talking points are positively riddled with them.

If it were only pundits and the conservative base who were making outlandish claims about Obama's intentions, origins, and loyalties, it might be possible to claim that Republican lawmakers have remained above the mud slingers and those who follow them, but such is not the case. The Tea Party movement brought to power a wave of elected officials who have pulled Republican politics toward what was once regarded as the far-right fringe.

With a seemingly unending series of gaffes, Tea Party Republicans have let the veil of political correctness fall away, either for a moment or in some cases completely. Racist epithets and caricatures that have been widely recognized as wildly inappropriate for half a century or more have been brought wholesale out of racist backwoods and

Bumper sticker warned America not to re-elect a Nigger to the White House in 2012

into state capitols, and even to the Hill itself. I cite just two illustrative examples. Marilyn Davenport, an elected official in Orange County with Tea Party roots, sent an email to constituents depicting Obama as a chimpanzee, which, in case the image didn't make her point clearly enough, she tagged with the following: "Now you know why—no birth certificate!"[37] A few months later, another official from a district with deep Tea Party roots, Rep. Doug Lamborn (R-CO), said, in reference to the President, "I don't even want to be associated with him. It's like touching a, a tar baby and you get it ... you know, you're stuck and you're part of the problem and you can't get away."[38] Neither of the politicians has offered a *mea culpa*, perhaps because racist caricatures and language have become something of a fixture on the far right of the political spectrum, and, as that far right enters the mainstream (which it has), it feels that transposing racist caricature and critique from the fringe of our political discourse into the mainstream is, if not appropriate, then at least excusable.[39]

The result of all this is a complete lack of respect on the part of Republicans, not only for the President himself, but also for his office. During a speech before Congress in September 2009, Rep. Joe Wilson (R-SC) shouted "You lie!" in the midst of the President's speech when Obama claimed that undocumented immigrants would not receive free health care under the *Affordable Care Act*.[40] While there has been plenty of eye rolling and snickering into sleeves during presidential addresses in the past, for a member of the House to heckle the President during a speech was unprecedented.

Though the disrespect Wilson showed to the office was widely condemned by all but the most rabid Obama haters, Obama's second term has seen Republicans (sometimes *en masse*) crawl under the low bar set by Wilson in 2009. The message is the same, whether it is Republicans' frequent invocation of words like "tyrant" and "dictator," Speaker Boehner taking the unprecedented step of inviting the leader of a foreign nation, Benjamin Netanyahu of Israel, to help make the case against a sitting president's acts of diplomacy, or Sen. Tom Cotton (R-AR) penning a letter to the Supreme Leader of Iran reminding him that once the President leaves office all bets are off (undermining ongoing and fragile nuclear negotiations), a letter that was then signed by an astounding 47 Republicans. What is the message? Obama is not only a bad president; he is an illegitimate one, a usurper who ill deserves his position or the dignity it affords him. This position is, however, a poor reflection of reality. Obama is a centrist Democrat. His policies are no more pulling this country into socialist territory than Bush's policies made America a fascist state. This unprecedented disrespect—and, as I will discuss in the next section, Republican obstruction and disrespect *are* unprecedented—has little to do with the President as a politician. The issue that Republicans have with Barack Obama (and have always had with him) is the fact that he dares to simultaneously be President and a Black man.

Not Politics as Usual

Casual political observers tend to shrug off much of the anti-Obama furor as politics as usual. It's only natural, they say, for those who sit on the side opposite the governing party to do everything in their power to discredit their opponents, to cast aspersions on their abilities, motivations, and allegiances, with a bit of racist side-eye thrown in for good measure when the politician belongs to a visible minority. In a political age that has come to place more emphasis on ideological adherence and re-election than on actual governance, dogged refusal to compromise with the enemy's factions seems to endear officials to their constituents; in deeply conservative districts, refusal to govern can be dressed up to look like a legitimate political strategy. Red states aren't sending politicians to Washington; they're sending combatants loaded for bear, who have run on promises of disrupting the establishment, not with fresh ideas, but with recalcitrance and truculence.[41]

In the Obama Age, this tactic has blossomed like never before, making hatred and vocal condemnation of the president a veritable mainstay of Republican strategy. In 2013, the Editorial Board of *The New York Times* wrote a column critiquing House Republicans for ignoring the mission that they have been given by the majority of the electorate: "the House," they wrote, "has retreated from the national mainstream into a cave of indifference and ignorance,"[42] and it does not appear they have stepped into the light since then. If anything, they've only retreated farther into their caves, refusing to recognize just how important it is for them to do something—anything—besides gum up the Washington machine. In a Gallup poll from the same year as the *Times* editorial, almost three-quarters of polled Americans expected some sort of compromise from those they had sent to Washington. Only 25 per cent of them said that adhering to one's values should outweigh cooperation (this number was a perhaps-unsurprising 40 per cent among Tea Party supporters).[43] House Republicans have, to all intents and purposes, listened only to those who shout loudest and most often, refusing precisely the kind of bipartisan compromise that basic governing (and many of their constituents, to boot) demands. They've used the filibuster a record number of times; scuttled nominees and delayed votes, in some cases for years on end; used the debt ceiling as a weapon and then proceeded to blame those they used it against for forcing their hand. Examined individually, the examples of Republican obstruction during Obama's tenure could fill volumes. While a single action is enough on its own to indict Republicans for sabotaging our government, in aggregate the evidence is damning.[44]

Those who believe that Republican obstruction is merely politics as usual tend to make their point with reference to either the last Democratic president or the last Republican one. Whether it was the rabid Bush hatred displayed during that President's two terms or the Republican smear campaigns waged during the Clinton years, the tone of political discourse has always, they say, been vitriolic, with Obama being no exception to this rule. But this neglects not only the record numbers of filibusters but also the new depths to which our political discourse has sunk since Obama took office. Not since the Cold War has an inflexible ideology so poisoned the political debate, and, at least in living memory, no sitting president has been so vilified (not Bush, not Clinton, not even Nixon has been subject to criticism in the tone of that which has been leveled at Obama). It is sheer deafness to hear nothing new in this.

Democrats and liberal media figures, of course, frequently attacked the character of George W. Bush and his associates during the Bush years—the almost comically Machiavellian vice-president Dick Cheney being frequently compared, in jest and in earnest, to Satan himself. Some of this criticism, particularly from those firmly in the anti-war camp, was undeniably rabid and ideologically cemented. "The anti-war faction," said the late Christopher Hitchens, "has subordinated everything to its hatred of Bush."[45] He was referring to one member of the anti-war camp in particular: a former attorney general of the United States, Ramsey Clark, who had taken it upon himself to defend the "demonized" Iraqi despot Saddam Hussein. The polarization of the debate and the vilification of the President and his advisors virtually assured that left-wing characterizations of hawks were overblown and uncharitable, while portraits of doves (or even occasionally overthrown dictators) might as well have used stained glass as a medium. For those on the right, this formula was reversed.[46]

Undeniably, political critique during Bush's presidency was more emotional than it was rational. Like Obama (though for different reasons), "Dubya" was compared to fascist dictators and there were suggestions that he was trying to erect some kind of world government of Orwellian proportions. Liberal commentators seemed to be in a race to outdo each other in how dark a portrait of the President they could paint: he was in bed with the terrorists (or at the very least those who financed them); he was a war profiteer (big-oil and security contractors apparently guiding his hand in the lead-up to war); he was somehow schemer and dupe at once, and he was frequently described as the worst president America had ever had.

Before Bush, the Republicans had whetted the rage machine with savage and unrelenting attacks on Bill Clinton. On his *Old Time Gospel Hour*, Rev. Jerry Falwell hawked tens of thousands of copies of *The Clinton Chronicles*, a documentary that claimed to prove that the Clintons were the shadowy figures behind a number of murders; when Vincent Foster, friend and aide to Bill Clinton, committed suicide in 1993, Pat Robertson, Rush Limbaugh, and columnists for the *Wall Street Journal* and the *New York Post* all attempted to paint Foster as the victim of a Clinton-led conspiracy; in *High Crimes and Misdemeanors: The Case Against Bill Clinton*, Ann Coulter went so far as to suggest that the debate should not be whether to impeach or to not impeach but, rather, "whether to impeach or assassinate."[47]

If politics teaches us anything, it's that what is good for the goose is good for the gander. An escalation of tactics on one side rarely leads to a détente; rather, when the shoe is on the other foot, the accused becomes the accuser. During Obama's inauguration, the outgoing president was met with a loud chorus of boos from the crowd. These boos represented the tail end of eight years of Bush hatred; eight years earlier, protesters had pelted the newly elected president's limousine with an egg and a tennis ball during his inauguration parade.[48] After enduring eight long years of liberal slings and arrows, is it any surprise that Republicans and the media outlets that endorse them were quick to move from defense to offense?

Obama was, therefore, an almost immediate lightning rod for conservative invective. What was a surprise, though, was the depths to which conservatives quickly sank in their attempts to make this new Democratic president as deeply unpopular as the Republican one he had just replaced. As luck would have it, Obama inherited an economy that was hemorrhaging jobs at nearly record levels. Thanks to stimulus packages made necessary by his predecessor's lax approach to financial regulation, Republicans found it easy to paint a picture of a president who had opened the public purse to all comers. His early advancement of a number of liberal causes (universal health care and equal pay for women in the workforce being notable examples) allowed conservatives to suggest that the country had been tipped so far to the left that the entire nation was in danger of sliding into the Pacific Ocean. Consider the fact that, at the time President Obama took office, the country was in the midst of the worst and sharpest economic downturn since the Great Depression, and there was a very real fear that it was headed for a deep economic depression. While Obama was taking measures to shore up the economy, Republicans in Congress were opposing him at every turn. The stimulus package received zero Republican votes in Congress, and Dodd-Frank, the *Wall Street Reform and Consumer Protection Act*, which was designed to eliminate the problems that had led to this severe downturn, also received no support from Republicans. In fact, the 111th Congress saw the minority Republicans set a record for filibusters, effectively shutting down the Democratic majority.[49]

Early on, Republicans alighted upon what could, were it not so childishly simple, almost be called a political strategy. In October 2010, Senate Minority Leader Mitch McConnell made it clear what the Republican mission in Washington was, saying, "The single most important thing we want to achieve is for President Obama to be a one-term president."[50] Light on remotely appealing ideas, the GOP seemed already to have grasped that they could not win another general election unless they could take some or all of the bloom off the rose. All of their efforts focused on one thing: discrediting the President (discrediting his policies was, for the most part, an afterthought).[51] It was his person (and all that included), his audacious vision for a more inclusive and equal America, and his symbolic stature that were the early targets for conservative pundits and politicians.

This was the only option for a White House that refused to give Republicans any grist for the rage mill. While Clinton gave Republicans Whitewater and Lewinsky and Bush gave Democrats the lead-up to the Iraq War and all its subterfuge and misdirection, Obama's presidency has, from the outset, been largely scandal-free. The IRS targeting of conservative groups certainly raised a few eyebrows and inspired a few Taxed Enough Already placards, but, try as they might, conservative commentators could not place a smoking gun of any kind in Obama's hand, and, since it was the President himself, not his administration, that was the target, Republican attempts to manufacture a scandal have been almost entirely ineffective. Not that they have not tried. The 2012 Benghazi attack, like the IRS scandal, could not be connected in any tangible way to the President, but conservative media outlets have doggedly refused to give up the bone, burying it in shallow ground and placing a marker over it designating it for future use. Having gnawed it down to a nub already, it is doubtful it will prove even remotely useful in the next election cycle— though, if redacted and deleted emails don't prove useful, Benghazi is almost sure to be dug up and dusted off in 2016.

After seven years without a scandal to really sink their teeth into, without anything concrete that conservative critics of Obama can point to and say, "This is why I hate Obama," the question remains: What is it about Obama that has inspired such vitriolic critique from the right? Why this escalation from politics as usual to unprecedented invective? In 2011, Kansas House Speaker Mike O'Neal forwarded an email to his constituents, which contained a quotation from Psalm 109:

> Let his days be few; and let another take his office
> May his children be fatherless and his wife a widow.
> May his children be wandering beggars; may they be driven from their ruined homes.
> May a creditor seize all he has; may strangers plunder the fruits of his labor.
> May no one extend kindness to him or take pity on his fatherless children.

O'Neal added his own message at the bottom of the email, saying, "At last—I can honestly voice a Biblical prayer for our president! Look it up—it is word for word! Let us all bow our heads and pray. Brothers and Sisters, can I get an AMEN? AMEN!!!!!!"[52]

For an elected official to wax reverential at the thought of a dead president, as there is no other way to read the passage,[53] shows more than just the kind of disrespect that has long characterized political debate. This is something new. Every president has had his critics, and some of these critics have pushed the boundaries of taste and decency, but elected officials, if occasionally nodding in silent assent, have not joined their own voices to the cries of "*sic semper tyrannis*" that have been dimly heard on the extreme edges of the political wings. The election of a visible minority to the highest office in the land opened the floodgates in an instant, and the onrushing flood has swept away all respect for the office of the President and all traces of civility in our political discourse. Elected officials from deeply conservative districts have positively relished in appallingly racist caricatures and gross mischaracterizations of Obama as a radical or even a tyrant, trading them back and forth like children do playing cards, each trying to outdo the other. "Did you hear the one about ...?"

In 2014, a number of right-wing militias sought to organize a rally they called Operation American Spring, which aimed to establish the foundation of a "second American Revolution," one that, like the first American Revolution, would overthrow the existing power structure.[54] One organizer, Erik Rush, has openly called for a "military coup" against Obama, and the way this call and many others like it are phrased is most revealing. It is not the government that is tyrannical; it is not the DNC (let alone the GOP) that needs to be swept out of office. No, it is Obama himself. Were they to gain traction (which is, at best, doubtful) these proposed revolutions would not be political; they would be a pre-emptive strike made by a group that considers itself to be on the losing end of an ongoing race war.

Again, it's not Obama's politics that elicit this kind of response. It's the man himself and what he stands for. Liberal voters and activists see in the President's person something to be celebrated; since his election, they have celebrated the color of his skin and made the man himself a symbol of a society-wide movement of promise and progress. No such powerfully symbolic status could possibly be claimed for any of the presidents before Obama (Kennedy, as the first Catholic president, comes perhaps the closest). Shortly before Obama's inauguration, Congressman John Lewis, a leader of the Selma to Montgomery Freedom March, said, "Barack Obama is what comes at the end of that bridge in Selma." It's telling that Lewis said at the end of the bridge, and not the highway upon which the Freedom Marchers walked. Whether they stand beside all of his policies or not, liberals see in Obama a symbol of America's direction. He does not represent the destination, but merely an important milestone along the way. The President is no less a symbolic figure for Republicans. When the Freedom Marchers first met the line of Alabama state troopers on the Edmund Pettus Bridge in 1965, they were met with billy clubs and tear gas, but, shortly thereafter, the troopers were made to stand down and allow the marchers passage without state-sanctioned violence upon them. That momentous gesture is one that must be repeated day in and day out until prejudices no longer infect our democracy, our social and economic lives, and our political discourse. Republicans see that repeated gesture as a constant reminder of the defeat of a worldview—especially in terms of its racial hierarchies—that history time and again refuses to vindicate. Though the bigots' weapons have changed, the prejudices they hold have not. *President* Barack Obama is *A Bridge (Gone) Too Far.*

Why have the floodgates opened for this president, if not for the obvious reason that conservatives find a Black president the stuff of nightmares? The argument could be made that Republicans, recognizing that their chances at a general-election victory in the next decade are rapidly slipping through their fingers, are desperate to make the Democrats (and Obama chief among them) look bad, and they will stoop as low as they need to in order to aggravate existing or awake dormant prejudice in white voters, but this would suggest that these prejudices and those who exploit them are somehow separate. The casual racism that typifies so much of the right-wing take on this president is no subtle ploy: the simplest reading of the often-racist Republican characterizations of Obama as an un-American radical with one Black fist raised high in the air and one open hand doling out benefits to his lazy brethren is not entirely a political strategy.[55] Republicans just can't help themselves. They find the specter of a Black man in the White House so utterly terrifying that their prejudices rush to the surface. Obama represents the sounding of the death knell of their worldview. He's the living embodiment of America's shifting demographics and increasingly progressive social attitudes.

Hence, when Rand Paul and Donald Trump pound the podium during campaign speeches and say that it's time to *take our country back*, they can leave the oblique object of the sentence unstated. Their audiences know full well who needs to be taken down a peg and what "our" country is (or, at least, once was): a predominantly white, Christian America. As progressive attitudes take hold around the country, the views they replace are beginning to become more transparent for what they are: antiquated hierarchies and ideologies that have run their course. Obama embodies this movement, so in denigrating him, Republicans are attempting to restore what they see as the natural order. Power, they feel, belongs to them; the Black man in the White House has reversed this natural order. Since they believe his skin color ought to disqualify him from holding such a powerful position, he must be a usurper.

Rather than subsiding as the President nears his final year in office, Republican attacks on Obama seem to have reached new lows in recent months, with the Tom Cotton–led obstruction of the negotiations with Iran something of a low point in partisan politics (not just during Obama's two terms, but during the long and often-ridiculous history of cross-aisle bickering). Such provocation in the twilight of Obama's presidency can mean only one thing: Republicans have wanted to do more than oppose the President at every turn. They want to delegitimize his time in office, to paint him as the "black spot" (pun intended) on American democracy. As Hughey and Parks state, they want him wiped away, cleansed, expunged. They want his name gone in much the same way that Egyptian pharaoh Amenhotep II systematically removed the image of his grandmother, Queen Hatshepsut, from monuments in the fifteenth century BCE. These anti-Obama powers have been employing a contemporary imperial gangster move reminiscent of what German Egyptologist Jan Assmann calls "acts of intentional and violent cultural repression,"[56] or what scholars have now termed similar actions within Roman history as *damnatio memoriae*.[57] Perhaps they are doing this in an effort to make the electorate think twice about voting for what NRA head Wayne LaPierre recently referred to as a "demographically symbolic"[58] president again, or to discredit him based on the fact that he's Black. They believe, if they tarnish his legacy enough, that no other Black man will ascend to the presidency any time soon. The symmetrical, though not equivalent, overlap between Obama and Hillary Clinton here shows a GOP that's switching, not gears, but targets. If the kind of critiques that are already being leveled at Hillary Clinton on the basis of her gender is any indication, conservatives are as adamantly opposed to her as they have been to Obama. However, missing has been any attempt to paint Clinton as some kind of outsider, as a radical ready to wage war with American values. One can't help but assume that the color of her skin has a great deal to do with this restraint.

Notes

1   See Enck-Wanzer.

2   Obama, "A More Perfect Union." For a full, book-length analysis of this speech and its social, historical, and political dimensions, see Sharpley-Whiting.

3   See also "Transcript: Illinois Senate Candidate Barack Obama," *The Washington Post* 27 July 2004, http://www.washingtonpost.com/wp-dyn/articles/A19751-2004Jul27.html.

4   That choice was made after the Republican Party's preferred candidate, Jack Ryan, was forced to pull out of the race because of a child-custody dispute that became nasty and revealed a little too much information.

5   Whatever the actual reason, Republicans didn't put any muscle behind Keyes. According to the Center for Responsible Politics, Obama's Senate campaign spent $14.3 million, while Keyes spent only $2.8 million. As a result, Obama won by the largest margin in Illinois Senate election history. See http://www.opensecrets.org/politicians/elections.php?cycle=Career&cid=n00009638&type=I.

6   Audie Cornish, "Rare National Buzz Tipped Obama's Decision to Run," NPR, 19 November 2007, http://www.npr.org/templates/story/story.php?storyId=16364560.

7   "Obama Declares He's Running for President," CNN, 2 May 2007, http://www.cnn.com/2007/POLITICS/02/10/obama.president/.

8   Ibid.

9   Chris Isidore, "America's Lost Trillions," CNN, 9 June 2011, http://money.cnn.com/2011/06/09/news/economy/household_wealth/.

10   Rev. Wright stepped down in 2008, after 36 years of pastoralship, and was replaced by Otis Moss III, son of prominent 1950s–60s civil rights–era religious activist Otis Moss Jr.

11   I witnessed this first hand. Some of my family belonged to Wright's church, and, on the day of a family wedding, they were surrounded by a throng of reporters who wanted some comment on the Reverend.

12   See Obama, "A More Perfect Union."

13   From a sermon given the Sunday after 9/11 (16 September 2001).

14   From a sermon, "Confusing God and Government," delivered on 13 April 2003.

15   President Obama discusses Trinity in his book *Dreams from My Father*, saying, "Like other predominantly black churches across the country, Trinity embodies the black community in its entirety—the doctor and the welfare mom, the model student and the former gang-banger. Like other black churches, Trinity's services are full of raucous laughter and sometimes-bawdy humor. They are full of dancing and clapping and screaming and shouting that may seem jarring to the untrained ear. The church contains in full the kindness and cruelty, the fierce intelligence and the shocking ignorance, the struggles and successes, the love and, yes, the bitterness and biases that make up the black experience in America."

16   "Mr. Obama and Rev. Wright," *The New York Times* 30 April 2008, http://www.nytimes.com/2008/04/30/opinion/30wed1.html?_r=0.

17   *Henry IV Part 2*, 3.1.31.

18 "Face the Nation Full Transcript," 4 January 2015, http://us3.campaign-archive2. com/?u=468d5dc43334640650b81443f&id=4355e64a4b&e=6d7cef570b.

19 Libby Quaid, "McCain Rejects Endorsements from 2 Controversial Pastors," AZCentral.com, 22 May 2008, http://www.azcentral.com/news/articles/2008/ 05/22/20080522mccain0522pastor.html.

20 Dr. Orly Taitz et al. vs. Democrat Party of Mississippi et al., "Memorandum Opinion and Order Dismissing Plaintiffs' Complaint," United States District Court for the Southern District of Mississippi, Northern Division, 31 March 2015, http://www.obamaconspiracy.org/wp-content/uploads/2015/04/Taitz-v-Mississippi-Democrat_117-Dismissal.pdf.

21 Andy Barr, "Poll: 51 percent of GOP Primary Voters Think Obama Born Abroad," *Politico* 15 February 2011, http://www.politico.com/news/stories/ 0211/49554.html.

22 Justin Bank, "John McCain's Presidential Eligibility," FactCheck.org, 25 February 2008, updated 16 June 2008, http://www.factcheck.org/2008/02/ john-mccains-presidential-eligibility/.

23 "Fact Check: Is Obama 'palling around with terrorists'?" CNN, 5 October 2008, http://politicalticker.blogs.cnn.com/2008/10/05/fact-check-is-obama-palling-around-with-terrorists/.

24 "Four-Star Admiral Makes HUGE Announcement about Obama and the Muslim Brotherhood," The Political Insider, n.d., http://www.thepoliticalinsider. com/breaking-four-star-admiral-makes-huge-announcement-obama-muslim-brotherhood-video/.

25 Jeffrey E. Jones, "Obama Averages 63% Approval in His First Quarter," Gallup, 17 April 2009, http://www.gallup.com/poll/117598/Obama-Averages-Approval-First-Quarter.aspx.

26 Karl Frisch, "Fox News: 100 Days of 'Opposition' to Obama," Media Matters for America, 29 April 2009, http://mediamatters.org/research/2009/04/29/ fox-news-100-days-of-opposition-to-obama/149632.

27 Ibid.

28 See Wise.

29 Bill O'Reilly, "Mistreating Black Americans," Fox News, 12 November 2014, http://www.foxnews.com/transcript/2014/11/12 bill-oreilly-mistreating-black-americans/.

30 Kelly Phillips Erb, "Crazy for 'Obama Phones'—but Are They for Real?" *Forbes* 28 September 2012, http://www.forbes.com/sites/kellyphillipserb/2012/09/28/ crazy-for-obama-phones-but-are-they-for-real/.

31   John Fund, "Obama's 'Free Stuff for Everyone' Speech," *National Review*
     20 January 2015, http://www.nationalreview.com/corner/396796/
     obamas-free-stuff-everyone-speech-john-fund.

32   "2007 Video Shows the Real Barack Obama: Angry, Race-Baiting
     Fear-Mongering Liberal," Rushlimbaugh.com, 3 October 2012, http://www.
     rushlimbaugh.com/daily/2012/10/03/2007_video_shows_the_real_barack_
     obama_angry_race_baiting_fear_mongering_liberal.

33   Ryan Grim and Luke Johnson, "Is the Tea Party Racist? Ask Some Actual,
     Out-of-the-Closet Racists," The Huffington Post, 24 October 2013, http://www.
     huffingtonpost.com/2013/10/24/tea-party-racist_n_4158262.html.

34   T. Jefferson, "Glenn Beck: Is Massive Health Care Plan Reparations?"
     glennbeck.com, 23 July 2009, http://www.glennbeck.com/content/articles/
     article/198/28317/.

35   "Gingrich: 'Obama Is the Most Successful Food Stamp President in
     History,'" Real Clear Politics, 29 June 2011, http://www.realclearpolitics.com/
     video/2011/06/29/gingrich_obama_is_the_most_successful_food_stamp_
     president_in_american_history.html.

36   Michael D. Shear, "Gingrich: President Exhibits 'Kenyan, Anticolonial Behavior,'"
     The New York Times 23 September 2010, http://thecaucus.blogs.nytimes.
     com/2010/09/13/gingrich-president-exhibits-kenyan-anti-colonial-behavior/.

37   Francis Martel, "Orange County, CA GOP Official Sends Email Saying
     Obama's Parents Were Monkeys," Mediaite, 16 April 2011, http://www.mediaite.
     com/tv/orange-county-gop-official-solves-birther-mystery-presidents-parents-
     were-monkeys/.

38   David Sirota, "Rep. Lamborn Likens Obama to a 'Tar Baby,'" Salon, 1 August
     2011, http://www.salon.com/2011/08/01/doug_lamborn_tar_baby/.

39   See Williamson, Skocpol, and Coggin.

40   "Rep. Wilson Shouts, 'You Lie' to Obama During Speech," CNN, 10 September
     2009, http://www.cnn.com/2009/POLITICS/09/09/joe.wilson/.

41   See Street.

42   "In the House, a Refusal to Govern," *The New York Times* 11 July 2013, http://
     www.nytimes.com/2013/07/12/opinion/in-the-house-a-refusal-to-govern.html.

43   Frank Newport, "Americans' Desire for Gov't Leaders to Compromise Increases."
     Gallup, 23 September 2013, http://www.gallup.com/poll/164570/americans-
     desire-gov-leaders-compromise-increases.aspx.

44   See Sabato.

45   Christopher Hitchens, "Saddam's Chief Apologist." *The Los Angeles Times*
     8 December 2005, http://articles.latimes.com/2005/dec/08/opinion/oe-hitchens8.

46   See Barreto et al.

47   Steve Rendall, "Bush-Hating Nation: Anatomy of an Epithet," FAIR: Fairness and Accuracy in Reporting, 1 June 2006, http://fair.org/extra-online-articles/bush-hating-nation/.

48   See Plouffe.

49   Josh Smith, "Majority Does Not Rule in Filibuster-Filled 111th Congress," National Journal, 16 December 2010, http://www.nationaljournal.com/daily/majority-does-not-rule-in-filibuster-filled-111th-congress-20101216.

50   Glenn Kessler, "When Did McConnell Say He Wanted to Make Obama a 'One-Term President'?", *The Washington Post* 25 September 2012, http://www.washingtonpost.com/blogs/fact-checker/post/when-did-mcconnell-say-he-wanted-to-make-obama-a-one-term-president/2012/09/24/79fd5cd8-0696-11e2-afff-d6c7f20a83bf_blog.html.

51   Inexplicably, with the economy beginning to recover in late 2010, the election handed the House of Representatives to the Republicans, who proceeded to turn the 112th Congress into a legislative body that set records for futility, with a modern record for the fewest laws passed. One would think that such a record would embarrass them, and get Republicans to work better with Democrats and the White House, but that just wasn't the case, as the 113th Congress was pretty much just as bad, beating out the 112th by only a hair in the number of laws passed. See Mark Murray, "Unproductive Congress: How Stalemates Became the Norm in Washington DC," NBC News, 30 June 2013, http://firstread.nbcnews.com/_news/2013/06/30/19206400-unproductive-congress-how-stalemates-became-the-norm-in-washington-dc. See also David Knowles, "The 113th Congress Was the Second-Least Productive in History," Bloomberg Politics, 21 December 2014, http://www.bloomberg.com/politics/articles/2014-12-21/the-113th-congress-was-the-second-least-productive-in-history.

52   Marie Diamond, "Kansas GOP House Speaker 'Prays' That 'Obama's Children Be Fatherless and His Wife a Widow,'" Think Progress, 13 January 2012, http://thinkprogress.org/justice/2012/01/13/403911/kansas-gop-house-speaker-prays-that-obamas-children-be-fatherless-and-his-wife-a-widow/.

53   O'Neal might have missed the fact that, in the biblical context, David presages his request by asking God to "appoint someone evil to oppose my enemy."

54   Brian Tashman, "Militias All Across the Nation Are Mobilizing for Anti-Obama Rally," Right Wing Watch, 17 January 2014, http://www.rightwingwatch.org/content/militias-all-across-nation-are-mobilizing-anti-obama-rally.

55   See Haney-López.

56   Cited in Harriet Flower, *The Art of Forgetting: Disgrace and Oblivion in Roman Political Culture* (Chapel Hill: University of North Carolina Press, 2006), xx.

57   Flower, xix–xx.

58   Alexandra Jaffe, "NRA's Wayne LaPierre: Obama, Clinton 'demographically-symbolic,'" CNN.com, 15 April 2015, http://www.cnn.com/2015/04/15/politics/nra-wayne-lapierre-obama-demographically-symbolic/.

Chapter Three

RACISM:
THE LONG MARCH
TO FREEDOM
AND THE
NEW JIM CROW

FOR MANY OF US, OBAMA'S ELECTION FELT LIKE A CULMINATION OF the Black struggle for freedom and equality in America, but the nature of the response he has received during his presidency (not to mention the spate of state-sponsored violence with Black bodies as its target) has forced many of us to look with new eyes upon American Blacks' long and tortuous path from bondage to freedom. This book would not be complete without a look back over our shoulder at this movement, its great figures, and its powerful lessons. Let us go then, you and I, to church, vicariously to Chicago's New Nazareth Church. Let us go back to April 9, 1965, a night when the Staple Singers, on the verge of massive crossover success, hold a concert. That night, they debut a song, "Freedom Highway," which Pops Staples tells the crowd is both about and dedicated to Alabama's Freedom Marchers, who marched less than three weeks earlier from Selma to Montgomery.

The congregation, having just been led in a stirring rendition of "We Shall Overcome," is in perfect concert with the Staples; it begins to clap its hands almost the moment the insistent drum beat first rolls from the stage, and the ecstatic clapping continues to echo through the room for the duration of the song.

The unedited recording of this performance (re-released earlier this year after spending decades out of print[1]) captures a portrait in sound, an intimate and unguarded Kodachrome of a nation standing at its racial crossroads. The previous year had seen the passage of the *Civil Rights Act* of 1964, undeniably a watershed moment in the Civil Rights Movement, and, at the end of the year, Martin Luther King Jr. had been awarded the Nobel Peace Prize in Oslo. America's reputation as a hypocritical and racist backwater was ebbing, albeit slowly; every inch of progress was a battle, as dug-in segregationists, who felt "their America" slipping through their fingers, pushed back, often in violent ways. Nonviolent sit-ins and marches were met with unconscionable and brutal violence in the South (some state-sponsored, some not). The North also saw flare-ups of racial violence. In Rochester, Harlem, Chicago, and North Philadelphia, the summer of '64 was marred by bloody race riots.[2]

Early in 1965, in Selma, Alabama, groups of Black would-be voters, led by the Dallas County Voters League, the Student Nonviolent Coordinating Committee (SNCC), and Dr. King's Southern Christian Leadership Conference, attempted to register at the county courthouse.[3] Dallas County officials did everything within their power to erect barriers between these Black citizens and their constitutionally guaranteed right to participate in the political process. They operated with a skeleton crew and with severely attenuated opening hours,[4] and when the lines grew, officers bullied and harassed the crowds. Here was the bigotry of the South writ large: news crews captured video of the bigoted local sheriff, Jim Clark, using the butt end of his billy club to jostle and jab the young Black men who stood on the courthouse steps—he muttering abuse through clenched teeth; they, with almost placid faces, the very picture of stoicism, their heads bowed and their hands clasped together at waist level. The mayor of Selma, Joseph Smitherman, when speaking to the press about these agitators, laid the blame for the confrontations at the feet of Black civil-rights leaders, referring to the most prominent among them as "Martin Luther Coon."[5]

The palpable outrage and the protests that these verbal and physical confrontations engendered spread to nearby Marion, Alabama, and on February 18, 1965, during a night-time march, Jimmie Lee Jackson, a deacon in the local Baptist church, was shot point-blank by Alabama state trooper James Bonard Fowler in a small café. Jackson died eight days later, but the man who shot him wouldn't see the inside of a jail cell for another 45 years: Fowler pleaded guilty to second-degree manslaughter in 2010 and served five months of a six-month sentence.[6]

The death of Jackson proved something of a catalyst, and activists planned a march along the highway that connected Selma and Montgomery. As 600 of them marched across the Edmund Pettus Bridge, they were met by a line of Alabama state troopers and Sheriff Jim Clark's deputies, who, declaring the marchers to be assembling illegally, met them with force, shooting tear gas into the crowd and beating them with clubs, ultimately hospitalizing more than 50 of them.[7] Two days later, King led a second march himself, which was turned back at the same spot without violence, but Selma had become a magnet for those on both sides of the issue, and that night a white Unitarian preacher, James Reeb, was clubbed to death on the streets of Selma by a group of white supremacists.[8]

If Jackson's death was a spark that had grown to a glowing ember among the Black community and its sympathizers, the death of a white preacher turned this smoldering ember into a conflagration—one that spread through Black and White America alike. Less than a week later, on March 15, 1965, President Lyndon Johnson made his famous voting-rights speech: "Their cause," he said, "must be our cause too, because it is not just Negroes but really it is all of us, who must overcome the crippling legacy of bigotry and injustice, and *we shall overcome*."[9] According to eyewitnesses, Dr. King wept hearing these words, which so strongly echoed those of the Movement, its great orators, and musicians.[10] Less than a week later, the ban on marching was lifted and, without serious incident, King began his march in Selma with almost 6,000 followers; he ended it a few days later in Montgomery with a train that had swelled to more than 25,000 people.[11]

When Pops Staples penned "Freedom Highway" shortly after the march, the gospel legend certainly took inspiration from the unqualified success of the marchers, but the song did not celebrate a victory won so much as it signaled and impelled the momentum of an ongoing journey. The destination was elsewhere, farther down the road, on the visible but still distant mountaintop. There is, to be sure, a jubilatory note in both Mavis Staples's voice and those of the congregation as they lift them to the rafters, but there is still a lingering frustration as well, encapsulated in the song's lyrics, which indict the continued, blatant presence of systemic racism in the nation: "The whole wide world," Mavis belts, "is wonderin' what's wrong with the United States."

Black gospel music had long been a vehicle for the vocalization of the struggle for freedom, but, for the most part, the injustices of the present were but dimly alluded to. In the half-decade leading up to 1965, something of a corner had been turned, and the struggle bubbled to the surface (where it would remain). Coded references and deep metaphoric connections to the Gospel's jeremiads gave way to frank discussions of the plight of Black America and calls for tangible change in the here and now reached a crescendo. The highway was no longer merely metaphoric—it was a very real place, and as the Staple Singers moved the congregation in Chicago, the shoulder of that road still bore the footprints of the thousands of Black brothers and sisters who had marched in King's train. These steps brought Black America closer to realizing its vision, and King made this tangible progress clear in his speech delivered immediately after the march: "How long?" he asks the crowd. "Not long!" he answers.[12]

These words were prescient. Not long after the marches, on August 6, 1965, President Johnson signed the *Voting Rights Act* into law—an act he would later claim as the high-water mark of his presidency.[13] The act abolished, in a stroke, practices (literacy tests and other similar voting prerequisites) that disproportionately affected Black voters. It also prevented states with a history of discriminatory practices (Alabama, Georgia, Louisiana, Mississippi, South Carolina, North Carolina, and Virginia) from changing their election laws without federal oversight.[14] The act's clear intention was to prevent the kind of flouting of the fourteenth and fifteenth amendments that had been taking place throughout the South, and, in very real ways, the act was a spectacular success. By the summer following its enactment, 9,000 Blacks had registered to vote in Selma.[15] In many of the counties in which less than 1 per cent of Blacks who were eligible to vote had registered to do so, the *Voting Rights Act* removed the barriers that stood between them and the democratic process. Within four years, almost all of the Southern states saw Black registration numbers around 60 per cent; in those same four years, 12,000 Black officials, a third of whom came from the South, were elected to office in the United States.[16]

The year 2015 marked the 50th anniversary of the Selma to Montgomery Freedom March, and we have, let nobody doubt it, much to be proud of as a nation. That year, 1965, was a pivotal moment in the history of American race relations, but it was not an isolated one. Other leveling legislation followed in its wake, and perhaps more importantly, massive social shifts have forced all but the most vocal racists into the closet. At every level we are better represented by those who govern us. Blackness is no longer an alien pigment even in the upper echelons of the halls of power. And yet saying that as a nation we have somehow transcended our racist past (which some among us claim to be perfectly true) is like hitting a sour note during the national anthem. While the utterly tone-deaf might not hear the dissonance, those with any ear for injustice can hear little else. For those with any understanding of historic racism and its legacy, and particularly for those who have encountered (and continue to encounter) the racism that still pervades American society, any claims that we live in a nation that has atoned for its racist past are patently false.

The self-assured tone-deafness persists, though—and is most immediately apparent in the Supreme Court's recent gutting of the *Voting Rights Act* and the justifications it gave for doing so. Despite the fact that in 2006 Congress passed, with an overwhelming majority, a 25-year reauthorization of the *Voting Rights Act* after a public campaign that included more than 100,000 petitions and 15,000 phone calls to congressional offices,[17] challenges to the constitutionality of Sections 4 and 5 found purchase in 2013, and, in a 5–4 decision, the Supreme Court ruled that the preclearance sections were unconstitutional.[18]

In the Court's decision, written by Chief Justice John Roberts, the two sections that demand federal oversight for states with a history of racist voter suppression are defined as "extraordinary and unprecedented features" that were thoroughly products of their racist times.[19] The four renewals of the act since 1965 were, according to the Court's majority decision, ahistorical—those who renewed the act were apparently acting as though "nothing ha[d] changed" since 1965: "History," writes Roberts, "did not end in 1965.... Coverage today is based on decades-old data and eradicated practices [and on] 40-year-old facts having no logical relation to the present day."[20] What Roberts and the other majority justices failed to realize is the extent to which the *Voting Rights Act* (and particularly the preclearance sections) has stood between those who would suppress minority voters and their ability to do so with impunity. The existence of democratic parity in the United States—and especially in the South—is not the result of some natural erosion of racism in America. There is substantial evidence which shows that, even in the last two decades, without the preclearance sections to prevent them from doing so, Southern states would have frequently erected barricades between minorities and the voting process. For instance, while covered under Sections 4 and 5, Alabama's Shelby County failed preclearance some 240 times when it tried to introduce new voting restrictions;[21] between 1999 and 2005, 153 changes to voting laws proposed by states that required preclearance were withdrawn when the Department of Justice requested that the states provide them with more information on the law's intended effects.[22]

What, Then, Is the Law?

Section 5 of the *Voting Rights Act* requires that states receive federal approval, also known as "preclearance," before making changes to their election laws. The burden of proof for ensuring that the change will not have any negative impact with respect to suppressing voters falls on the jurisdiction itself. The scope of this section of the *Voting Rights Act* was first interpreted at the federal level by the Supreme Court in 1969 in the landmark case *Allen v. State Board of Election*. That case found that any change in a jurisdiction's voting practices, even if local officials perceive that change to be minor, has to get preclearance. The Court doesn't decide the merits of any proposed changes and is not involved with approving them. Still, so long as a relevant case is on the docket, the Court does verify whether a proposed change has obtained the requisite preclearance.

Under this provision, jurisdictions were eligible to go about pre-clearance in two separate ways: seeking a declaratory judgment from a three-person D.C. District Court panel or by submitting the proposed change to the U.S. Attorney General. If the jurisdiction went the latter route, the A.G. had the right to object to the change for up to 60 days. In an interview, political science professor J. Robert Baker explained, "while Section 5 has garnered considerable attention due to its preclearance requirement, Section 2 has also been instrumental to how the VRA has been applied in practice. This section prohibits vote denial and vote dilution."[23] He later explained that "in 1982 Congress amended it, clarifying that for minority plaintiffs to win suits they needed to show that changes to electoral procedures resulted in the denial or dilution of their voting rights." When the Supreme Court initially construed this in *Thornburg v. Gingles* (1986), it was widely understood that jurisdictions were encouraged to draw majority-minority districts in order to improve the electoral chances of minorities. After the 1990 census, several states drew these types of districts, which resulted in some minority candidates winning for the first time ever. However, in order to pack minorities adequately together and create majority-minority districts, some odd-shaped districts had to be created. Baker later surmised that "this prompted white voters to sue, claiming that the long-standing districting criterion of compactness had been violated. In *Shaw v. Reno*, the Supreme Court agreed and struck down positive racial gerrymandering, i.e., the drawing of majority-minority districts. The result has been a re-emergence of minority vote dilution."

As in the *Shelby County* case, there are dozens of similar examples. In an instant, states that have time and again proven themselves, in both the recent and the remote past, to be keen to suppress minority voters were placed on an equal footing with those who had long since passed what Jelani Cobb calls "the litmus test of discrimination."[24] But Justice Roberts used an entirely different set of criteria. With an oblique reference to the 1965 Freedom March, he cited Black elected officials as evidence enough that America has almost entirely left its racist past behind it: "Today," he wrote, "both [Selma and Birmingham] are governed by African-American mayors. Problems remain in these States and others, but there is no denying that, due to the *Voting Rights Act*, our nation has made great strides."[25] The implication is that the barriers that once stood between African Americans and the democratic process were swept away (presumably along with the attitudes that informed them) in the years following the passage of the *Voting Rights Act*. The protections may have been valid when America was first coming to grips with its past, but now, with Black mayors in the South and a Black president in the White House, these protections have apparently run their course. American democracy, to Justice Roberts's way of seeing things, is as equal and even-handed as it needs to be. In her strongly worded dissent, Justice Ruth Bader Ginsburg challenged the premise that informed Roberts's decision, noting that as late as 2006, Congress reauthorized the law, with 390 votes in the House and a unanimous vote in the Senate:

> Beyond question, the VRA is no ordinary legislation. It is extraordinary because Congress embarked on a mission ... to realize the purpose and promise of the Fifteenth Amendment [which barred racial discrimination in voting and authorized Congress to enforce it]....
> In my judgment, the Court errs egregiously by overriding Congress' decision.[26]

Surprising nobody, in the months following the Supreme Court's decision, North Carolina, South Carolina, Texas, Florida, Virginia, Mississippi, Alabama, and Arizona all enacted measures that disenfranchised voters, eliminating same-day voter registration, redistricting along racial and political lines, shortening (often dramatically so) opportunities for early voting, and, of course, demanding much more rigorous identification requirements—all in the name of combating the chimerical problem of voter fraud.[27] In the state of Ohio, for example, Secretary of State Jon Husted trumpeted the 17 cases of ballot fraud that occurred during the 2012 presidential elections, but in this case the meager statistic may have had the opposite effect to what he intended. After all, 17 votes were entirely inconsequential, as President Obama won the state by a grand total of 166,272 votes.[28] With all the incidents, furthermore, a valid state ID was used, so basic ID laws would have had a negligible effect.

December 10 march for voting rights. https://flic.kr/p/bfTsKg. Credit: Michael Fleshman, 10 December 2011.

And yet voter fraud gets so much attention in the news that the federal government found it worthy of its time and money to research. One such example is the community group ACORN, which received a lot of press in 2009 on allegations of voter fraud. Although investigations later found that the organization had not done anything criminal and that it had used federal funds appropriately, the damage was already done: the group filed for bankruptcy in 2010. The Department of Justice reviewed 197 million votes cast in federal elections between 2002 and 2005 and uncovered a whopping 40 cases of voter fraud.[29] How great it is to see our tax dollars at work conducting studies with results we already knew.

When called into question, the GOP has gone out of its way to rationalize voter suppression by arguing that it's necessary to keep integrity in the election process. In reality, that's very far from the truth. Alleging that voters and members of the general public are the problem, rather than the potential for the solution, downplays the vital purpose of voting, namely to empower the demos and to keep those seeking election accountable to the people. Many GOP leaders argue that it's about unity and uniformity, but that is not the case. The real goal is to divide people as much as possible, especially on class and race lines. But grouping people into categories, and then taking whatever action is possible to limit those "unwanted" people from voting, has nothing to do with uniformity. It's about empowering the few at the cost of the many. Certainly the right to vote should be uniform, but that's something we could not get right for so many years on our own. Go ahead and see just how far back you'd have to look to talk to relatives who were in some direct way discriminated against with regard to voting. I'd wager it's not too far. The only thing that should be uniform about voting is the ability to access that right. Outside of that, all people have an individual right to express their opinion and play a crucial role in the political process. Even different communities approach voting in various ways, and Republican leaders know this. They know that just as voters can be "divided" into racial and class lines, geography factors into the story as well. So those communities that need the most when it comes to voter access do not need uniformity at all; they need to be able to use best-practice programs and approaches to allow whoever wants to vote to do so. Anything short of complete access is in itself tantamount to suppression.

The claim that our racist past is behind us—repeated loudly and frequently by the GOP and its mouthpieces since Obama's election—is a fallacy without a shred of supporting evidence. The reason for its propagation is obvious enough: American exceptionalism may grudgingly recognize its racist past, but it is less inclined to recognize the *legacy* of that past. It seems that as the Civil Rights Movement crossed the half-century threshold, this marked, for some, a period at the end of a sentence that, they feel, had long ago reached its conclusion. They admit that America may not have always been the land of opportunity it presented itself to be, but, in the twenty-first century, they say, nothing of any substance stands between men and women of color and the American Dream (such is the view frequently propagated by conservative pundits such as Bill O'Reilly and mercilessly skewered by his satirical doppelganger Stephen Colbert). It is what Eduardo Bonilla-Silva calls "color-blind racism," a postmodern and putatively post-racial manifestation of prejudice. It presents itself as innocuous, "otheriz[ing] softly," because it doesn't get hung up on

racial distinctions; it is "ideological armor for a covert and institutionalized system in the post-Civil Rights era" (3). It may be killing us softly with sweet songs, but make no mistake, this brand of
racism is killing us. Hiding behind seemingly progressive attitudes,
it entirely ignores historical context—in this case the long history
of racism in states like Alabama and Mississippi. The telltale trade-
mark of this blinkered view of America is its "rhetorical incoherence,"
which manifests in everything from literal incoherence (false starts,
self-corrections and contradictions, sentences littered with "ums" and
"uhs") to ideological incoherence—failed attempts to frame blatantly
racist positions in politically correct ways and to claim to be color-
blind or post-racial even while highlighting how Blacks are, to cite a
few of the examples from Bonilla-Silva's study, more violent, lazy, or
immoral than whites (54).

   This kind of "racism lite" is a product of the polarization of racist
attitudes and sociopolitical standards of correctness. The old guard
stubbornly refuses to release its tenacious grip on racist ideologies, so
rather than changing its mind, it has changed the way it presents these
ideologies. It has found ways to cloak its prejudice in the raiment of
enlightened modernity. Watch conservative mouthpieces when they
discuss the issue of race in America; it is clear that they desperately
want to call a spade a spade—to shift the blame away from the power
structure and its privileges and onto those whose putative obstinacy
and obsession with America's racist past are the only barriers to their
political, economic, and social success.

It's All about Resources: How Voter Suppression
Comes Down to Money

In the spring of 2014, the Supreme Court struck down limits on campaign contributions, making it easier for private money to be stream-
lined directly into federal elections, and giving the wealthy 1 per cent
greater influence over what happens inside the Beltway.[30] As if the
average American needed one more barrier to vote or one more piece
of legislation designed to make him or her feel unimportant. The
decision was a close one at 5-4, but it took down decades of campaign
finance law that had restricted campaign funds. Many people began

protesting as soon as the decision was handed down, arguing that the new rules violate First Amendment rights. Some are already comparing this decision to Citizens United, in which the Supreme Court held that the government didn't have the right to regulate free speech with regard to forbidding corporate spending on elections.

The wealthiest people in this country earn the majority of the money.[31] In 2012, the wealthiest 10 per cent actually held more than half of the country's money (see Chapter 6). Isn't democracy supposed to protect the minority from the tyranny of the majority? But the opposite is now occurring. A very small sliver of the population is controlling increasingly higher amounts of money and power, while many others struggle to get by. In the meantime, the rich can flex their power through donations, supporting lobbying groups, or getting involved in politics themselves. There are few to no barriers for these people to grab more power, even though their numbers are small. Their wallets are big enough to make an impact, quashing the rights of the many other people living in our great nation. While America is all about being the land of opportunity, I'm not sure that's meant to be at the expense of most of our citizens.

Rather than remaining the land of opportunity, we're widening the gap between the haves and the have-nots. Those empowered with money have all the opportunity at the fingertips, but it's increasingly difficult for a typical American to achieve something in politics. With money comes power, and, sadly, this power sometimes crushes the interests of the majority in favor of the goals of the donor class. Instead of paving the way for future freedoms, this is all the proof needed to convince some people that their vote just doesn't matter. Even though their one vote might matter in a few races, it's hard to convince these single voters that all the behind-the-scenes action isn't really dictated by the wealthy.

The sad, unmistakable truth is that voter suppression becomes subtler and more insidious with each passing year, and many voters do not even realize the extent to which it occurs. While the current brand of suppression might not be as obvious as showing up to the polls only to learn that you'll be turned away after failing a literacy test, the result is the same. With power being taken away from the people and with voting being made more difficult, voters might not even

realize that their power is being eroded. As younger individuals realize that without money they have limited power, the novelty of voting
will eventually wear off. This is exactly what those pushing for voter
suppression want. If people begin to believe that their one vote has,
at most, a negligible impact and the process of registering to vote or
voting itself becomes too difficult, they may just stop voting altogether.
It may have taken centuries to reach this point, but sadly, we are well
on our way to seeing a world where unwanted voters are so oppressed
as to be voiceless in the democratic process.

The systematic, incremental degradation of voting rights is most
apparent in the Deep South, where states are resurrecting an attack
on the franchise that has been correctly identified by Reverend Jesse
Jackson as "The New Jim Crow."[32] Nowhere is this assault more blatant than in the state of Alabama. The (new) story began in 2011,
when the state legislature passed a law requiring citizens to produce
photo identification before voting. The pre-clearance language of the
VRA applied to any state with a history of racial discrimination, and
Alabama, a state that was forced at gunpoint—President Kennedy
had to call out the National Guard to guarantee the integration
of the University of Alabama in 1963—clearly had to seek federal
approval before making any changes in its election procedures. This
all changed, however, with the Supreme Court's gutting of the VRA
in 2013 and its determination that the pre-clearance language was
unconstitutional.[33]

With this decision, the floodgates opened. The very next day,
Alabama Attorney General Luther Strange instated the new photo
ID law, which had previously been blocked by the pre-clearance pro-
visions of the VRA.[34] Then, in October 2015, the State of Alabama
announced the closure of 31 offices of the Department of Motor
Vehicles—the majority of which are located in counties where over
75 per cent of voters are African-American.[35] These closures clearly
target minority voters in Alabama, and the endgame is obvious: make
it nearly impossible for poor, rural African Americans to vote.

When questioned about the DMV closures and their disproportionate effect on the ability of certain segments of Alabama's citizenry
to secure the documents needed to cast a ballot, Alabama Governor
Robert Bentley replied, "As far as voting rights, this has nothing to

do with that."[36] He further refuted the idea that the closings were racially motivated. For my part, I'd love to give Governor Bentley the benefit of the doubt. But the facts fly in the face of his position, which is simply not credible. Let's recap the story: 1) in 2011, Alabama passes voter ID laws which can't be implemented because of the pre-clearance language in the VRA; 2) in 2013, the *day after* that language in the VRA is deemed unconstitutional, the state implements the law; 3) and in 2015, the State closes DMV offices in counties that are largely poor and African-American.

But if the closures weren't racially motivated, there's no getting around the fact that they were politically motivated. They were a bald-faced attempt to restrict the rights of a group of people who are demographically more likely to vote Democrat than Republican. The fact that the group of people just *happened* to be African-American is just coincidence. If it looks like racism and feels like racism and it happens in state with a history of racism, then it's ... not racism. No, it can't be. Obama was elected and racism is over. You're right, Governor Bentley. We'll just close our eyes and take your word for it: it's all just a big coincidence.

Such post-racial claims ring as true when we discuss voter suppression as they do when we discuss police violence and wildly uneven incarceration rates. We know that racism is alive and well in America; we know that the Freedom Highway still stretches far into the distance. Though many would have us believe otherwise, it has not reached its destination yet. At an outdoor concert in 2011, Mavis Staples sang, as she often does, her father's song, "Freedom Highway." Her voice is far huskier and the effortless power that it had in the 1960s is fading ever so slightly, but when she sings that song, she still sings to our hearts. She's doing more—much more—than going through the back-catalog motions. There remains a distinct note of urgency and revolution in her voice. As she introduced the song, she talked about the palpable momentum of the 1960s and the slow, steady march toward freedom. It was this figurative march that inspired her father to write "Freedom Highway"; but, more than that, it was those who, risking their very lives to do so, literally marched arm in arm with their brothers and sisters in the name of freedom and democracy early in 1965 that quickened his pen. Enthusiastically, she reaffirmed the song's contemporary relevance: "I'm still on that

President Barack Obama speaking at the 50th anniversary of the Selma–Montgomery march at the Edmund Pettus Bridge, 7 March 2015 (front row, right to left: long-time civil-rights activist and current Georgia Congressman John Lewis; Michelle Obama; former president George W. Bush; Laura Bush). https://commons.wikimedia.org/wiki/File:50th_Anniversary_of_the_Selma_Marches_-_Former_President_George_W_Bush_listens_as_President_Obama_delivers_remarks_at_the_foot_of_the_Edmund_Pettus_Bridge_%28cropped_to_height_of_bridge%29.jpg. Credit: Wikimedia Commons.

highway," she told the assembly, "and I will be there until Dr. Martin Luther King's dream has been realized."[37]

As Common and John Legend accepted their 2015 Academy Award for "Glory," which, like "Freedom Highway," gestures toward the ongoing nature of our long march to the mountaintop, they drew parallels between the events of 1965 and those in the present. We are, it seems, fated to fight the same battles against the same prejudices, and, despite what pundits and politicians may tell you, we have yet to reach the mountaintop. Common and John Legend were right: "Selma is now." We all continue to walk that highway with Mavis, and the question is as pertinent now as it was then: How much longer? We still hope—not long. We can do this, of course. But that will require us to change our way of thinking in many respects. We can change policy, but we will also have to change hearts and minds. If the passage of the *Civil Rights Act* taught us nothing else, it's that giving people legal civil rights is only half the battle. But changing the politics would be an excellent start.

The New Jim Crow

- In March 2014, Glenn Ford was released from prison. Despite his complete innocence, an all-white jury convicted him of murder in Louisiana in 1984. Ford spent 30 years on death row before his exoneration last year after credible evidence emerged proving that he could not have committed the murder.[38]
- Jonathan Fleming spent 24 years in prison before his wrongful conviction was overturned in April 2014. Although he was vacationing at Disney World at the time of the murder (he had a time-stamped receipt from a Florida hotel in his pocket when he was arrested), Fleming was convicted of murdering his friend in Brooklyn. None of the exonerating evidence was ever turned over to the defense, and Fleming was sentenced to life in prison.[39]
- In Ohio, Ricky Jackson and Wiley Bridgeman spent 39 years behind bars after being wrongfully convicted of murder in 1975. The Ohio Innocence Project took up their case, and in 2014 a Cleveland judge exonerated both men.[40] Their conviction had rested on the testimony of a 12-year-old witness, who admitted in 2013 that he had been coerced by detectives into implicating the two men.
- Joseph Sledge, wrongfully convicted in 1976, was released earlier this year after almost 40 years in prison on trumped-up charges. The testimony of a jailhouse informant, when scrutinized, was recanted—the authorities had made promises of leniency to the informant in exchange for his damning testimony. To this was added DNA evidence, which made it clear that Sledge was not the "Black male" the authorities had sought in connection with the murder.[41]

These are just a few of the examples taken from the long list of Black men who have been wrongly convicted and incarcerated. There have been so many of them, in fact, that the media find little worth reporting about when yet another wrongfully convicted Black man is set free. At most, they are presented as human-interest stories, the reunion with family members serving as the soft heart of the story. But much is left almost entirely unexamined: the system that resulted in these wrongful

convictions; the skewed conviction rates for young Black men that continue today; the many ways in which the young Black man (especially
one who cannot afford legal representation), upon entering the justice
system, is assumed to be guilty long before he is proven so. The Office
of Juvenile Justice and Delinquency Prevention has collected youth-
incarceration data for years, and the numbers speak rather clearly about
the ways in which minorities are disproportionately caught in the gears
of the justice system. Minorities accounted for more than half (54%)
of all juvenile arrests for violent crime and over two-fifths (41%) of all
juvenile arrests for property crime offenses.[42]

In New York, the alarming way in which juvenile minorities are
unfairly targeted by law-enforcement officials and disproportionately
convicted by the courts has come under the microscope recently, as
five Latino and Black New York City council members have written
a scathing open letter to Mayor Bill de Blasio, charging the NYPD
with unfair and discriminatory practices, especially in their handling
of marijuana arrests. Although arrests for possession dropped in the
city in the previous two years, an appallingly high percentage of these
arrests targeted young minorities (most of them male). While white
males are just as likely to use cannabis as their Black counterparts,
minorities make up 85 per cent of possession arrests.[43] When convictions follow these arrests (as they often do), the individual is weighted
with a criminal record that makes it all but impossible for them to lead
completely fulfilling lives. Councilman Ritchie Torres wrote in the
letter that many young, male minorities come to him for help when
they find it difficult or even impossible to find satisfying employment
(in some cases, any employment at all) or a bank loan due to their permanent criminal records.[44] Torres's letter made sure to note that the
NYPD "made 15,324 such [marijuana] arrests from March of last year
to August of this year, exceeding the number of arrests made during
the same time period last year, under the Bloomberg Administration."
By associating de Blasio with the Bloomberg Administration, Torres
tried to highlight the fact that despite de Blasio running on a platform opposing Bloomberg's NYPD policies, his administration had
not actually made any significant changes. Neither de Blasio nor the
NYPD made an official response to the letter.[45]

Two months after the open letter was sent to de Blasio, the mayor
faced intense criticism from the New York City Police Union for

his rather frank—too frank for their tastes—discussion about racial profiling and the NYPD in the·wake of the unsurprising but still-disheartening grand jury decision not to indict the NYPD officer who choked Eric Garner to death. He said at a press conference on December 7, 2014, that he (like so many other Black or Latino parents) has sat his biracial son down for serious talks about what precautions he needs to take when he deals with New York's finest. Mayor de Blasio ruffled yet more feathers when he said what few politicians are willing to state outright: "It's different for a white child," he said. "That's just the reality in this country."[46] The head of the city's police union said that de Blasio was throwing "cops under the bus," yet a growing consensus of people (both white and black) believe that the mayor was merely giving voice to what others have long known to be true. Michael Brown and Eric Garner and the public outcry that is still ongoing in their names have, if nothing else, made the conversation about racial profiling a national one. Since he's white himself, de Blasio's words reached white Americans in a way that might have not been possible had he been African American. This brings to mind the plight of James Reeb, discussed above, the white minister who marched with Martin Luther King Jr. in Selma in efforts to produce equal rights for Black people and who was clubbed in the head, leading to lethal injuries. While much of White America was content to stand idly by while African Americans were subject to bigotry and violence, when a white minister was subjected to the same, it prompted national outcry and even a statement from President Lyndon Johnson. Today, the plight of African Americans fighting against police brutality and discrimination in the legal system has largely fallen upon deaf ears. But de Blasio, both because of the color of his skin and his position as mayor of America's most popular city, is in a unique, yet precarious, position to bring these issues to the forefront.

Is the Drug War Really a Race War?

The United States has the best universities, the most powerful military, and the highest level of personal earnings in the world, and it is the largest contributor of foreign aid. We also, however, consistently have an appalling number-one spot year after year: our incarceration rate. Since 2002, the U.S. has maintained the highest incarceration rate in the world—more than Russia, more than North Korea, more than China. Although the U.S. accounts for 5 only per cent of the world's population, it has almost 25 per cent of the world's prisoners. More than two million people are behind bars in the U.S.,[47] paired with 4.7 million on parole or probation would then mean that the figure (nearly 7 million) is more than the populations of Los Angeles and Chicago combined. Thanks to America's ongoing War on Drugs, a full 50 per cent of America's prison population is serving time for drug offenses.[48] Thanks to a majority of police attention being directed toward inner-city neighborhoods, young Black males have been rounded up and sent up the river; they are an astonishing six times more likely to be incarcerated than young white men.[49]

For the last few decades, America has been conducting an experiment with its criminal justice system—with the unwitting and unwilling subjects of this experiment being millions of young Black men. America's incarceration rate is ten times higher than other democracies around the world, and, like our failing education system, our deplorable inequality, and our dysfunctional govern-ment, it gives our critics around the world ammunition and makes us play the hypocrite on the world stage when we demand that other countries respect the life and liberty of all their citizens. From an outsider's perspective, we have no room to censure the way another country treats its minority populations, since we treat ours so poorly. According to the NAACP, one in three Black males should expect, at some point in his life, to spend time behind bars.[50] What is glaringly obvious to the international community must become just as obvious to us, domestically: minorities in the United States are being ground under the heel of a privatized, profit-driven justice system—one that seems to be more concerned with keeping grist flowing into the mill than it is with reforming or punishing offenders with any measure of proportionality.

America's politicians have recently broken a long period of silence on this matter. Obama and other political leaders have shone a spot-light on America's prisons as a major site of justice in desperate need of reform. At the root of the issue is America's now decades-old and completely ineffective War on Drugs, conceived by Ronald Reagan and continued by his successors. Due to the number of Black men this ill-advised, wasteful charade has put behind bars, social justice advocates have long wondered if the drug war is a race war in disguise. History answers with a resounding "Yes."

The very first drug law implemented in the United States, which occurred during the 1870s, was clearly racially motivated. On November 15, 1875, San Francisco passed a landmark ordinance banning opium in the city.[51] At the time, opium dens were absolutely legal and operated chiefly by the Chinese. Opium was not considered a threat. For local white residents, the real threat was the skyrocketing Chinese population, which inspired fear and caused a crisis among whites along the West Coast. They found themselves unable to quell the population, and so they resorted to incarceration.

The first anti-marijuana laws also had sinister and manifestly racist beginnings. After the Mexican Revolution of 1910, Mexican immigrants flooded into the U.S. and introduced White America to marijuana as a recreational drug. For the next two decades, Americans enjoyed smoking marijuana without police interference, but that would change during the Great Depression. As unemployment skyrocketed, so too did public resentment and hatred of Mexican immigrants. Marijuana was labeled a drug used by the "racially inferior," and it was deemed illegal by 1931.[52] Incarceration rates for Mexicans skyrocketed, and by 1937 some 458,000 Mexicans had been arrested and deported without due process.[53] Once all was said and done, the Mexican-American population had been cut in half; those who remained were pushed into the margins of society and forced into dilapidated barrios where they were treated as second-class citizens.[54]

The Civil Rights Movement forced many Americans to re-evaluate their views on race, but, thanks in no small part to firmly entrenched pockets of white supremacy all over the nation that would not be swayed by reasonable arguments and nonviolent resistance, the Movement had something of an unintended effect. It exacerbated racial tensions and fears, which changed the landscape of the prison system. Longer sentences for drug crimes and property crimes, coupled with determinate sentencing, started to play a role in racial disparities between inmates. The trend escalated in the 1980s. The rights and freedoms granted to Black Americans through the Civil Rights Movement seemed almost to compel the remaining reactionary factions in the government to adopt a new strategy to stop the upward mobility of the African-American community. The holdouts could no longer rely on Jim Crow, so they resorted to a different method: the prison industrial complex.

Sentencing policies introduced during Reagan's presidency caused incarceration rates among Black men to skyrocket—of today's level of 2.2 million inmates, 1 million are African-American. This is a 500-percent increase over the past 30 years. There were about 200,000 inmates in 1980, when Reagan was elected, a figure that had remained steady since the late 1940s. By 1988, Reagan's last year in office, that number stood at 600,000. In 1992, the year Reagan's former vice-president George H.W. Bush finished his single term as president, the number was 800,000.[55] Throughout the 1980s and 1990s, drug laws would become increasingly draconian, and harsh sentencing laws with mandatory minimums kept people in prison longer; in 1986, drug offenders were spending an average of 22 months in federal prison, but by 2004 they were serving three times that length.[56] And America's War on Drugs "has incarcerated Black men at a rate six times higher than South Africa did during apartheid."[57]

The War on Drugs, as we know it, started in the 1980s. Its target: young Black men living in America's inner cities. The drugs made their way into the Black community—some believe through the CIA—and ate away at Black culture, prosperity, and unity like a cancer.[58] Former cocaine kingpin "Freeway" Rick Ross had long alleged that he worked with the CIA in his drug operations. Links that the American government, and the CIA in particular, had supported funding the Nicaraguan rebels with drug trafficking were reported by journalists such as Gary Webb. The federal government went through major efforts to silence such journalists.[59] Many believed that the public wouldn't be moved by money raised selling drugs in the Black community, especially with the anti-Black, "anti-crime" sentiment coming from Republican leaders at the time. The United States government made it blatantly clear that the War on Drugs was really a war on Black men by implementing a five-year mandatory minimum sentence for anyone with simple possession of crack cocaine. The courts treated powder and crack cocaine entirely differently, a disparity that wouldn't be fully addressed until 2010, when Obama signed into law the *Fair Sentencing Act*. The act eliminated the five-year mandatory sentence for crack possession and closed the gap between crack and powder cocaine in terms of the amounts needed to trigger stiff federal penalties (100:1 became 18:1 under the new rules).[60] Despite these changes, hundreds of thousands of Black men remain behind bars in crack-cocaine limbo, waiting for the Justice Department to determine if the law applies to those sentenced before 2010 or only to those sentenced after the new laws took effect. In the case of *US v. Blewett*, the Justice Department struck down a motion that could have ended unfair prison sentences for Black men jailed for crack-cocaine offenses before 2010,[61] even though the U.S. Court of Appeals for the sixth circuit held that the *Fair Sentencing Act* should be applied retroactively to those sentenced prior to 2010. Even the Obama Administration has stood between the Black community and the equal justice it has long sought.

The Obama Administration and Black Incarceration

In February 2015, Obama was asked by members of the Congressional Black Caucus to use Executive Action to reduce incarceration rates for the Black community. Obama told the caucus that he understood the need for justice-system reform and made promises that he would work to reform institutions that have long underserved Black Americans.[62]

These pledges, like all political promises, should be taken with a grain of salt, but there is strong evidence to suggest that Obama is making good on his vow to do something to improve the relationship between minorities and the state (especially in terms of policing). President Obama and Attorney General Eric Holder made the following moves, all of which have had a great impact on U.S. incarceration rates:

> 1. The Administration allowed the states of Colorado and Washington to make history in November 2012 when they voted to allow their people to use marijuana recreationally. Legal, judiciary, and political experts were waiting to see how Obama would respond and if he would allow the states to implement their new marijuana laws. The Obama Administration stated openly that it would not challenge laws legalizing marijuana in Colorado and Washington as long as the states maintained regulations involving the sale and distribution of the drug.[63]

Eric Holder personally called and informed the governors of the two states that the Department of Justice would allow them to legalize marijuana without resistance from the Obama Administration. In late February 2015, D.C. overwhelmingly approved the limited possession and cultivation of marijuana by anyone 21 or older. Obama told the *New Yorker* that "weed" was no more dangerous a substance than alcohol. In the same interview, he also said that he smoked marijuana when he was younger, and, unlike Bill Clinton, he was transparent: he did inhale.[64]

2. During a meeting of the Western hemisphere's security ministers held in Colombia in November 2013, Holder emphasized that the Obama Administration would scale back mandatory minimum-sentencing policies.[65] The old legislation, he said, was outdated, unjust, and unsustainable. He admitted that the Administration didn't have the money to build more prisons to support unfair laws and also highlighted the non-financial costs: "The human and moral costs," he said, "are too much to bear."[66]

3. In late December 2013, Obama granted eight clemencies for people serving life-long sentences for crack-cocaine–related crimes, and the next December granted clemencies for eight more. Shortly afterwards, he encouraged defense lawyers to step up and suggest further inmates that he might consider for early release.[67]

While the actions of Obama and his Administration leave much to be desired, it's clear that the issue of incarceration is on the Administration's radar. It's also clear that Obama is not a modern embodiment of Martin Luther King Jr., despite Melissa Harris-Perry's attempt in January 2010 to convince readers that he has inherited King's legacy.[68] The chances that he will live up to the mountain of expectations placed on his shoulders since his first election are, to say the least, slim. Several prominent African-American intellectuals and leaders have ridiculed the President for not doing enough to change the way that race is talked about (or not talked about) in this country. Michael Eric Dyson, for instance, critiqued the President's seeming unwillingness to speak frankly about race. Obama, he said, "runs from race like a Black man runs from a cop."[69] During Obama's first term, Cornel West decried Obama as a "Black mascot of Wall Street oligarchs and a Black puppet of corporate plutocrats." But the Princeton professor's most stinging rebuke was when he called Obama a counterfeit and claimed that he "posed as if he was Lincoln, but ended up as a brown-faced Clinton."[70] And Tavis Smiley derided Obama for going on BET to give Black folks a lecture while going on Stephen Colbert's show to tell white people jokes.[71] He's been criticized (by no less a figure than Colin Powell) for his handling of the Trayvon Martin verdict, for speaking in what many felt was a condescending tone to graduates at a historically Black college in Atlanta,[72] and, though the President's office embodies the definition of not being able to please all the people all the time, Obama's staunchest defenders had to admit that, during Obama's first term, he waded only gingerly into the waters where matters of race were concerned, at times even downplaying its obvious significance.

But Obama supporters' waning enthusiasm has been given a shot in the arm during the President's second term. Since his re-election, the President has spoken candidly about racial issues. The theme of "Hope and Change," which occasionally rang false during his first term, is taking tangible shape as the President begins to let his frustration with systemic racism and the ugly legacy of America's long history of inequality show. His speeches on race no longer feel like puppet theater, and this has raised hopes in the Black community that he will address racial inequality in tangible and lasting ways. Doing something—anything—about the Black incarceration rate would be an excellent place to start. If his actions on immigration reform are any indication, Obama has learned that the conventional channels of governance are obstructed. Senate and House Republicans will cry foul and gnash their teeth no matter what the President does, and it looks as though the President, with no more campaigns to run, having won both of them, has regained some of his former swagger. If anything is going to be done to help young Black men in this country, the time is now, during the last year and a half of his second term.

Obama's Attorney General, Eric Holder, can be seen as something of a model for the President. Whereas Obama has spoken on matters of race reticently, Holder has been reluctant to hold his tongue. During a visit to a St. Louis courthouse, Holder said that when he was a judge he watched lines of young people—most often young Black men—stream through his courtroom. He spoke openly and passionately about the destructive effects that incarceration is having in Black communities.[73] Early in 2014, he called for the repeal of the law that bars former felons from voting. These laws, he said, are built upon "centuries-old conceptions of justice that were too often based on exclusion, animus, and fear."[74] Thanks to the disproportionate numbers of Black men that find themselves behind bars early in their lives, this law, which excludes 5.3 million Americans from the voting process, disenfranchises an outrageously high percentage (13%) of African-American men.[75] Like the voter ID laws that were recently green-lighted by the Supreme Court, laws that disenfranchise ex-cons target minorities (arguments that claim that such is not the laws' *intended* purpose are transparently false in the light of their *actual* effects). A study conducted in late 2013 by the University of Massachusetts found that the states that enacted voter ID laws also happened to be the states in which minorities and lower-income voters were showing up at the polls in increasing numbers.[76] Voter ID laws put a burden on low-income voters for obvious reasons, which are intentionally ignored by the lawmakers who propose them: it's difficult for working-class people to make the time or allocate the money to get the ID cards. The lower the economic class, the more votes tend to trend Democratic. Furthermore, these laws, which are clearly discriminatory, are eerily similar to laws that existed in the Jim Crow era, which is particularly troubling for people of color. Like Jim Crow, voter ID laws are designed to red-line minorities, using discriminatory practices with the effect of keeping them in a place where they have no voice, no power, and no political vehicle through which to address their grievances.

When Holder was in office, he became Obama's leading voice on civil-rights issues, and he took that role seriously. He made it clear that civil rights and criminal justice are intertwined, and his goal was to overturn any legislation that corroded both sides. Holder always said that he believed in the "conscience of the Justice Department."[77] He understands that racist police officers, coupled with sentencing disparities, ensure that Black male offenders receive sentences nearly 20 per cent longer than whites convicted of similar crimes.[78] He has called the injustice unacceptable and shameful; however, only time will tell how the Administration handles what it has singled out as shameful. During a speech about his My Brother's Keeper initiative, Obama said, "We can reform our criminal justice system to ensure that it's not infected with bias." But those who look and listen carefully to his words know that there is a difference between "we can" and "we will."

The School-to-Prison Pipeline

The school-to-prison pipeline is an American phenomenon that has received an increasing amount of scrutiny in recent years. Researchers have found that in addition to the militarization of police that has taken place over the past several decades, there have also been new trends of school systems scaling back or eliminating security guards and using city or state police forces in public and charter schools. These police forces have a similar effect on school populations as they do on the public at large—minorities, Black students especially, are targeted for arrests in greater numbers, even though they commit infractions at the same rates as their non-minority peers. This is similar to the statistic that Blacks smoke weed at the same rate as whites but are cited, arrested, and charged at far higher rates. When school systems opt to use state or city police forces for their security systems, students don't just get a demerit. Instead, they get an arrest record and are sent to the courts, with potentially long-lasting consequences that affect their chances at getting a job or securing a loan. Getting an arrest record in school, even for a minor offense, means that any subsequent offense is likely to be viewed in the prism of a "repeat offender," with harsher penalties or longer sentencing.

Various statistics compiled on state policing in public-school systems show a clear pattern of discrimination against people of color. Below are data collected by the Department of Education's Office of Civil Rights in the 2011–12 school year:

- Twelve per cent of all Black girls in school were suspended, compared with just two per cent of White girls.
- In New York City schools, Black students made up 28 per cent of the student body and White students 14 per cent. But

Black girls constituted 90 per cent of all girls expelled, and no White girls were expelled that school year.

- In Boston, Black students made up 35 per cent of the student body and White students 14 per cent, 63 per cent of all girls expelled were Black, and no White girls were expelled that school year.
- The arrest rate for Black students was one-third higher than for White students.
- In Chicago, nearly three-quarters of all arrests were of African-American students, even though they comprised less than half of the total number of public-school students.
- When it comes to policing and disciplining students, race played a significant factor.[79]

Tanzina Vega reported, in a *New York Times* piece, that researchers found that darker-skinned students were typically issued harsher punishments even when committing the same crime as lighter-skinned students. Biases about race and gender are part of the American public consciousness, so they inevitably manifest themselves in the school system, where Black students can be perceived as "violent" or "hypersexual" or "loud and rowdy." In order to counter these perceived behaviors, teachers and administrators often dole out harsh punishments, regardless of merit. The charges for which Black students are being arrested largely aren't serious crimes such as robbery or assault, but simple infractions that schools should be able to handle themselves, such as vandalism, smoking, disrespect of authority, or obscene language. Because these minor infractions, when committed by Black students, are viewed as violent threats, police are called, and arrests are made that could change the trajectory of a student's life.

African-American students face bigger problems than just trying to learn while at school. They also must face discrimination from teachers and administrators and a school security system that has increasingly turned away from traditional security guards and is now using more state and city police forces. Arrests for something as petty as "talking back" to a teacher can stay on a student's record for years, especially if their parents don't have the economic means to hire a lawyer to help the process of expunging a record. Not only that, being labeled a criminal has a devastating emotional and psychological effect on the young mind. Imagine sitting in civics class one day, and county jail the next, for nothing more than an ill-advised moment of adolescent impulsivity. A teenager can go from the right type of education—school—to the wrong type of education—incarceration—in the blink of an eye. The criminalization of Black youth in schools has led to a direct pipeline from classrooms to prisons, as small infractions that used to merit a detention now merit an arrest for African-American students.

In *The New Jim Crow: Mass Incarceration in the Age of Colorblindness*, Michelle Alexander explains that the nature of the criminal justice system has changed. It is no longer primarily concerned with the prevention and punishment of crime, but rather with the maintenance of the new caste system kept in place by incarceration and its manifold effects on Black men and women and their communities; it manages and controls the dispossessed and the alienated. The mass incarceration that has taken place in the new Jim Crow era isn't a problem that is likely to vanish any time soon. Even if the disastrous policies that have led to the skyrocketing incarceration rates and the disproportionate number of young Black men being placed behind bars were amended overnight to ensure that policing and justice serve Black and White America in identical ways, the disastrous effects of decades of the New Jim Crow will continue to be felt in Black communities and families for generations to come. Although our progress is excruciatingly slow (glacial even), this is no reason to lose hope or to allow our sails to droop. Though it may still be trying to avert its eyes, America is slowly facing the truth: our justice and policing systems are conflating race and criminality, and young men of color are paying the price (some with their very lives) of these racist policies and practices. As long as society continues to believe the fallacy that it is post-racial, an authentic resolution to this issue isn't possible. In February 2015, the Brennan Center for Justice issued a new report that discovered mass incarceration over the last two decades has had little to no effect on crime. Simply put, mass incarceration is a failure.[80] Mandatory minimum sentences have backfired. The War on Drugs has been lost; the War on Race has been won. The policies initiated in the Reagan era have failed the American public, and have certainly failed the thousands of Black families that they have torn (and are still tearing) apart.

As a system that erects and maintains firm barriers between the classes and the races, the privatized, profit-driven prison industrial complex is not something that can be dismantled overnight. Racial and class interests are at stake, but so is a tremendous amount of revenue for those who own and operate these prisons. Wide-reaching reform is at odds with the powerful industries that profit from mass incarceration, which include not only the organizations that own the prisons themselves but also those that profit from the cheap labor that they provide: health-care companies, food-supply companies, clothing manufacturers, and many more.[81]

Mass incarceration and voter suppression are not just political issues, social issues, or even intra-race issues—they are American moral issues. They are *the* civil-rights issues of our day. It's not just the Black community that has to fight a system that seems purposefully designed to incarcerate young Black men and disenfranchise Black voters; all of America has to join in the fight if we are to seek greatness. Otherwise, there is no way to bend the moral arc toward justice.

Notes

1   Staple Singers, "Freedom Highway," *Freedom Highway Complete* (1965), re-released March 2015 (Chicago: Legacy).

2   Alan Taylor, "1964: Civil Rights Battles," *The Atlantic* 28 May 2014, http://www.theatlantic.com/photo/2014/05/1964-civil-rights-battles/100744/.

3   National Voting Rights Museum and Institute, http://nvrmi.com/?page_id=43.

4   Callie Crossley and James A. DeVinney, "Bridge to Freedom (1965)," *Eyes on the Prize: America's Civil Rights Years, 1954-1965*, DVD (Blackside Inc., 2009).

5   Ibid.

6   Robbie Brown, "45 Years Later, an Apology and 6 Months," *The New York Times* 15 November 2010, http://www.nytimes.com/2010/11/16/us/16fowler.html?partner=rss&emc=rss&_r=0.

7   Crossley and DeVinney, "Bridge to Freedom (1965)."

8   Ibid.

9   "Lyndon B. Johnson: Voting Rights Act Address," Great American Documents, http://www.greatamericandocuments.com/speeches/lbj-voting-rights.html.

10   Crossley and DeVinney, "Bridge to Freedom (1965)."

11   Ibid.

12   Ibid.

13   See Davidson 7.

14   Ibid. 19.

15   Crossley and DeVinney, "Bridge to Freedom (1965)."

16   "Civil Rights, Voting Rights, and the Selma March," Amistad Digital Resource, Columbia University, 2009, http://www.amistadresource.org/civil_rights_era/ civil_rights_voting_rights_selma_march.html.

17   Scott Simpson, "Civil Rights Coalition Celebrates Renewal of Landmark Voting Rights Act," The Leadership Conference, 27 July 2006, http://www.civilrights. org/press/2006/civil-rights-coalition-celebrates-renewal-of-landmark-voting-rights-act.html.

18   *Shelby County v. Holder*, The Supreme Court of the United States 12–96, 25 June 2013, http://www.supremecourt.gov/opinions/12pdf/12-96_6k47.pdf.

19   Ibid. 3.

20   Ibid. 3–4.

21   Jelani Cobb, "The Voting Rights Act: An End to Racism by Judicial Order," *The New Yorker* 25 June 2013, http://www.newyorker.com/news/news-desk/ the-voting-rights-act-an-end-to-racism-by-judicial-order.

22   Myrna Pérez and Vishal Agraharkar, "If Section 5 Falls: New Voting Implications," Brennan Center for Justice, New York University School of Law, 12 June 2013, http://www.brennancenter.org/publication/ if-section-5-falls-new-voting-implications.

23   Personal interview, 11 May 2015.

24   Cobb, "The Voting Rights Act."

25   *Shelby County v. Holder* 16.

26   Ibid. 36–37.

27   Kara Brandeisky, Hanqing Chen, and Mike Tigas, "Everything That's Happened Since Supreme Court Ruled on Voting Rights Act," ProPublica, 4 November 2014, http://www.propublica.org/article/voting-rights-by-state-map.

28   David Weigel, "Did 17 Illegal Voters in Ohio Steal the 2012 Election?" *Slate* 19 December 2013, http://www.slate.com/blogs/weigel/2013/12/19/did_17_ illegal_voters_in_ohio_steal_the_2012_election.html.

29   Ryan Beckwith, "Voting Rights Is a Hot Topic Again," *Denver Post* 17 January 2014, http://www.denverpost.com/nationworld/ci_24933786/ voting-rights-is-hot-topic-again.

30   *McCutcheon v. Federal Election Commission*, 572 US (2014), 134 SC 1434.

31   David A. Love, "Poor People Lose Out when Elections Are Bought and Sold," theGrio.com, 3 April 2014, http://thegrio.com/2014/04/03/ poor-people-lose-out-when-elections-are-bought-and-sold/.

32   Jesse Jackson, "Jesse Jackson: Alabama's New Jim Crow Far from Subtle,"
     The Chicago Sun-Times 5 October 2015, http://chicago.suntimes.com/
     opinion/7/71/1014049/jesse-jackson-alabamas-new-jim-crow-far-subtle.

33   Ibid.

34   Dana Leibelson, "The Supreme Court Gutted the Voting Rights Act.
     What Happened Next in These 8 States Will Not Shock You," *Mother
     Jones* 8 April 2014, http://www.motherjones.com/politics/2014/04/
     republican-voting-rights-supreme-court-id.

35   Aaron Morrison, "Alabama Voting Rights: Congressional Black Caucus Blasts
     State's DMV Closures as Discriminatory and Racist," *International Business
     Times* 2 October 2015, http://www.ibtimes.com/alabama-voting-rights-
     congressional-black-caucus-blasts-states-dmv-office-closures-2125471.

36   Charles J. Dean, "Governor Bentley Says Decision to Close Driver's License
     Offices Not Race-Based," AL.com News, 6 October 2015, http://www.al.com/
     news/index.ssf/2015/10/gov_bentley_says_decision_to_c.html.

37   Kot 3.

38   Andre Cohen, "Freedom after 30 Years on Death Row," *The Atlantic* 11
     March 2014, http://www.theatlantic.com/national/archive/2014/03/
     freedom-after-30-years-on-death-row/284179/.

39   Chris Boyette, "Jonathan Fleming, Convicted in Killing despite Vacation Alibi,
     Freed after 24 Years," CNN, 9 April 2014, http://www.cnn.com/2014/04/08/
     justice/new-york-wrongful-conviction/index.html.

40   John Caniglia, "Ricky Jackson Leaves Prison," Cleveland.com, 21
     November 2014, www.cleveland.com/court-justice/index.ssf/2014/11/
     ricky_jackson_leaves_a_life_be.html.

41   Scott Neuman, "DNA Exonerates Man Who Served Nearly 40 Years for
     Murder," NPR, 23 January 2015, www npr.com/setions/thetwo-way/2015/
     01/23/379417126/dna-exonerates-man-who-served-nearly-40-years-for-murder.

42   Office of Juvenile Justice and Delinquency Prevention, *Statistical Briefing Book*,
     http://www.ojjdp.gov/ojstatbb/crime/qa05104.asp?qaDate=2011&text=.

43   Rocco Parascandola, "Five City Council Members Charge NYPD of
     Unfairly Targeting Minority Men for Marijuana Arrests," *New York Daily
     News* 31 October 2014, http://www.nydailynews.com//news/politics/5-city-
     council-members-charge-nypd-targeting-minority-men-marijuana-arrests-
     article-1.1993956.

44   Ben Chapman, "City Council Members Want to Overhaul School Discipline
     Policies to End Race Gap," *New York Daily News* 3 February 2015,
     http://www.nydailynews.com/new-york/educationpush-made-overhaul-school-
     discipline-policies-article-1.2101240.

45   Parascandola, "Five City Council Members."

46   Dave Jamieson, "Bill De Blasio Explains Why His Son Needs to Be Careful around Cops," The Huffington Post, 7 December 2014, http://www.huffingtonpost.com/2014/12/07/bill-de-blasio-son_n_6283774.html.

47   "Incarceration," The Sentencing Project, n.d., http://www.sentencingproject.org/template/page.cfm?id=107.

48   Kathleen Miles, "Just How Much the War on Drugs Impacts Our Overcrowded Prisons," The Huffington Post, 10 March 2014, http://www.huffingtonpost.com/2014/03/10/war-on-drugs-prisons-infographic_n_4914884.html.

49   National Association for the Advancement of Colored People, *Criminal Justice Fact Sheet*, http://www.naacp.org/pages/criminal-justice-fact-sheet.

50   Ibid.

51   Dale Gieringer, "125th Anniversary of the First U.S. Anti-Drug Law: San Francisco's Opium Den Ordinance," Drugsense.org, November 2000, http://www.drugsense.org/dpfca/opiumlaw.html.

52   Oscar Pascual, "Marijuana and Immigration: A Common History," *San Francisco Gate* 7 June 2013, http://blog.sfgate.com/smellthetruth/2013/06/07/marijuana-and-immigration-a-common-history/.

53   See Massey, http://www.ncbi.nlm.nih.gov/pmc/articles/PMC2931357/.

54   See Jaffe, Cullen, and Boswell.

55   See Nunn, excerpted at http://racism.org/index.php?option=com_content&view=article&id=820:crime09-1&catid=142&Itemid=155. The full article can be found at http://scholarship.law.ufl.edu/cgi/viewcontent.cgi?article=1178&context=facultypub.

56   Pamela Oliver, "Racial Disparities in Imprisonment," University of Wisconsin Madison, http://www.ssc.wisc.edu/~oliver/RACIAL/Reports/meparticledraft3.pdf.

57   Milosh Marinovich, "A Change Has Gotta Come," *The Harlem Times* n.d., http://theharlemtimes.com/culture/a-change-has-gotta-come.

58   "Decades-Old CIA Crack-Cocaine Scandal Gains New Momentum," *Russia Today* 11 October 2014, http://rt.com/usa/194992-cia-crack-scandal-webb/.

59   Ryan Grim, Matt Sledge, and Matt Ferner, "Key Figures in CIA-Crack Cocaine Scandal Begin to Come Forward," The Huffington Post, 10 October 2014, http://www.huffingtonpost.com/2014/10/10/gary-webb-dark-alliance_n_5961748.html.

60   Jesse Lee, "President Obama Signs the Fair Sentencing Act," The White House, 3 August 2010, https://www.whitehouse.gov/blog/2010/08/03/president-obama-signs-fair-sentencing-act.

61   Alec Karakatsanis, "Why US v Blewett Is the Obama Justice Department's Greatest Shame." Common Dreams, 23 July 2013, http://www.commondreams. org/views/2013/07/23 why-us-v-blewett-obama-justice-departments-greatest-shame.

62   Nick Chiles, "Congressional Black Caucus Pushes Obama to Use Executive Action to Reduce Poverty and Incarceration Rates for Black Community," Atlanta Blackstar, 12 February 2015, http://atlantablackstar.com/2015/02/12/ congressional-black-caucus-pushes-obama-use-executive-action-reduce-poverty-rate-incarceration-rate-black-community/.

63   Brady Dennis, "Obama Administration Will Not Block State Marijuana Laws if Distribution Is Regulated," *The Washington Post* 29 August 2013, http://www. washingtonpost.com/national/health-science/obama-administration-will-not-preempt-state-marijuana-laws--for-now/2013/08/29/b725bfd8-10bd-11e3-8cdd-bcdc09410972_story.html.

64   William M. Welch, "Obama: Pot No More Dangerous than Alcohol," *USA Today* 20 January 2014, http://www.usatoday.com//story/news/ politics/2014/01/19/obama-marijuana-not-so-bad/4649883/.

65   Victoria Bekiempis, "Eric Holder Moves Against Mandatory Minimum Drug Sentencing," *Newsweek* 13 March 2014, http://www.newsweek.com// eric-holder-moves-against-mandatory-minimum-drug-sentencing-231818.

66   "Attorney General Eric Holder Slams U.S. Mass Incarceration at Security Ministers Conference in Medellín, Colombia," Drug Policy Alliance, 22 November 2013, http://www.drugpolicy.org/news/2013/11/attorney-general-eric-holder-slams-us-mass-incarceration-security-ministers-conference-.

67   "Obama Grants Clemency to Just 8 Federal Prisoners," *The Clemency Report*, 18 December 2014, http://clemencyreport.org/obama-grants-clemency-8-prisoners/.

68   M. Harris-Perry, "How Barack Obama Is like Martin Luther King, Jr," *The Nation* 18 January 2010, http://www.thenation.com/article/how-barack-obama-martin-luther-king-jr/.

69   See https://www.youtube.com/watch?v=WA3oqycCBvQ; originally broadcast on MSNBC, 11 January 2010.

70   Oren Yaniv, "Cornel West Decries Obama as Counterfeit," *New York Daily News* 25 August 2014, http://www.nydailynews.com//news/politics/cornel-west-decries-president-obama-counterfeit-article-1.1916726.

71   Greg Richter, "Tavis Smiley: Obama Lectures Blacks, Jokes with Whites," Newsmax.com, 9 December 2014, http://www.newsmax.com/Newsfront/ BET-Colbert-Show-Obama-race/2014/12/09/id/611920/.

72   Eyder Peralta, "Two Excerpts You Should Read from Obama's Morehouse Speech," NPR, 19 May 2013, http://www.npr.org/sections/thetwo-way/ 2013/05/19/185348873/two-excerpts-you-should-read-from-obamas-morehouse-speech.

73   Sari Horwitz, "Reforming Justice System Is Personal Goal for Holder," *The Washington Post* 14 November 2013, http://www.washingtonpost.com/ world/national-security/reforming-justice-system-is-personal-goal-for-holder/2013/11/14/134554bc-4c7e-11e3-be6b-d3d28122e6d4_story.html.

74   Ryan J. Reilly, "Eric Holder Backs Restoration of Voting Rights for Former Felons," The Huffington Post, 11 February 2014, http://www.huffingtonpost.com/2014/02/11/eric-holder-felon-voting_n_4762863.html.

75   Sophie Kerby, "The Top 10 Most Startling Facts about People of Color and Criminal Justice in the United States," Center for American Progress, 13 March 2012, https://www.americanprogress.org/issues/race/news/2012/03/13/11351/ the-top-10-most-startling-facts-about-people-of-color-and-criminal-justice-in-the-united-states/.

76   Tom McKay, "This Study Confirms Everything You Suspected about Voter ID Laws," Policy Mic, 18 December 2013, http://mic.com/articles/77049/ this-study-confirms-everything-you-suspected-about-voter-id-laws.

77   Brentin Mock, "Eric Holder's Racial Justice Legacy," Colorlines, 29 September 2014, http://www.colorlines.com/articles/eric-holders-racial-justice-legacy.

78   Josh Gerstein, "Eric Holder: Some Prison Terms Too Long," *Politico* 5 April 2013, http://www.politico.com/politico44/2013/04/eric-holder-some-prison-terms-too-long-160897.html.

79   Dani McClain, "This Is How Black Girls End Up in the School-To-Prison Pipeline," *The Nation* 5 February 2015, http://www.thenation.com/blog/197257/ too-many-black-girls-school-prison-pipeline#.

80   "New Report: Increased Incarceration Had Limited Effect on Reducing Crime for Over Two Decades," Brennan Center for Justice, New York University School of Law, 12 February 2015, https://www.brennancenter.org/press-release/ new-report-increased-incarceration-had-limited-effect-reducing-crime-over-two-decades.

81   Alex Henderson, "9 Surprising Industries Getting Filthy Rich from Mass Incarceration," Salon, 22 February 2015, http://www.salon.com/2015/02/22/9_ surprising_industries_getting_filthy_rich_from_mass_incarceration_partner/.

Chapter Four

XENOPHOBIA: AMERICA INSIDE OUT

LIKE AMERICA'S PERSISTENT PROBLEMS WITH RACISM (SO APPARENT in the gulf separating our theoretical from our practical equality), the nation has long struggled to reconcile its self-representation as a safe harbor for freedom seekers with its treatment of those who come to America in search of the bounty the country promises. Since 1886, Lady Liberty has stood at her post at the entrance to the New York Harbor. All that time, we have claimed her as a symbol of the freedom promised by the land of liberty and opportunity. Her upraised torch is, we say, a beacon of hope for those fleeing oppressive and corrupt regimes, interminable and often-deadly poverty, the constant threat of violence, or some combination of these three (and many others besides). "Her name," says the plaque in the statue's base: "Mother of Exiles." Her cry to the world and its citizens who would seek shelter from the darkness in her light:

Give me your tired, your poor,
Your huddled masses yearning to breathe free,
The wretched refuse of your teeming shore.
Send these, the homeless, tempest-tost to me,
I lift my lamp beside the golden door!

As America grew into a superpower, that call was answered, as through her shadow passed millions of immigrants, each of them touching American soil for the first time on Ellis Island. Whatever their reasons for coming, immigrants were implicitly promised two things: opportunity and equality. If they arrived penniless, a can-do spirit would be enough to turn rags to riches—or, if not riches, at least a degree of middle-class comfort; Old World economic and social castes were not—or so it appeared—a significant feature of the New World. Under the watchful eye of "The New Colossus," the free market, that great leveler, putatively sorted Americans according to their relative merits.

For many of these third- and fourth-wave immigrants, we can safely assume that their first glimpse of Lady Liberty was accompanied by the thought, "I made it. I'm safe. *America. A new beginning.*" But this unbridled optimism ran headlong into widespread racism and a class system only marginally less rigid than those they had left behind. Conditions in America's ghettoes (the beaches onto which many of the third- and fourth-wave immigrants rolled) were deplorable, good work with fair pay was out of reach for many new Americans, and institutional racism represented a nearly insurmountable barrier between many of these immigrants and the equality and opportunities they had been promised. This, however, did not prevent them from contributing in both small and large ways to the building of America into the superpower it would so quickly become. The concrete, steel, glass, and marble of which our great cities are composed all bear the fingerprints of these new Americans. Our entrepreneur-built middle class bears the same traces—as do countless many of the cultural traditions that we have appropriated as our own from those who brought them from every corner of the globe. As the world's great melting pot, we seem positively eager to forget that the stuff of which we are forged is not homogenous.

Now, as then, there is a distinct note of hypocrisy in Lady Liberty's words. For immigrants, America is, at times, an incredibly hostile and opportunity-starved place. The bigotry and xenophobia that once targeted Irish, Catholic, Jewish, and Asian immigrants are now focused largely on Hispanic and Middle Eastern immigrants (we'll examine the latter in the next section). Politicians (largely, but not exclusively, Republicans) parrot the xenophobia of America's conservative base, who seem to fear nothing as much as the gradual "browning" of America.[1] Highly emotional, vitriolic, and irrational arguments are made at town halls and in campaign ads, and, when these campaigners are elected, they make good on their promises to "do something" about America's immigration problem: they call for, write, and pass legislation that treats immigrants (especially Mexican ones) as though they actually were the criminals and morally bankrupt freeloaders that anti-immigrant crusaders paint them to be.

Rep. Steve King (R-IA), with apparent seriousness, said that for every child of illegal immigrants "who's a valedictorian, there's another 100 out there who weigh 130 pounds and they've got calves the size of cantaloupes because they're hauling 75 pounds of marijuana across the desert."[2] Such wildly inaccurate factoids and inflammatory rhetoric are widely trafficked on conservative media outlets, and, laughably ridiculous as these claims are,[3] it would seem that both state legislators and local voters find them convincing. Consider the spate of recent anti-immigrant legislation, including Arizona's SB 1070, which allows officers to demand that Latinos present documentation to prove they are in the country legally (five other states quickly passed copycat legislation), and the notorious stop-and-frisk laws in New York, which allow police to stop, interrogate, and search anybody they suspect of carrying contraband or weapons (not surprisingly, the vast majority of those forced to submit to such indignities are Black or Latino— between 2003 and 2014, 53–56% of them were Black, 29–34% Latino).[4] Anti-Latino sentiment swept the U.S. after an uptick in migrants (many of them unaccompanied minors) from El Salvador, Honduras, and Guatemala. Buses crossing the southern border were met with protesters who waved placards and hurled abusive language at those aboard the buses, many of whom were fleeing escalating gang violence and predatory child-prostitution rings in their home countries.[5]

If the content of their signs is any indication, xenophobes in this country feel that the ground is shifting beneath their feet, and, to their credit, they're absolutely correct. America is becoming "browner" by the moment. To keep pace, the reactionary, conservative politicians resort to immigration-based fear mongering. This leads to an abundance of emotional arguments that escalate an already vitriolic and irrational discourse on the subject, breeding more anger and prejudice. Those on the right do their best to portray immigrants as criminals and leeches, without being intellectually honest or attempting in any way to foster a discussion on the deeper socioeconomic, geopolitical, and cultural issues at play. They completely ignore the fundamental facts of the situation—one of these facts being that very few undocumented immigrants who are apprehended are actually criminals.[6] The vast majority are simply regular people who want a better life and will do what is needed to attain it. They are productive and routinely contribute a great deal to our country. Often, the debate on immigration is lowered to the level of prejudice, xenophobia, and white supremacy. As a matter of numbers and demography, the racial landscape of the United States is, indeed, changing. Within thirty years, white people will be in the minority, and current minorities, including immigrants of minority backgrounds, will become the majority. This fact, frequently produced as evidence that something has to be done to secure America's borders, has galvanized into action those who see America as a "white" nation. For a country founded by white individuals who enslaved Blacks and oppressed other minorities, this shift has likely put even the least racist of white people on the defensive for fear of what such a demographic shift could mean for laws, public policies, and, more fundamentally, societal treatment of the soon-to-be minority population. Pat Buchanan, for example, sees America as a once-proud nation that has been utterly ruined by a combination of godlessness and unchecked immigration; the country has, apparently, lost sight of its white, Christian heritage altogether.[7] For the most part, those who find his view compelling are, like Buchanan himself, of an older generation, yet they still exercise an undue influence in Washington and are pandered to on conservative media as though their viewpoints had any value in our pluralistic, twenty-first-century world.

So eager are conservatives to pander to those obsessed with the past that they would have us roll our clocks back nearly a century and a half. In 2010, members of Congress actually considered repealing the Fourteenth Amendment, which guarantees citizenship to anyone born in the United States.[8] The amendment was originally crafted to ensure that former slaves would have all the rights and titles of American citizens, but, due to manufactured outrage over "anchor babies," a pejorative term referring to children born in the United States to undocumented workers who, due to the Fourteenth Amendment, are "anchored" as citizens, have been heavily politicized by Donald Trump, Jeb Bush, and others during the 2016 presidential cycle. The insensitivity and outright hate have even created an even more ridiculous term, "terrorist babies," which refers to anchor babies who go back to their parents' country and learn to hate America, with the expectation of returning as citizens and waging war upon the U.S.[9] Congress actually considered rewriting the rules to make citizenship even more exclusive than it already is. This type of language is not only offensive; it also distracts us from the real need we have to fix our immigration system. It also violates one of the most fundamental of Constitutional rights: that there shall be no government-sanctioned judgment until after due process of law.

Much of this inflammatory anti-immigrant rhetoric has little effect on most people. However, there is nevertheless danger in these base, outdated ideas. Arizona's 2010 "papers, please" law created a constitutional crisis in which the federal government, particularly the judicial branch via the Supreme Court, was charged with balancing the needs of law-enforcement agencies to protect the sovereignty of the U.S. by protecting its borders and verifying the permission of suspected illegal immigrants, with the need to treat all people as equal before the law by not racially profiling.[10] While the Court empathized with law-enforcement agencies in Arizona, it found on both procedural and substantive grounds that the state had overstepped its authority. It had acted unconstitutionally by stopping people suspected of being illegal immigrants. The Court wisely found that while searches and seizures are important in ensuring the public safety, neither Arizona nor other states could arbitrarily racially profile suspected immigrants without any substantive reasonable suspicion and probable cause.[11]

The Court also ruled that while some previsions could remain, assuming probable cause existed, the crux of the law, which was essentially to intimidate minorities suspected of being Latino, could not stand. In addition to the already mentioned legal rationales for striking down SB 1070, the majority argued that the issue at hand revolved around the Supremacy Clause and the fact that Arizona could not merely interject itself in immigration matters that it lacked the knowledge and authority to handle. Ultimately, the Court rightly put Arizona's state government in its place, which served as a reminder that immigration is not an evil but a human and civil right. Whereas the larger issue of immigration certainly ought to be argued with the goal of formulating a strategic approach to ensure that the country has the resources to welcome large groups of people, it nevertheless stands that the story of immigration is fundamentally the story of the American Dream. The immigrant's story is truly the American story: almost every American is descended from an immigrant, yet immigrants continue to face discrimination from those whose few generations on this land make them feel exclusively entitled to its bounty. Less than a century ago, Irish immigrants (like conservative commentators Sean Hannity's and Bill O'Reilly's recent ancestors) were still considered unworthy of the same opportunities as Americans descended from the English. Many native-born Americans in the eighteenth and nineteenth centuries were fervently anti-Catholic, and Irish immigrants—thanks in no small part to centuries of Catholic/Protestant antagonisms and racist caricature in England—were painted in the least flattering colors imaginable.[12]

In time, Irish immigrants became an important part of the American landscape (and were recognized—albeit grudgingly at first—as Americans entitled to the same dignity as those with English ancestry). The election of John F. Kennedy (an Irish Catholic) in 1960 proved that America was able to let at least some of its prejudices drop. It's hard to overstate how important this moment was for those of Irish ancestry. It was their Barack Obama moment—and they've forgotten it. Now, it would seem, this history is being intentionally ignored, and those whose ancestors assimilated with more than their share of difficulty are, hand over fist, pulling up the ladder behind them.

Nobody is denying that comprehensive immigration reform is necessary; but at issue is the shape this reform will take. Nobody can deny that the U.S. needs the labor that immigrants provide. We employ documented and undocumented immigrants heavily in the hospitality, agriculture, construction, food services, health care, and information technology fields.[13] Without their contributions, these sectors would be starved for workers. Whether their income is taxed or not, immigrants stimulate the economy with their spending, which is exactly what governments the world over have been trying to do since the Great Recession. According to Ian Goldin of Oxford, immigrants (with new access to technology and education) inject significant amounts of intellectual capital into their host countries, lifting lower- and middle-class wages across the board as industry capitalizes on this new labor.[14] Giovanni Perri of the University of California, Davis, has used sophisticated mathematical models to study the effects of legalizing as opposed to deporting undocumented workers. His findings make mincemeat of conservative claims that an unobstructed pathway to citizenship for immigrants is a road to financial ruin for this country:

> More deportation resulted in fewer jobs for native-born U.S. citizens by preventing migrants from stimulating job creation by U.S. firms. Legalizing these undocumented people increased the number of migrants, boosting the economic stimulus and creating more jobs for migrants and locals alike.[15]

In 2010, the United Farm Workers union made this point all the clearer by starting a "Take our Jobs" campaign, offering the kind of work that migrants have long made do with in this country to all comers. How many of the hard-working, white Americans whose jobs were being stolen by migrant workers showed up to fill the half-million positions that were available? No more than a few dozen.[16] Debates surrounding immigration reform, especially when undertaken in bad faith or without any trace of intelligent thinking, put more than just the livelihood of millions of undocumented workers at risk; the kind of strict immigration laws that are being floated by those purporting to stand up for middle-class Americans would be nothing short of disastrous for the economy if they were to be uniformly implemented. Without the massive, inexpensive labor pool needed at harvest time, America would soon be facing serious food shortages. It is abundantly clear that the jobs done by migrant workers have not been stolen; quite the contrary, they are the jobs (due to back-breaking working hours and wages often below state minimums) that even unemployed

Americans feel are somehow beneath their dignity.[17] If nobody is willing to take these jobs when they are freely offered, who exactly are immigrants stealing them from?

Even in less economically measurable ways, the influx of immigrants from every corner of the planet enriches this country. Our culture teems with their art, film, music, and literature; as their worldview enters the mainstream it enriches our own, providing new perspectives and a truly global context. We laud the accomplishments of immigrants like Andrew Carnegie, Albert Einstein, Wyclef Jean, and Yao Ming, but too many of us fail to connect these undoubtedly exceptional immigrants with those who cross our borders every day hoping to make a new and better life here.

Deportations have increased dramatically over the last six years,[18] earning President Obama the moniker "Deporter in Chief" from many immigration activists. According to the Pew Research Center, the Obama Administration had deported more than two million immigrants by the end of the first year of Obama's second term (setting a record of 438,421 deportations in 2013 alone).[19] The inflammatory and xenophobic rhetoric in Congress has created a toxic miasma that hangs over the issue of immigration reform. Witness, for example, the verbal knots into which Senator Marco Rubio ties himself to appear even remotely appealing to conservative voters riding the immigration hobbyhorse. His erstwhile moderate stance on immigration reform (surely informed by his own experience as the son of Cuban immigrants) has been pushed so far to the right by xenophobic sentiment within his party that his attempts to reconcile his former statements with the ones he is making on the campaign trail would be comical, were the situation not so tragic.[20] The GOP had a chance to learn from the drubbing that minority voters handed Romney in 2012, and Rubio seemed like the party's best chance at showing that they had learned their lesson. Instead, the Tea Party has dragged Rubio (hardly kicking and screaming) to the fringe, where he has become virtually indistinguishable from the immigrant-vilifying field.

Elected representatives (and especially those in conservative districts) seem to be convinced that any leniency, no matter how slight, will be the death knell of their re-election hopes. President Obama attempted to cut through this fog, instituting through executive action his Deferred Action for Childhood Arrivals. Republicans were quick to paint Obama as a tyrant for this decisive step, but this has not affected his resolve. Though it may not be a permanent solution, and though it certainly does not go as far as the *DREAM Act*, Obama's movement toward immigration reform (like his signature health-care act) shows a willingness to defy Republican rhetoric and the threats it carries with it.

The next step is to push for more comprehensive reform—either the *DREAM Act* or something very much like it. The Dreamers, undocumented immigrants who came to the U.S. before the age of 16 and have lived here for at least five years,[21] are, indeed, entitled to some share of the benefits that American citizenship has to offer. Many of them came to this country without any say in the matter, and there is no reason that the sins of the parents (if immigrating illegally can even be counted as such) should be visited on the next generation. The lion's share of Dreamers have meaningful and productive lives; they are integral parts of their communities, their cities, and their country (for such it deserves to be called). They work hard (harder than many) for what they earn, and they deserve the official status they have long sought. Opening pathways to citizenship and to everything this citizenship entails (education, health care, and tax-paying status) will enrich this nation beyond imagining. Giving young immigrants legal status through the *DREAM Act* would result in at least $1.4 trillion in higher earnings, with some estimates at $3.6 trillion.[22] Why should we keep them in limbo and threaten them with deportation when they are such a valuable resource?

Every era has its own huddled masses yearning to breathe free. Conflict arises when they huddle too closely together, unite, and transform into a viable competitor to the reigning demographic. Every major clash between the marginalized and the majority can be traced to the rising power of the oppressed. From the Irish to the Asians to the Hispanics, they all had their hour of solidarity that defined a moment in history. For the Muslims, that moment was September 11, 2001.

Islamophobia in America: Who Is to Blame?

One very contentious issue that America faces—informed by the same xenophobic prejudices that inform the out-and-out bigotry it displays toward those with brown skin who dare to immigrate to America—is Islamophobia. Similar to xenophobia and anti-Semitism, Islamophobia has deep historical roots; it isn't just a post-9/11 phenomenon. Various factors and events have led to the twenty-first-century version of Islamophobia, a more violent one than before. Most important among them are post–World War II immigration, the Iranian Revolution, the Iran hostage crisis, and the terrorist events from the 1980s onwards, culminating in the 9/11 attacks and followed by other terrorist acts in Europe.[23] The fear of all things associated with Islam skews the way it is represented in our media, which seems hell-bent on exaggerating fear and stoking the ancient fire of hatred. It distorts Islam into a movement synonymous with violence and terror, leading many Americans to insist—in veiled or unveiled ways—that those who practice (or even appear to practice) the Muslim religion must be excluded, pre-emptively, from our society.

In 1991, the Runnymede Trust released a damning report on the West and the ways in which it viewed and represented Islam, citing widespread and "unfounded hostility" toward either particular Muslims or Muslims in aggregate. The report assigned the following opinions to the belief system they referred to as Islamophobia:

- Islam is monolithic and cannot adapt to new realities.
- Islam does not share common values with other major faiths.
- Islam as a religion is inferior to the West. It is archaic, barbaric, and irrational.
- Islam is a religion of violence and supports terrorism.
- Islam is a violent political ideology.[24]

This uninformed and prejudiced view of Islam is derived from centuries-old racial and religious hierarchies that dictated the way in which the European West approached and attempted (or did not attempt) to understand the Muslim East. Twenty-first-century American Anti-Muslim sentiments dovetail neatly with this kind of thinking—the same that underpinned centuries of religious wars and pogroms in Europe.

Noam Chomsky traces the beginning of the demonization of Islam in America back to 1958,[25] but it didn't hit full stride until the U.S.S.R. ceased to be a threat large enough to frighten the American public. The Middle East, which had long been something of an also-ran in terms of capturing the public's complete attention, took center stage as American tanks rumbled across the Iraqi desert. Saddam Hussein became the new villain, and the entire Arab world—except, of course, for our allies like Saudi Arabia, upon whom we depend for oil—became the new monolithic enemy. Along with the saturated coverage of Operation Desert Storm came a new brand of Middle East experts, many of whom betray atrociously simplistic understandings of the region and its variegated inhabitants. Edward Said, one of the first to ring alarm bells about how Western media outlets cover the Middle East (particularly its coverage of the Palestinian/Israeli conflict), urged a degree of skepticism when exposed to Western images of the Middle East: "A corps of experts on the Islamic world has grown to prominence, and during a crisis, they are brought out to pontificate on formulaic ideas about Islam on news programs or talk shows." These so-called experts, he continues, have revived "canonical, though previously discredited, Orientalist ideas about Muslim, generally non-white, people" (xvi). The result is widely accepted forms of caricature and demonology based on the false belief that West and East are diametrically opposed and the differences can never be resolved. We're sold a bill of goods that claims the values, religions, cultures, and civilizations of the East are incompatible with our Western notions of freedom, democracy, and self-determination.

For Muslims living in the United States, this overt, unabashed demonization has thrown up massive barriers to assimilation. Consider, for instance, the difficulty that Muslims encounter when they want to do something as innocuous as construct a house of worship in their communities. In 2010, *Time* published an article that gave a first-hand account of daily life for a Muslim in America. Their subject, Dr. Mansoor Mirza of Sheboygan County, Wisconsin, had been a resident of the community for many years, working at the nearby hospital for five of them. Since there were no houses of worship nearby where he could practice his faith, he sought permission from the county planning commission to construct a mosque on a piece of property he owned. Perhaps naïvely, Dr. Mirza expected his application to be little more than a formality. However, when the commission opened the floor to debate, the men and women of the community, given the opportunity to voice their concerns, let loose a barrage of xenophobic views on Islam and Muslims. A few of the statements made by concerned community members:

- Islam is a religion of hate.
- Muslims are determined to wipe out Christianity.
- There are 20 jihadi training camps hidden across rural America, busy even now producing the next wave of terrorists.
- Muslims murder their children.[26]

This incident shows how racist, xenophobic, and irrational Americans can be, even when surrounded by practicing Muslims who are upstanding members of their communities.

Though the response to the planned mosque in the American Midwest was a nauseating look into deeply ingrained American prejudices, it was relatively minor in scope when compared to the national uproar that followed the media's sensational coverage of the plan to build a Muslim cultural center and mosque in lower Manhattan, just a few blocks from Ground Zero. The proposal, called Park51, sought permission to renovate a derelict Burlington Coat Factory retail store that had been empty for almost a decade. The project, with support from Mayor Michael Bloomberg, had already received approval from the New York City Council. Unfortunately, even that level of support wasn't enough to keep the Islamophobes at bay. While some of the project's critics had quasi-legitimate concerns about what the Muslim center would mean to the families of 9/11 victims (that some of these victims were themselves Muslims seemed not to factor into these concerns), much of the criticism was rabidly Islamophobic.

In the wake of widespread conservative media coverage of the issue, there were a number of protests featuring the usual flag-waving freedom lovers with racist invective printed on placards, and speakers who vacillated wildly between patriotic platitudes and patent falsehoods. The largest of these was organized by right-wing blogger Pamela Geller, the founder of Stop Islamization of America (SIA). SIA uses high-profile advertising to spread its message, which boils down to little more than the fact that Muslims are un-American savages who want nothing more than to destroy this country and take away its God-given freedoms. She told reporters, "Building the Ground Zero mosque is not an issue of religious freedom, but . . . an effort to insult the victims of 9/11 and to establish a beachhead for political Islam and Islamic supremacists in New York."[27] What she and most other protesters failed to note, however, was that the location had already served as a de facto Muslim cultural center for more than a year before the protests started. Muslims had been praying and gathering in that building for quite some time without any complaints from anyone in the neighborhood.[28]

Geller and many of those who took the time to scrawl their concerns on cardboard made no attempts to conceal the fact that the protests were anti-Muslim (they had less to do with the proposed cultural center than they did with the perceived encroachment of Islam into "American" life). The crowd seemed most concerned that the mosque and community center would stand as some kind of monument to the victory won by Islam when the towers fell. Geller was particularly insistent on this point: "This," she said, "is Islamic domination and expansionism. The location is no accident. Just as al-Aqsa was built on top of the Temple Mount in Jerusalem."[29] Geller conflates events a millennia and a half apart, but her followers aren't exactly known to be concerned with rhetorically valid arguments grounded in historical fact. Islamophobia is built upon a foundation of ignorance and fear, and inflammatory rhetoric spewed by Geller (and even by some of the right's less incendiary ideologues) stokes the fires of resentment and revanchism among those who can, thanks to their blinkered or non-existent readings of history, be easily convinced that they have lost or are losing something precious. All the better if that something is as intangible and airy a thing as the American way of life—which need never be defined so long as the receptive listener catches the speaker's drift.

Islamophobia is by no means new in America. 9/11 merely gave ideologues the ideal cover for anti-Muslim sentiment, which many Muslim Americans contend has long been bubbling beneath the surface. The terrorist attacks on the World Trade Center and the Pentagon merely opened the floodgates for those with an ax to grind with Islam and gave them legions of new followers. Few would doubt, though, that the particular strain of Islamophobia that infects America today is far more virulent than the late-twentieth-century one.

Immediately following the 2001 terrorist attacks, President George W. Bush attempted to stem the swelling tide of anti-Muslim sentiment that followed in the wake of the attacks by visiting an Islamic center in Washington, D.C. He assured Muslims that there would be no reprisals against them. While I cannot speak to the inner recesses of the former president's heart, this address was counterproductive, given that America's growing army of Islamophobes leaped into action despite this ceremonial visit. While being stirred up by leading Christians like Pat Robertson and Jerry Falwell, who questioned Islam's legitimacy and called Mohammed a robber and a terrorist, and by countless conservative anchors and radio personalities, our nation's moral conscience was deliberately duped and became hopelessly blurred. The Muslim Public Affairs Council reports that, in the aftermath of the 9/11 attacks, anti-Muslim hate crimes skyrocketed by 1600 per cent.[30] Anti-Muslim sentiment was suddenly everywhere. Even state representatives got in on the act. In Georgia, Representative Saxby Chambliss (now a senator) opined at one point that his state should "arrest every Muslim that comes across the state line."[31]

Following the attacks, such remarks were stunningly commonplace in political discourse and the media in general, and they continue to be, almost a decade and a half later. Many of the most egregious comments tend to be isolated to a few individuals or media outlets, but thanks to the instant connectivity allowed by the Internet, their viral potential is nearly limitless. So eager have we become to have our worst suspicions confirmed that discredited experts with highly questionable readings of either history or current affairs are given a national platform. In 2011, for instance, Florida Rep. Allen West commemorated the tenth anniversary of the 9/11 terrorist attacks by holding a screening in congressional offices of *Sacrificed Survivors: The Untold Story of the Ground Zero Mega-Mosque*, a thoroughly discredited anti-Muslim "documentary" film produced by the Christian Action Network (CAN) that makes nauseating claims about "the radical Muslim agenda" and posits a secret alliance between liberals and Muslims that will implement sharia law as soon as it is powerful enough to do so.[32]

This strange conflation of mainstream liberal values with radical religious doctrine makes the political game played by activists and conservative politicians like West somewhat more transparent. As the country changes around those who remain fixated on the past, those who represent that change are fused into a single body that is identifiably foreign, liberal, menacing, and, worst of all, un-American. Rep. Keith Ellison (D-MN), one of only two Muslims ever to be elected to Congress, has faced rabidly anti-Muslim opposition from the Tea Party, which has made no attempts to conceal the fact that it is Ellison's religion that makes him a soft target. One of his recent opponents, Chris Fields, sent out a mailer accusing Ellison of being "militantly anti-American."[33] Another Tea Party–backed candidate, Lynne Torgerson, who ran an entire campaign against Ellison's religion, called him a "radical Islamist" as she was in the midst of announcing her candidacy for his seat.[34]

Perhaps the worst of all the political stunts that betrayed the clear anti-Muslim bias that has taken firm root in the far right of the political spectrum is the veritable witch hunt that Minnesota Rep. Michele Bachmann led in 2012. She, along with fellow Republican Representatives Trent Franks, Lewis Gohmert, Thomas Rooney, and Lynn Westmoreland, sent letters to the inspectors general of five different government agencies, asking them to investigate the possible "deep penetration" of Muslim Brotherhood operatives "in the halls of our United States government."[35] They strongly suggested that Huma Abedin, a top aide to then-secretary of state Hillary Clinton and the wife of former Congressman Anthony Weiner, was suspect due to (entirely specious) connections between the Muslim Brotherhood and Abedin's late father, her mother, and her brother.[36] Intense criticism from both sides of the aisle didn't change Bachmann's position in the slightest. In fact, she doubled down, addressing a letter to Keith Ellison, who had demanded she produce "credible, substantial evidence" to bolster her claims.[37] The 16-page letter that Bachmann responded with, which included footnoted references to a host of discredited Muslim conspiracy theorists, was most definitely not the "credible" evidence that Ellison had asked for, but her letter is widely circulated on right-wing websites that traffic (as Bachmann still does) in Muslim conspiracy theories.

Given the ubiquitous and vitriolic anti-Muslim rhetoric coming from conservative pundits and politicians, perhaps it is no surprise that the American public (especially those who rely on conservative media for information) has increasingly soured on Muslims in the last few years. A poll released on July 29, 2014, by the Arab-American Institute showed that there has been a marked decline in positive attitudes toward Muslims among Americans. Favorable attitudes toward Arabs declined from 43 per cent in 2010 to 32 per cent in 2014, and for Muslims as a whole the favorability rating declined from 35 per cent in 2010 to 27 per cent in 2014.[38]

Behind this decline is the willingness of conservative commentators and pundits to use fear as a campaigning tool. Their strategy is to twist the justified fear of Islamist terror groups (particularly ISIS as of late) into a generalized, undiscriminating suspicion of all Muslims: behind every mosque, a terrorist training camp; beneath every burqa, a suicide vest. U.S. Rep. Joe Walsh (R-IL), while trying to win re-election in 2012, scared nearly everybody in the room during a town hall when he was asked about the threat of radical Islam:

> One thing I'm sure of is that there are people in this country—there is a radical strain of Islam in this country—it's not just over there—trying to kill Americans every week. It is a real threat, and it is a threat that is much more at home now than it was after 9/11. ... It's here. It's in Elk Grove. It's in Addison. It's in Elgin. It's here.[39]

The Chicago Council on American-Islamic Relations (CAIR) issued a statement expressing fear that Muslims in the area could become the targets of violence. Due to Walsh's remarks, a man named David Conrad fired two shots at the Muslim Education Center while nearly 500 Muslims were inside observing Ramadan.[40] Nobody was injured (Conrad was armed only with a high-powered air rifle), but the connections between the speech and the shooting, if not concrete, are at least suggestive. Hate speech (whether delivered from atop a soapbox or published anonymously online) can have (and has had) precisely the effects one would expect it to. In March 2014, FBI agents arrested Robert James Talbot Jr., a regular reader of Geller's Atlas Shrugs blog and other anti-Muslim sites, who, they alleged, was plotting to blow up a number of mosques and other buildings.[41]

America's new and distinct brand of Islamophobia has found receptive audiences all over the world. In one particular instance of this, the results were, to say the very least, chilling. In July 2011, a bomb exploded inside a van parked next to a government building in Oslo, Norway. That explosion left eight people dead. But the mayhem didn't end there: a few hours later a man, Anders Breivik, dressed in a police uniform, killed 69 people (most of them teenagers) at a political youth camp on an island near the Scandinavian capital. While the details were still unclear, American media outlets outdid each other, jumping to conclusions before the facts were in. Whether implied or suggested outright, the prevailing assumption was that Muslim extremists were behind the attack. Furious with the "Muslimization" of Norway, Breivik imagined himself as something of a crusader fighting the swelling tide of Muslim immigration; his stated mission was to "save Europe from Muslim immigration."[42]

One of the most troubling aspects of the tragedy was Breivik's 1500-page manifesto, much of which either cites or copies and pastes entire passages from writings found on anti-Muslim Internet sites. If these borrowings and citations are any indication, Breivik was heavily influenced by many of the American "experts" on Islam—the same experts that are regularly cited by many of our more vociferously anti-Muslim politicians. Robert Spencer, the director of Jihad Watch and a regular interviewee on Fox News, is cited in Breivik's manifesto more than 160 times. Breivik also cites David Horowitz, the chief organizer behind America's charmingly named Islamofascism Awareness Week, and Pamela Geller, whom I discussed above. Though the blame for the tragedy in Oslo can't be laid entirely at the feet of American Islamophobes, there is a rather clear connection between the ink spilled here and the blood spilled there. Breivik was by no means acting under their direction. Nevertheless, it would appear as though some of their words struck a chord with him.

And their words are definitely striking a chord here in America. In 2011, just before the tenth anniversary of the 9/11 terrorist attacks, the Center for American Progress conducted an in-depth investigation into American Islamophobia and its tributaries. It found that a surprisingly small network of propagandists and "misinformation experts" were behind many of the movement's messages.[43] This relatively small network has been able to reach millions of Americans with very carefully crafted falsehoods about Muslims and the Islamic religion. It narrowed down the sources of most of the misinformation to five individuals:

- Frank Gaffney of the Center for Security Policy
- David Yerushalmi of the Society of Americans for National Existence
- Daniel Pipes of the Middle East Forum
- Robert Spencer of Jihad Watch and Stop Islamization of America
- Steven Emerson of the Investigative Project on Terrorism[44]

This network crisscrosses the country and attends state legislature hearings and conferences, where they plant and water the seeds of the Islamophobia.[45] These five experts, who received more than $42.6 million in funding between 2001 and 2009, are being bankrolled by seven deep-pocketed organizations:

- Donors Capital Fund
- Richard Mellon Scaife Foundations
- Lynde and Harry Bradley Foundation
- Newton D. & Rochelle F. Becker foundations and charitable trust
- Russell Berrie Foundation
- Anchorage Charitable Fund and William Rosenwald Family Fund
- Fairbrook Foundation[46]

As might be expected, all of these groups donate large sums to conservative political campaigns and lobbying groups that are working in Washington to advance socially and fiscally conservative causes (with a pronounced emphasis on the latter).[47] They all donate heavily to Republican campaigns, rewarding those who are the most vociferously anti-Muslim in their stump speeches or campaign ads. While this certainly doesn't mean that all Republicans think negatively of Islam as a religion in general, and practicing Muslims in particular, according to a recent poll substantially more than half of Republicans (57%) profess negative views of Muslims (a marginally better 47% when you ask them how they feel about "Muslim Americans").

The demonization of Islam (like the demonization of Black Americans and Hispanic immigrants) is something of a bulletproof political strategy when one is reaffirming pre-existing biases and long-standing antipathies. Non sequiturs, straw men, slippery slopes, and appeals to emotion all hit the mark when they light upon our seemingly inbuilt confirmation bias, which leads us (liberals and conservatives alike) to mistake misinformation for truth, even in the light of contradictory evidence. Our sense of self is so wrapped up in what we take to be true that we instinctively prefer the guidance of our guts over that of our senses. We ignore the intellect and default to the heart. That the evidence doesn't support their claims doesn't matter; they *feel* true, so they *are* true. When psychologist Drew Westen of Emory University conducted a test that presented both liberals and conservatives with examples of political hypocrisy, conservatives were more likely than their liberal counterparts to engage in "biased political reasoning," which activates those parts of the brain associated not with logical thinking, but, rather, as Mooney puts it, with "emotional processing and psychological defense.... These people weren't solving math problems. They were committing the mental equivalent of beating their chests" (41). In another, similar study, researchers found that, when factually corrected, the conservative mind actually backfires, believing and defending false claims even more strongly and vigorously than before (45). Surprisingly, this tendency does not decrease when the partisan in question has received tertiary education; on the contrary, when asked about the legitimacy of climate-change science, well-educated Republicans—presumably better equipped to accurately assess climate-change data—were actually more skeptical about the science than less educated ones, probably because they are more exposed to the knowledge distorted by conservatism than their uneducated fellows (48).

This helps to explain the effectiveness of Islamophobic propaganda campaigns. They build upon a foundation of xenophobic suspicion an edifice constructed of half-truths and patent falsehoods. The truth of their claims, once established as absolute in the minds of the Republican faithful, justifies all manner of ludicrously Islamophobic responses to perceived threats. State legislatures in all but sixteen states have considered (and eight of them have passed) laws banning the use of sharia law to settle legal disputes—an almost entirely chimerical threat that has been grotesquely exaggerated by concerned Christians like Pat Robertson, Ralph Reed, Rush Limbaugh, Glenn Beck, and Sean Hannity.[48] Invoking their faith at every opportunity,

conservatives claim that Muslims (around 1 per cent of the population) and Christians (around 84 per cent of the population) are
locked in a mortal power struggle, one that will determine whether
America remains a Christian nation or will be turned instead into
a Muslim theocracy. There is no evidence to support this position,
but that has not prevented it from taking firm root in conservative
circles (even mainstream ones). It's no wonder that many conservative "patriots" get up in arms whenever Muslims seek or are granted
any kind of foothold within American civic life (be it a new place
of worship, the right to cover their bodies or faces according to the
guidelines of their faith, or the right to swear on their own holy book
instead of the Bible). Such patriots seem to see freedom as a limited resource (see, for instance, their defense of traditional marriage):
an increase in freedom for a minority somehow carries an implicit
decrease in the freedom of the majority. Ask them how it will do so,
and they'll lead you down a fire-and-brimstone-filled slippery slope
to a hellscape of Dantean proportions.

On January 7, 2015, two masked gunmen armed with assault
weapons stormed the Paris offices of *Charlie Hebdo*, a controversial
satirical magazine. The two men, asking for the editors of the magazine by name, started shooting, killing 12 people and wounding 11
others. The attacks were, they claimed, retribution for a series of offensive cartoons depicting the Prophet Muhammad. In both Europe and
the United States, Islamophobes were apoplectic. The military-style
incursion, some of which was caught on video, was evidence that
Islamist extremists were firing the first shots in what was presumed to
be an all-out war with the West.

The Paris attacks came on the heels of several months of international handwringing in the face of the undeniably growing threat of
ISIS in the Middle East. In September, Senator Lindsay Graham went
on Fox News to warn Americans about the impending apocalypse:
"They [ISIS] will open the gates of hell to spill out on the world....
They're intending to come here, so I will not let this president suggest
to the American people we can outsource our security.... This president needs to rise to the occasion before we all get killed back here
at home."[49] For months, Republican demagogues fired salvo after
salvo at the President, who, they said, was leaving America vulnerable
thanks to his stance on immigration (ISIS, with the help of Mexican

drug cartels, was apparently planning to enter the U.S. through the Mexican border, though no tangible evidence was ever offered to support this claim).[50] Muslim leaders were called upon to denounce ISIS and the terrorists in Paris; when they did so, their critics moved the goalposts, demanding that they declaim them more vigorously.

The images of masked gunmen on the streets of a Western capital, of uniformed officers killed in broad daylight, were equally effective as propaganda tools for both Islamist terror organizations like Al-Qaeda and ISIS and for America's Islamophobic pundits and policy makers. For the former, the images terrified millions of global witnesses to the carnage, making the threat more immediate and tangible, and for that reason all the more unnerving; for the latter, the propaganda proved that the beast could still be attacked directly in its belly. Islamists and Islamophobes are both entirely convinced that we are in the midst of an all-important clash of civilizations, a clash of religions of apocalyptic proportions, a clash of incompatible ideologies between which compromise is impossible. This combatant's propaganda becomes the weapon of his or her enemy, and vice versa.

It must be said that mainstream American Islamophobia is not as blatantly racist as it is in its European varieties. It tends to wear a thin (very thin) veil of political correctness when it appears in high-profile public forums, but the same cannot be said of much of Europe, where anti-Muslim sentiment has come to something of a head in recent years, resulting in official practices of discrimination that would never pass muster in America. In France, for instance, the burqa (along with all other religious clothing) has been banned in public schools; in the UK, a ban on the building of any new mosques was proposed by a United Kingdom Independence Party (UKIP) member who subsequently received 27 per cent of the vote.[51] Perhaps most troubling, the membership of one particularly nasty Dresden-based German group, Patriotic Europeans Against the Islamization of the West, which had held a 17,000-member-strong demonstration the week before the Paris massacre, swelled to 25,000 people a week later.[52] Unfortunately the hate-spewing by the West is only surpassed by ISIS's continuing terror being waged upon the West. From the recruiting of Westerners, to the growing of their own "home-grown soldiers," they are intent upon the radicalization of young men and women who are prepared to die while exacting pain and death on those in the Western Hemisphere in an apocalyptic fashion. While the vast majority of Muslims and Christians oppose such violence within ISIL's land reach (ISIL stands for Islamic State in Iraq and the Levant), they are being persecuted and even driven out of their homeland by these terrorists.[53] I maintained hope that such outwardly racist displays of anti-Muslim sentiment will not swell to such proportions on this side of the Atlantic. But after the violent weekend of November 14th, 2015, where ISIS claimed responsibility for the 130 who were killed in Paris and 43 killed in Lebanon, American Governors have pledged, amongst a growing politics of fear, to abort their "ALL LIVES MATTER" mantra (created in response to Black Lives Matter causing a de-centering of white privilege and appropriation) and fight President Obama's plan to allow Syrian refugees (escaping ISIS's violence) into the U.S.

No matter how strong the argument against Islamophobia is, it can never succeed in conveying the visceral sufferings that ordinary Muslims undergo daily in America and the rest of the West. Ordinary Muslims are punished for the deeds of a very few extremists. They're held accountable for the actions of murderers and madmen, while all they want to do is live their lives in peace. These Muslims are not interested in jihad; they are simply people trying to find solace in, and stay faithful to, their religion. They want to love their god and be left alone—just like the founders of the United States. I'm also hopeful that with the publication of more and more scholarly works that unravel media tactics and agendas, increasing numbers of Americans will take media misrepresentations—not just of Islam and Muslims— with a grain of salt. That said, if we wish to avoid following the same trajectory as European Islamophobia, if we wish to avoid its infiltration into our public institutions (as its already begun to rear its head in our state legislatures), we need to come to a firm (and relatively unanimous) decision about whether we believe that the freedoms we value for ourselves are one and the same as the ones we offer to others.

Notes

1　William A. Henry III, "Beyond the Melting Pot," *Time* 135.15 (1990): 28–31.

2　Juliet Lapidos, "Steve King Still Stands by 'Cantaloupe' Comments," *The New York Times* 12 August 2013, http://takingnote.blogs.nytimes.com/2013/08/12/steve-king-still-stands-by-cantaloupe-comments/?_r=0.

3   "Misplaced Priorities: Most Immigrants Deported by ICE in 2013 Were a
     Threat to No One," American Immigration Council, http://www.immigration
     policy.org/just-facts/misplaced-priorities-most-immigrants-deported-ice-2013-
     were-threat-no-one.

4   "Stop-And-Frisk Data," New York Civil Liberties Union, http://www.nyclu.org/
     content/stop-and-frisk-data.

5   Matt Hamilton, "Immigration Rallies Wait for Buses of Immigrants in Murrieta,"
     The Huffington Post, 4 July 2014, http://www.huffingtonpost.com/2014/07/04/
     immigration-bus-murrieta_n_5559113.html.

6   "Misplaced Minorities."

7   See Buchanan.

8   Jimmy So, "Kyl: Illegal Aliens' Kids Shouldn't Be Citizens," CBS News,
     1 August 2010, http://www.cbsnews.com/news/kyl-illegal-aliens-kids-shouldnt-
     be-citizens.

9   Joe Tacopino, "Texas Rep. Louie Gohmert Warns of Baby-Making Terrorists
     Coming to US," New York Daily News 27 June 2010, http://www.nydailynews.
     com/news/politics/texas-rep-louie-gohmert-warns-baby-making-terrorists-
     coming-article-1.182787.

10   See Andreas.

11   See Dzidzienyo and Oboler.

12   See Hout and Goldstein.

13   Audrey Singer, "Immigrant Workers in the U.S. Labor Force," Brookings
     Institution, 15 March 2012, http://www.brookings.edu/research/papers/2012/
     03/15-immigrant-workers-singer.

14   Cited in Debora MacKenzie, "Opening the Door to Immigrants Is Good for
     the Economy," New Scientist 24 November 2014, http://www.newscientist.com/
     article/dn26605-opening-the-door-to-immigrants-is-good-for-the-economy.
     html#.VQ61j1yn-68.

15   Cited in ibid.

16   Aaron Smith, "Farm Workers: Take Our Jobs, Please!" CNN, 10 July 2010,
     http://money.cnn.com/2010/07/07/news/economy/farm_worker_jobs.

17   See Portes and Rumbaut.

18   John F. Simanski and Lesley M. Sapp, "Immigration Enforcement Actions:
     2012," Department of Homeland Security, December 2013, http://www.dhs.gov/
     sites/default/files/publications/ois_enforcement_ar_2012_1.pdf.

19   Ana Gonzalez-Barrera and Jens Manuel Krogstad, "U.S. Deportations of
     Immigrants Reach Record High in 2013," Pew Research Center, 2 October
     2014, http://www.pewresearch.org/fact-tank/2014/10/02/u-s-deportations-of-
     immigrants-reach-record-high-in-2013/.

20   Simon Maloy, "Marco Rubio's Existential Flip-Flop," *Salon*, 27 August 2014, http://www.salon.com/2014/08/27/marco_rubios_existential_flip_flop_why_he_demonized_dreamers_to_win_over_south_carolina_conservatives/.

21   Jeanne Batalova and Margie McHugh, "DREAM vs. Reality: An Analysis of Potential DREAM Act Beneficiaries," Migration Policy Institute, July 2010, http://migrationpolicy.org/research/dream-vs-reality-analysis-potential-dream-act-beneficiaries.

22   "No DREAMers Left Behind: The Economic Potential of DREAM Act Beneficiaries," North American Integration and Development Center, University of California, Los Angeles, http://www.naid.ucla.edu/uploads/4/2/1/9/4219226/b67_hinojosa_2010_no_dreamers_left_behind_6.pdf.

23   See Esposito and Kalin, xxii.

24   "Defining 'Islamophobia,'" University of California, Berkeley, Center for Race & Gender, http://crg.berkeley.edu/content/islamophobia/defining-islamophobia.

25   See Chomsky and Bidwai.

26   Bobby Ghosh, "Islamophobia: Does America Have a Muslim Problem?" *Time* 30 August 2010, http://content.time.com/time/magazine/article/0,9171,2011936-4,00.html.

27   "Protesters Descend on Ground Zero for Anti-Mosque Demonstration," CNN, 7 June 2010, http://www.cnn.com/2010/US/06/06/new.york.ground.zero.mosque.

28   Ibid.

29   Daniel Denvir, "Islamaphobe and Conspiracist Pamela Geller to Speak in Philly," *Philadelphia CityPaper* 16 March 2012, http://citypaper.net/Blogs/Islamaphobe-and-conspiracist-Pamela-Geller-to-speak-in-Philly.

30   "Statistics: What You Need to Know," Muslim Public Affairs Council, http://www.mpac.org/programs/hate-crime-prevention/statistics.php.

31   See Ghosh, "Islamophobia."

32   Alyssa Rosenberg, "Rep. Allen West Commemorates 9/11 by Screening Muslim-Bashing Film," Think Progress, 7 September 2011, http://thinkprogress.org/alyssa/2011/09/07/312488/the-muslim-bashing-movie-rep-allen-west-is-screening-today/.

33   Tim Murphy, "GOP Candidate: Rep. Keith Ellison Is 'Militantly Anti-America,'" *Mother Jones* 25 July 2012, http://www.motherjones.com/mojo/2012/07/gop-candidate-keith-ellison-militantly-anti-american.

34   Justin Elliott, "Muslim Rep. Ellison Draws Anti-Muslim Tea Party Challenger," *Salon*, 28 June 2011, http://www.salon.com/2011/06/28/keith_ellison_tea_party_challenge.

35   Alex Seitz-Wald, "Her Muslim Witch Hunt," Salon, 13 July 2012, http://www.
     salon.com/2012/07/13/bachmann%E2%80%99s_muslim_witch_hunt.

36   Ibid.

37   Ali Gharib, "Ellison Calls Bachmann's Evidence of Muslim Brotherhood
     Conspiracy '16 Pages Worth Of Nothing,'" Think Progress, 18 July 2012,
     http://thinkprogress.org/security/2012/07/18/537991/ellison-bachmann-
     muslim-brotherhood-nothing.

38   Taylor Wofford, "Islamophobia in America on the Rise, Poll Shows," *Newsweek*
     31 July 2014, http://www.newsweek.com/islamophobia-america-rise-poll-
     shows-262478.

39   "Rep. Walsh's Comments Infuriate Muslims," CBS Chicago, 10 August 2012,
     http://chicago.cbslocal.com/2012/08/10/rep-walshs-comments-infuriate-
     muslims.

40   David Edwards, "Chicago-Area Mosque Shot with Rifle after Rep. Walsh
     Warns Of 'Radical' Islam," Raw Story, 13 August 2012, http://www.rawstory.com/
     rs/2012/08/13/chicago-area-mosque-shot-with-rifle-after-rep-walsh-warns-of-
     radical-islam/.

41   Omar Sacierbey, "Report Says Internet Hate Speech Can Lead to Acts of
     Violence," The Huffington Post, 6 May 2014, http://www.huffingtonpost.
     com/2014/05/06/internet-hate-speech-violence_n_5273806.html.

42   Starla Muhammad, "Tragedy in Norway Borne out of Seeds of Racism
     and Intolerance in UK, EU," New America Media, 19 August 2011, http://
     newamericamedia.org/2011/08/tragedy-in-norway-borne-out-of-seeds-of-
     racism-and-intolerance-in-uk-eu.php.

43   Ali Wajahat, et al., "Fear, Inc.: The Roots of the Islamophobia Network in
     America," Center for American Progress, August 2011, http://cdn.american
     progress.org/wp-content/uploads/issues/2011/08/pdf/islamophobia.pdf.

44   Ibid., Chapter 3.

45   Ibid.

46   Ibid., p. 4.

47   Ibid.

48   Daniel Tutt, "Tennessee's Anti-Muslim Bill Is an American Disgrace," The
     Huffington Post, 17 May 2011, http://www.huffingtonpost.com/daniel-tutt/
     tennessees-antimuslim-bil_b_863032.html.

49   Brian Glyn Williams, "'They Will Kill Us All!' Critically Assessing ISIS Fear
     Mongering by US Politicians," The World Post 18 November 2014, http://www.
     huffingtonpost.com/brian-glyn-williams/they-will-kill-us-all-cri_b_6174566.
     html.

50   Ibid.

51   Sara Farris, "On Anti-Semitism and Islamophobia in Europe," Aljazeera, 5 June
     2014, http://www.aljazeera.com/indepth/opinion/2014/06/anti-semitism-
     islamophobia-europ-20146414191330623.html.

52   Dennis Lynch, "Dresden's PEGIDA Movement: How Germany's Anti-Muslim
     Protesters Are Using Charlie Hebdo to Recruit Followers," *International Business
     Times* 14 January 2015, http://www.ibtimes.com/dresdens-pegida-movement-
     how-germanys-anti-muslim-protesters-are-using-charlie-hebdo-1782442.

53   The Levant, better known as the entire region east of the Mediterranean, from
     Egypt to Iran and Turkey. The term "ISIS" refers specifically to the Islamic State
     of Iraq and Syria. See Jamie Fuller, "'ISIS' vs. 'ISIL' vs. 'Islamic State': The
     political importance of a much-debated acronym," *The Washington Post*
     9 September 2014, https://www.washingtonpost.com/news/the-fix/
     wp/2014/09/09/isis-vs-isil-vs-islamic-state-the-political-importance-
     of-a-much-debated-acronym/.

Chapter Five

POVERTY:
A LOAD TOO
HEAVY TO BEAR

MUCH OF THE GROUND WE COVERED IN THE PREVIOUS CHAPTERS deals with the ways in which the American experience is dramatically different for people of color (even the President) than it is for those of European descent. Social and political life is, however, only part of the picture. Economic life is a crucial component of the American experience, and in a capitalist society, money (or the lack thereof) can transform this experience. Poverty and income inequality (which I will address, respectively, in this chapter and the next) are issues every bit as pressing as America's treatment of people of color. Like America's long and checkered history of race relations (especially in terms of her stubborn refusal to address—or even admit the existence of—racial inequality), her history of economic inequality is a fresh source of grievances for progressives.

Of course, income inequality is not a distinctly American problem. Perhaps from the very moment that humans began to congregate in communities, the problems of poverty and inequality were born. There have always been—and, precluding the unlikely event of a global socialist revolution, there always will be—some degree of inequality separating the flush from the flat. The fact that this phenomenon seems to be part and parcel of our tendency to congregate socially justifies neither poverty nor inequality, but our sociability does explain many of the more salient features of each. Whether in small-scale communities or large ones, resources are, of course, finite, and human desires infinite. Free-market capitalism positively encourages those either motivated or equipped to do so to secure for themselves as many of the market's finite resources as they wish to possess. While it would be irresponsible to imply that those who are doing well are making others worse off as a consequence, I do maintain that it leads to a kind of dangerous gap between the rich and the poor that has grown to unconscionable proportions in the last four decades. This I will discuss at length in the next chapter, but for now I want to focus, not on the still-growing gulf between the haves and the have-nots in this country, but on America's invisible class: the poor.

For a brief time, America made strides toward reducing, even dramatically so, the pernicious effects of, and the stigmas attached to, poverty. These strides began during the Great Depression. In the aftermath of the stock-market crash and the drought that followed on its heels, poverty became something that could no longer be ignored; the issue grabbed America by the shirtfront and pulled its face, imprinted with suffering and want, close enough that the undeniably strong impulse to turn away was overpowered by the pull of human sympathy. Bread lines stretched for blocks, and the omnipresence of drudgery and misery stamped on the faces of the unemployed millions was a cause for tremendous and widespread concern. In the decades that followed, poverty was by no means eradicated, but it built itself a nest in America's collective conscience. It was no longer a problem to be ignored; it was seen as a problem to be solved.

By the beginning of the 1960s, though, our collective feelings about poverty had changed considerably. Things had noticeably improved for the middle class, and there was a widespread feeling that poverty as a problem in America had effectively been handled. The poverty level that was 22.4 per cent in 1959 came down to 16 per cent in 2012. In 1962, Michael Harrington published his exposé on

American poverty, *The Other America*, describing the day-to-day life of America's unemployed and working poor, rural and elderly, claiming that "tens of millions of Americans [he later claims the actual number to be around 50 million] are at this very moment, maimed in body and spirit, existing at levels beneath those necessary for human decency" (2). The rising tides of postwar economic progress had not, Harrington argued, lifted all boats. Harrington's book, with its cogent demands for policies to help the poor, helped along by a favorable review in *The New Yorker*, was widely read and discussed among intellectuals and, indeed, the public at large as well (a rarely duplicated accomplishment for a social-sciences text). John F. Kennedy, responding to some of the clamor the book raised, read it himself, which some claim directly influenced his later attempt to eradicate domestic poverty.[1]

Shortly after President Lyndon Johnson began his War on Poverty after Kennedy's assassination, the U.S. poverty rate fell precipitously. Large-scale intervention clearly had the kind of widespread effects that those who conceived the programs hoped they would. Since then, though, the U.S. has been surpassed by nearly all other advanced industrialized nations. Since the 1980s it has consistently ranked among the worst performers in terms of poverty levels among the wealthier industrial nations.[2] The fact that the United States has experienced higher poverty rates[3] than other industrialized countries keeps the problem in the national spotlight, spurring intense public debates and emotional responses from every corner.

The problem with the spotlight is its tendency to distort what it illuminates. Perhaps more than any other issue, poverty has been the object of fact manipulation and statistical cherry picking. On the one hand, you have a demonization of the poor—particularly the semi-mythical welfare queen who makes her perennial appearance in Republican discussions of the undeserving poor; on the other hand, you have a lionization of the destitute, which, like that to which it is opposed, uses largely anecdotal evidence to paint a monochromatic portrait of those living beneath the poverty line (a line that is itself a site of intense bickering). One thing is clear, however: America is confronted with the problem of poverty. The victims of poverty are both the poor and the taxpayers, as the latter have to foot the bill for the former's subsistence.

As might be expected when the issue is approached from viewpoints that so little resemble each other, widely disparate solutions to the problem of poverty are floated by policy makers, intellectuals, and pundits. My compassion for the suffering and my revulsion for the dehumanizing and humiliating rhetoric so often directed at the poor from the right make the ideas from the left more plausible, in terms of both the diagnoses of the issues and the proposed solution. I will try to avoid, wherever possible, the temptation that so many of the commentators on poverty (both left- and right-wing) find irresistible—namely, overstatement. A statistical portrait of poverty in the United States says that poverty levels, after a sharp decline in the 1960s, have not changed in any significant way in the last half-century,[4] but, like the media's coverage of violence (if it bleeds, it leads), pundits speaking for and from both sides of the aisle have been competing with each other to see who can ring the alarm bells the loudest. From the left, this coverage often claims that the media are largely ignoring poverty; from the right, the feeling is that the poor have been spoiled during Obama's tenure. In what follows, I will try to look at the issue of poverty with passionate eyes, but through a non-partisan lens.

The Middle-Class Squeeze

One need not look far to see the very real effects of poverty on society. Unforeseen urban migration and deeply entrenched poverty can be witnessed in America's once-great centers. According to the 2013 Annual Community Survey, 15.8 per cent of the U.S. population had income below the poverty level. The figure for Miami and Fort Lauderdale is 17.7 per cent, Los Angeles 17.6 per cent, Detroit 16.9 per cent, and Philadelphia 13.5 percent. In some of America's rural towns, the picture is even bleaker and the poverty rate is much higher.[5] Job cuts in the manufacturing sector—automobiles in Detroit and steel in Cleveland and elsewhere—partly because of expensive labor, are a significant factor in the increase in poverty. Michael Katz suggests that "Part of the blame rests on cuts in benefits that began in the mid-70s and accelerated during the Reagan years. Part rests on a legacy of policies that fail to attack the roots of poverty in unemployment, income distribution, and discrimination."[6] If there had been a continuation of not merely the policies of Johnson and Kennedy, but also the very spirit that animated the idea of the Great Society, rather than a changing of course in the 1970s and 1980s—which brought with it the tendency to extol the virtues of the business class and demean the already humiliated lower classes—perhaps then we would not have painted ourselves into the corner in which we now find ourselves.

As with the national problems with inequality, persistent, multi-generational poverty seems to be entirely incompatible with the American Dream. It is unfortunate that, in 2013, 45.3 million Americans[7] were stuck in an interminable cycle of privation, all but entirely cut off from the benefits enjoyed by the rest of society (access to basic commodities, health care, and education, to name a few). Sixteen million children born in poor families (six million of them under the age of seven)[8] are obviously in a disadvantageous position when compared to children of middle- or upper-class families. They are malnourished with little or no schooling, under stresses, subject to behavioral and emotional problems, and they take these disadvantages with them into adulthood.[9] As teenagers they are more likely to have children themselves,[10] be exposed to violent crime, be arrested for committing crimes of all sorts, and do jail time, and they are thus less likely to find meaningful work when they are released. Such dismal outcomes are creating a largely static underclass in this country, kept in place by predatory financial practices. Their chances of a life outside of the tightening noose of poverty are diminishing. Indeed, they are often prevented from having access to the opportunities that invest in human capital, those basic job-related skills and experiences that serve a company or organization. As investments in human capital have characteristics of public/marketable goods, their absence retards economic growth, and the government ought to do more in this area.

The increase in the general price level, particularly for housing, medical care, and education, as well as the rising standard of living, have also aggravated the poverty situation. While middle-class incomes and national productivity levels followed identical trend lines during the 1950s and 1960s, the only people who have seen significant income gains since the 1970s have been top-quintile wage earners, especially those in the top one per cent.[11] In an attempt at survival, the working poor—in most cases both husband and wife—are increasingly taking second and even third jobs to supplement their incomes. This practice continues even as the economy improves.

Labor statistics show that job openings have been slowly but steadily increasing since 2009, but the majority of these jobs are at the minimum pay level.[12] Employers both large and small use the uncertain atmosphere of possible unemployment as a weapon against the working poor. In labor markets, employers have enjoyed a buyers' market, especially since 2008. It is a simple situation of supply and demand. On average, in early 2014 there were 2.9 unemployed persons for each job opening in the United States.[13] Even if the economy continues to improve—and with it corporate profits—it seems unlikely that the benefit of gains will be passed on to the working class.

Traditionally, the way to get a good job in America and thereby to break out of the cycle of poverty has been to pursue postsecondary education, but that education, thanks to the skyrocketing price of tuition that I discuss in the next chapter, comes at a price—namely, debt that can hamstring graduates for years or longer if the degree or certificate does not translate into commensurate employment. Following larger anti-migration trends showing that individuals and families receiving social assistance are much less likely to move out of state,[14] poor students are much more likely to choose educational institutions relatively close to home; this tendency even extends to high-achieving students from poor families, who are dramatically more likely to settle for close-to-home institutions than they are to apply to the kinds of schools that can have a significant impact on their future economic success.[15] A recent Stanford/Harvard study estimated that as many as 92 per cent of poor, gifted academics are choosing to forgo the application process for America's prestigious institutions, even when their SAT scores are high enough to merit consideration.[16] As it is, only 9 per cent of college students come from the lowest-income families.[17]

Given that higher education can lead to better employment opportunities, this is disheartening, but it is important to note that there are no structures (at least not formal ones) in place that are keeping these students from either applying to or being accepted by America's top universities. Indeed, there are programs in place to allow academically gifted students from low-income families to attend the best schools in this country at a cost to the student and his or her family that is less than what it would cost to attend less prestigious institutions, and there is no discernible lack of effort on the part of admissions staff for these institutions to reach out to lower-income students. The only plausible reason for this abysmally poor application rate that the Harvard/Stanford researchers cautiously suggest is the fact that these students, as "one-offs," are dispersed through the country. Furthermore, school staff are reported to be neither well equipped nor experienced enough to help them navigate the more intensive application process for America's prestigious schools.[18] Whatever the reason, often low-income students, even when they are high achievers, are passing up on the opportunity that our best institutions offer in terms of lifting themselves out of the cycle of poverty.

To a certain degree, those in the grip of poverty must be afforded an opportunity to change their status through education, but such is, admittedly, not the path for everybody. For the high percentage of the working poor with, at most, a high-school education, the reality is that their standard of living is determined largely by the wages they earn. While there are not massive numbers of workers earning the minimum wage or less in the U.S. (3.3 million at last count),[19] the number of low-wage workers—that is, those earning less than $10.55 per hour—is staggeringly high: 35 million Americans, 26 per cent of the workforce, are getting by with the low wage levels, and even when they are working full-time hours, many of these workers are still not cresting the poverty line. Senator Elizabeth Warren has made this fact a cornerstone of her very public position on the sorry state of America's lower and middle classes, saying that "No one should have to work full-time and live in poverty"[20]—a sentiment repeated almost verbatim by the highly vocal and visible advocates for a substantial minimum-wage hike at 15Now.[21] The truth of this statement seems self-evident, but the status quo defenders—and their numbers are legion—either change the subject, keeping America's gaze focused elsewhere, or turn the debate into a defense of capitalism, frequently painting business owners as the "little guys" in the process. Instead of institutional reform, stopgap measures have become the norm, and our heel dragging has made our once globally competitive levels of wage disparity the worst in the developed world. Of the 22 countries in the Organization for Economic Cooperation and Development (OECD) that have a statutory minimum wage, the United States is the perennial lowest scorer in terms of the ratio of the minimum wage to the median wage.[22] By raising the minimum wage to $10 per hour (which would still only bring us into the middle of the pack in terms of global rankings), we would be giving nearly 23 million individuals and more than 11 million children in low-income households a shot at a more financially secure future.[23]

From the tone of the debate, it would be quite natural to think that advocates for a living wage were asking for nothing less than a complete reversal of the class structure. Much like the debate surrounding welfare reform, conservatives use a broad brush to paint those advocating for anything that would help the working poor raise their standard of living as anti-capitalist union thugs. This is the old zero-sum-game problem: any gains in the wages of this country's poorest workers must come from somewhere, and since it would be corporate blasphemy to cut into the profits of the corporations that pay these wages, these gains must be passed on to consumers in the form of massive price hikes. In the case of smaller businesses, higher wages will inevitably result in empty tills and, eventually, shuttered windows. Therefore, any rise in the minimum wage is, according to *Forbes* contributor and author of *Ending the Era of the Free Lunch*, Jeffrey Dorfman, "just an attempt by liberals to punish a subset of business owners by redistributing a share of their supposed wealth to their employees. It is just another attempt at class warfare."[24] Redistribution and class warfare, along with the slippery slope to socialism, are terms and phrases that are lobbed at the living-wage advocates as though they were standing atop barricades waving red flags emblazoned with the hammer and sickle. Class interests are being defended as though the very heads of their defenders were attached to them.

There is, to be sure, exaggeration and alarmism on both sides of the debate surrounding wages and entitlement reform in this country, but one thing in particular stands out as a point that we should not have to be debating as a country: single-digit hourly wages are not enough, and they are certainly not enough to maintain a decent standard of living for those who work in entry-level retail positions or in the fast-food industry, where these wages are particularly prevalent.[25] The sheer numbers of those who work in these positions while still relying on federal assistance to meet their bare necessities is enough proof that we still have a long way to go in terms of bridging the gap between the low wages paid by American employers, many of them enjoying record profits, and the living wages that America's lowest tier of employees need if they are to live with some measure of the human dignity to which they ought to be entitled. In the strong-performing northern European economies, this entitlement to human dignity has been recognized as a legitimate one, and wages have been adjusted to ensure that those working full-time are able to live in a moderate degree of comfort. They have seen through the claims of the corporations and their acolytes that government-mandated wage hikes hurt everybody in the short and long term; they have largely rejected America's "quarterly capitalism" obsession.[26] They have recognized that a better-paid lower class allows for the degree of class mobility promised by democratic capitalism; they have recognized that the much-vaunted consumer is an earner as well, and that more prosperous lower and middle classes can be the engine of economic growth. And, most fundamentally, they understand that there is a human element at the root of the wage debate that short-term, bottom-line-focused economic thinking almost entirely ignores. We should learn something from their example.

Poverty and Race

In *Racecraft: The Soul of Inequality in American Life*, Karen E. Fields and Barbara J. Fields discuss the double standard manifested in the way in which poverty is discussed in America. The double standard is especially evident in the national debate surrounding the use or abuse of welfare and food stamps in this country. Fields and Fields note that "the question 'Why food stamps?' has two stock answers, depending on the ancestry of the person using them, on the one hand, fecklessness; on the other, bad luck, plant-closing, and the like" (39). According to 2013 data, 42 per cent of those receiving SNAP assistance were white, 25 per cent Black, and the numbers are virtually identical for welfare recipients.[27] And yet the almost entirely mythical young bucks and welfare queens that Reagan introduced into the welfare conversations more than three decades ago have taken firm root in the collective consciousness. The problem with food stamps is problematically represented by the conservative media as a problem that White America has with Black America. In a recent interview with the Jackson *Clarion-Ledger*, state Rep. Gene Alday (R-MS) made a shockingly racist (and wildly inaccurate) claim about his home town in Mississippi: "I come from a town," he told the reporter, "where all the Blacks are getting food stamps and what I call 'welfare crazy checks.' They don't work."[28] While the grammar of the final sentence doesn't reveal whether he was talking about the federal assistance programs or the Black people in his hometown, his follow-up comments made his position clearer. He went on to say that when a severe bout of back pain brought him to his local emergency room, he "laid [*sic*] in there for hours because they [Blacks] were in there being treated for gunshots."[29] Alday attempted to walk back his comments when they quickly went viral, but it's hard not to see the unguarded moment as revealing in terms of the GOP's position on African Americans. Alday suggested, none too subtly, that Blacks are lazy criminals unworthy of the benefits and even of the hospital care they are receiving.

The picture of American poverty is wildly different when it frames white people. When conservative pundits and politicians are addressing the issue, there is a tendency to describe those with pale skin receiving welfare benefits as the victims of misfortune or even of Obama's apparently disastrous economic policies. When those within the frame are Black, they are masters of their own destiny; they are responsible, not only for the conditions that caused their poverty, but also for bringing about the conditions that will end it. Martin Gilens finds at the root of this issue the racially biased way in which poverty has been covered in the media in the last half-century: "[In the 1960s] Blacks began to appear in poverty coverage only as that coverage turned a critical eye toward the country's poor and toward the War on Poverty in particular" (6). Fiscal and social conservatives, and the media that address them, found an easy and highly visible target for their soapbox rage in America's inner cities: "The most salient contemporary images of the poor—the homeless beggar, the welfare queen, the teenage ghetto gang member, the heroin addict shooting up in an abandoned building, are strongly associated with minorities in both the mass media and the public imagination" (67).

The result of more than fifty years of media-perpetuated stereotypes and racialized representations of poverty is a severely skewed public perception of poverty. At the end of Clinton's presidency, the median response to a survey that asked respondents what percentage of America's poor they thought was Black was 50 per cent (almost double the actual figure).[30] During Obama's presidency, coverage of Black poverty has by no means improved; it remains condemnatory in its visual and verbal tone, the implication (or outright suggestion, depending on your news source) often being that the President created a culture of dependency, in the midst of the Great Recession, making it easier for the poor to apply for federal assistance. The thinly veiled argument behind so much of the coverage of poverty since Obama's election is that Obamaphone[31] recipients and salmon-eating SNAP beneficiaries are the inevitable outcome of outreached hands being filled to overflowing with government benefits. When Blacks experience poverty, they apparently do so willingly, even willfully.

This has, to say the least, poisoned the well of our political discourse regarding Black poverty. Without this conflation of blackness and the undeserving poor, we could speak about White and Black poverty in the same breath; we could discuss its effects on the individual, the family, and the community at large and perhaps even agree on some possible solutions. But this is the kind of broadly inclusive discourse that the stigma hanging over Black poverty stifles. We have known for a long time that race is a social construct, not a genetic one. And yet we hold onto it as something that divides us, as an all-too-easy way to tell friend from foe. Black poverty and White poverty cannot, at least not yet, be yoked together. This does no favor to the white poor in this country. In fact, it renders them all the more invisible—an issue we'll examine in more depth in the next section.

The Invisible Poor

As White America began to flee the inner cities in the middle of the twentieth century—a movement that Catherine Jurca aptly calls the "white diaspora"—the problem of poverty began to be more easily relegated to the back of one's mind (at least for those whose daily lives no longer featured a face-to-face encounter with the conditions of the inner city). Even in the early 1960s, Harrington recognized that the poor were "slipping out of the very experience and consciousness of the nation" (4). His book was intended as something of a wake-up call for the nation, and, for the most part, it was a success in this regard, but we seem to have been lulled back to sleep by the sedatives of consumerism and wall-to-wall infotainment. The gated community and its security guards have reinforced the sense of security once felt behind the picket fence (no longer an effective guard against the perceived danger posed by the black and brown menace that threatens every moment to invade the tranquility of compound life).

Besides relatively minor, street-level intrusions, poverty (and more importantly, the poor themselves) is something of an alien concept to America's legions of multi-generational suburbanites. Class segregation and ghettoization have effectively sanitized America's exclusive communities and even the corridors through which many of these residents move. Human engagement with the face of poverty has become entirely optional in today's America, and, if the language that is so often used to describe poverty and the poor is any indication, the option is not one that is being exercised frequently. As Katz has said, starting in the 1970s, poverty "slipped easily, unreflectively, into a language of family, race, and culture rather than inequality, power, and exploitation. The silence is, therefore, no anomaly."[32] This slippage is facilitated by the ease with which Americans can, if they so wish, dramatically limit their exposure to the lived experience of poverty happening beneath their feet and their notice. This, in turn, renders invisible, or nearly so, the gears within the jeweled watch casing; it makes it possible to hold fast to the meritocratic myth—the favorite of those who most loudly trumpet American exceptionalism, that takes within its purview America's successes, not her failures. Her successes are held up as proof positive that the American merit-rewarding system functions as it should, that it rewards ingenuity, integrity, and industriousness; poverty becomes, thus, a moral issue, and America has been reading her psalms: "I will set," she says, "no wicked thing before mine eyes."[33] We have averted our gaze and thereby allowed poverty, and particularly the poor who suffer from it, to slip from our consciousness. It is only once we have turned our backs on the poor that we can ignore what we all (to some degree or another) participate in: the countless "exploitative relationships" that are both root and branch of America's dramatic inequalities.[34]

The indignities of poverty are made exponentially worse when one suffers them in the shadows of the city's towers or the Appalachian mountains, into which the light of notice never penetrates. Self-determination, shackled as it is by reduced means, is close to nil for these invisible poor. As Harrington recognized more than 50 years ago, this deeply felt powerlessness represents a profound psychological crisis at the heart of the experience of impoverishment, one

When a Dream is deferred. The economic suffering in America is often silent, lonely, and ironic in the face of such a prosperous nation. Such a moral defect in the character of America would prompt Martin Luther King Jr. to say, "There is nothing new about poverty. What is new, however, is that we have the resources to get rid of it." https://flic.kr/p/4F891W. Credit: Alex Barth, January 2008.

that statistics can never capture: "If a group has internal vitality, a will, if it has aspiration, it may live in dilapidated housing, it may eat an inadequate diet, and it may suffer poverty, but it is not impoverished" (10). Destitution's most revolting feature is not, therefore, hunger or even substandard living conditions (undignified though these may be); it is the mask that poverty so often wears, one that renders its victims mute and utterly invisible. Man does not, it is true, live by bread alone, and the experience of late American poverty, particularly its more dehumanizing and humiliating features, is one in which dismal standards of living are made much worse by the further indignities of powerlessness and loneliness.

While doing research for his book *The American Way of Poverty: How the Other Half Still Lives,* Sasha Abramsky traveled to some of the areas hardest hit by recession, and to a great number of places where poverty is positively ancient—where it is as much a part of the landscape as the hills. He everywhere found that the American experience of poverty was virtually identical to the kind of deep-seated suffering that Harrington described half a century ago. Rather than addressing the issue of adequately granting these communities access to the opportunities for the advancement of human capital, we have merely pushed it out of view, and we resort to bashing the poor as being unproductive when, as economist David Wishart says, "we have not created access to physical capital,"[35] which is having a profound psychological effect on the poor. As Abramsky says, "profound economic hardship pushes people to the psychological and physical margins of society—isolated from friends and relatives; shunted into dilapidated trailer parks, shanties, or ghettoized public housing; and removed from banks and stores, transit systems and cultural institutions" (5). This creates an aura of shame that heaps indignity upon indignity. Our collective focus on individual success, coupled with our tendency to ascribe that success to the American can-do spirit—not to mention the outright demonization of the American underclass, has so stigmatized the poor in this country that the worry about "being judged failures in life" keeps many of the poor from making their presence felt. Abramsky shows that America's poor have not merely been ghettoized; rather, they have themselves retreated even farther into the margins, withdrawing from "all but the most necessary, unavoidable social interactions" (5). This represents our failure, not theirs.

By ignoring poverty as an issue and the poor as suffering individuals, we have opened the door to the predatory practices that have turned the poor into a source of profit for some of America's least scrupulous lenders. While they ostensibly offer assistance through short-term loans to those who lack ready capital, these lenders are trapping those living below the poverty line in interminable debt spirals. There seems to be no shortage of retailers, credit-card companies, for-profit colleges,[36] or payday loan companies that are more than happy to take on the added risk of lending money to the poor (their ads shamelessly target the unemployed and the working poor), so long as this risk comes with punitive interest rates. The subprime mortgage crisis opened America's eyes to the extent of this problem, but the majority of the focus was on the lenders, not the borrowers; they were lambasted in the media, but not for their predatory lending practices.[37] The real victims were the investors who bought the investment vehicles driven by these "high-risk" mortgages. There was a smattering of stories focusing on those whose mortgages were suddenly out of the reach of their budgets when they came up for renewal, but the lion's share of the media's interest was on these mortgages as bad investments that the banks should not have re-sold to investors. Whether or not they should have capitalized on the desire of the lower classes to join the ranks of the property owners was largely ignored, as were the consequences of these disastrous loans, not on the middle- and upper-class investors, but on those who were the dupes of the lenders' bait and switch: those whose reduced means had rendered them all but invisible.

The Deserving and the Undeserving

In the last four decades, fiscal and social conservatism has dramatically altered the way in which poverty and the poor are discussed in this country. A palpable disrespect for the working poor and a downright demonization of the welfare-receiving unemployed have bubbled to the surface in conservative rhetoric surrounding entitlement reform and a general tightening of the country's fiscal belt, something that, since the tax cuts began during Reagan's first term, has never seemed to include increased taxes on those who can most afford them. Perhaps unsurprisingly, Reagan introduced the term "welfare queen" into the conservative lexicon,[38] frequently using it to typify a broken federal benefits system during his 1976 and 1980 campaigns; he said he was the man to fix it. Reagan's choice epithet referred to a particularly chameleon-like woman, Linda Taylor, whose laundry list of criminal activities by no means stopped at welfare fraud. The discussion of Taylor's fraud in the *Chicago Tribune* made her infamous almost overnight. According to *Slate*'s Josh Levin, "There was evidence that the 47-year-old Taylor had used three Social Security cards, 27 names, 31 addresses, and 25 phone numbers to fuel her mischief, not to mention 30 different wigs."[39] As reporters dug deeper, the number of aliases climbed to more than 80. The amount of governmental assistance she had received under her many aliases swelled to more than $150,000 per annum (this was the figure that Reagan frequently cited during his campaign). The *Tribune* continued to turn up details about Taylor, implicating her in everything from kidnapping and baby-trafficking to voodoo curses and murder, yet her status as a "welfare queen" was the only line that journalists, and probably the aghast public as well, were interested in pursuing. It was, to put the matter quite simply, easier to produce frothy rage when the entire country (or at least the tax-paying public) could claim a share in victimhood: "A murder in Chicago," says Levin, "is mundane. A sumptuously attired woman stealing from John Q. Taxpayer is a menace, the kind of criminal who victimizes absolutely everyone."[40]

As something of a testing ground for the viability of welfare fraud as an issue around which conservative politicians could (and would) campaign, Illinois proved remarkably fertile soil. As Julilly Kohler-Hausmann reported, a poll of Illinois voters in 1978 found that "84% ranked controlling welfare and Medicaid fraud and abuses their *highest* legislative priority" (339; emphasis in original). The issue not only put down deep roots remarkably quickly, but it flowered in Reagan's successful 1980 campaign, and entitlement abuse and reform have remained conservative talking points ever since—frequently used to stoke the fires of resentment among white, working-class Americans. The effortlessness that an isolated case of welfare fraud in 1976 by Illinois resident, Linda Taylor, was made into a racially charged term, Welfare Queen, was in poor taste. But the term became plural, "welfare queens," and an infamous buzzword for Black women receiving federal assistance who have the audacity not to wear their poverty as a badge for all to see. The fact that Taylor was dark-skinned helped to further racially code the discourse surrounding welfare and its abuse. It dovetailed neatly with one of Reagan's other racially charged pet topics, food stamps. When campaigning in the South, Reagan spoke of a "strapping young buck" buying a T-bone steak with food stamps; this was later white-washed into "some young fellow," but for those who heard the unedited version, it was clear what Reagan was talking about: America's broken welfare system, the same one that honest (white) Americans depended upon, as a last resort to see them through occasional spates of joblessness, was broken because it was being sucked dry by Black America.[41] This message was barely concealed in the rhetoric surrounding the welfare queens; in his "strapping young buck" comment, racist undertones became overtones. At few moments has top-to-bottom white resentment of Black America been more transparent.

Whereas the portrait of American poverty had once been hued in Appalachian pinks and blues, such sympathetic images of the melancholy yet dignified poor were replaced by decidedly urban studies, ones painted in brown and black oils. Young men and women of color appear in the center of these portraits, painted as lazy and irresponsible criminals, drug users, and negligent parents, gamers of the system. As familiar as this portrait of American poverty is, it is not true to life. While poverty does disproportionately visit Blacks and Hispanics living deep within America's largest cities as well as the rural south and southwest, the demographics of poverty reflect the American patchwork in ways that are ill reflected in the conservative caricature of the American underclass. For one, poverty is more widespread in rural areas than it is in urban ones. The USDA split the nation into four quadrants—the Northeast, South, West, and Midwest—and in each area found that a higher percentage of the poor live in non-metropolitan areas.[42] The racialized nature of the caricature is also divorced from reality. Taken as a whole, 42 per cent of the nation's poor people are White, 21 per cent Black, and 28 per cent Hispanic.[43] Yet that doesn't stop the conservative establishment from focusing disproportionately on dark-skinned welfare recipients, and it certainly has not stopped them from reinvigorating the discussions regarding the deserving and the undeserving poor.

Because of the relentless application of the stereotype of the poor, especially the Black poor, as freeloaders or hucksters who are, at best, feeding off the government, or, at worst, defrauding taxpayers of their hard-earned dollars, it has become acceptable in some circles to divide the poor into two categories: the deserving and the undeserving. The former are those who are seen in a relatively positive light—as those who are simply down on their luck; the latter are those who are painted in less flattering colors, the drug addicts, the ne'er-do-wells, the Obamaphone recipients. Attempts to separate the deserving and the undeserving poor are problematic for a number of reasons, perhaps most of all because of the way they entwine the individual worth of a member of society with that individual's ability to either turn or grease the wheels of the capitalist economic machinery. The intellectually dishonest yoking of morality and poverty leads one to the inevitable conclusion that personal responsibility is at the heart of the condition of poverty. This dovetails nicely with the frequent willingness of those at the top of the food chain to cite their moral character or work ethic as the main reasons they have reached those heights. The unemployed and the working poor (Romney's 47%, for instance) are, therefore, poor by choice: they have chosen a path of government dependence because it suits them and their lack of work ethic down to the ground. This tendency to turn poverty into a moral issue is an act of class, often race as well, warfare waged not against poverty, but against the poor themselves. Let us note, however, that this dichotomy tends to turn into a single category for conservatives, who believe that all the poor have made bad choices.

Such acts of class and race warfare have always had their defenders, who, with conclusion-first thinking, justify the status quo by claiming that those who are unable to scale the social or economic ladder are somehow destined not to do so, thanks to genetic or psychological limitations. This kind of taxonomy of the lower classes, frequently bordering on pathology, is an offshoot of our meritocratic discourse—an attempt to justify our unjustifiable inequalities. They are yet another form of self-congratulation, a bedside sleep-aid for those who profit either socially or economically from inequality. Like meritocratic discourse, taxonomies of the poor deflect attention from Katz's "exploitative relationships" of American capitalism, mentioned above; poverty, in this formulation, is a product of "identity, morality, and patronage,"[44] and Nature herself—or more commonly, God—has vouchsafed the success of the successful few and blessed them with all the gifts in her command. Blessed are the principals; damned are their subjects.

When Oscar Lewis published *The Children of Sanchez* in 1961, he unintentionally gave life (albeit not entirely new life) to taxonomic studies of the pathology of poverty. Like Harrington (who took inspiration from Lewis's palpable outrage at the living conditions of America's lower classes), Lewis was attempting to critique the system that produced the dramatic inequalities that his research brought him nose-to-nose with. He noted the particular ways in which the poor were conditioned by the limited (often dismal) choices presented by their immediate environment. In his subjects from the lower classes, he frequently noticed "a strong present time orientation with relatively little ability to defer gratification and plan for the future, a sense of resignation and fatalism based upon the realities of their difficult life situation, a belief in male superiority which reaches its crystallization in *machismo* or the cult of masculinity, a corresponding martyr complex among women, and finally, a high tolerance for psychological pathology of all sorts" (xxxix). This was intended as an examination of the *effects* of poverty, not their causes, but the idea of a "culture of poverty" was transposed into a new key in the 1970s, and Lewis's ideas became utterly unrecognizable in the racist diatribes about pathological poverty (especially Black poverty) that followed.

Edward Banfield, who would later advise the White House during both Nixon's and Reagan's presidencies, was particularly adept at justifying the class system by positing a culture of poverty that, perhaps more transparently than anything written since, shows how White America was reaching back to (very) old ideas about the inferiority of non-Caucasians to push back against the perceived gains of Black Americans. In *The Unheavenly City*, published for the first time in 1970 and revised just four years later as *The Unheavenly City Revisited*, he noted: "Naturally, [the Negro] concludes that the same old cause—'Whitey'—is still producing the same old effects. That these effects are now being produced largely (not entirely, of course) by other causes, especially differences of education, income, and—in the case of those who are lower class—class culture is something he cannot be expected to see for himself or to believe if it is pointed out to him, especially when the pointing out is done by a white" (97). A little later, Banfield makes this push-back even more transparent: "The faster and farther the Negro rises the more impatient he is likely to be with whatever he thinks prevents his rising still faster and still farther" (232). This is white privilege in black and white. Bill O'Reilly and Rush Limbaugh, by no means isolated instances of this practice, continue to perpetuate the kernel of wisdom at the heart of Banfield's comments: Black America—and, by extension, almost the entirety of the American lower class—is, by their reckoning, mired in a self-perpetuating culture of poverty, crime, victimhood, and irresponsibility. Blaming the victim is not enough; it is the (racially coded) cultural milieu of the ghetto—violent, radically immoral, and antagonistic to American values—that is unfailingly located at the root of every issue pertaining to racial or class-based suffering. The individual is still to be blamed for either willingly immersing him/herself in this culture or choosing not to rise above it. This (moral) flaw is further complicated by their poor impulse control and inability to defer gratification.[45] What is lacking from all of these accounts is a discussion of the practices that led to the creation of the ghetto, the innumerable forces of institutionalized class-based and racial discrimination against poor and dark-skinned Americans (so often one and the same). It is the circular logic with a racist and fatalistic center that must go on perpetually spinning if we are to keep the meritocratic myth alive, and there is clearly no shortage of people willing to step forward and put their shoulder to the wheel.

The Moral Crisis

Whether one is looking at the issue of poverty from the left, the right, or the center, it is hardly controversial to say that America is in the midst of a moral crisis with respect to what to do about the poor and poverty. I'm not at all convinced that widespread poverty is yet another symptom (along with violence and its glorification) of an accelerating moral decline; quite the contrary, I think the outlines of the moral crisis have changed very little in the last few decades, and, while we have attempted to address the issue in effectual ways, it is difficult to claim any success in the arena while there are still 50 million Americans living below the poverty line. America's moral arc and its long bend toward justice (especially justice for the poor) have, for the time being at least, flattened out. Ironically, it is our moralizing about poverty, the yoking together of destitution and depravity, that represents as much as anything our moral failings as a nation. When Cadillac-driving welfare queens and thuggish males buying steaks with food stamps slipped unreflectively into our political discourse, when they became accepted and perpetuated images of poverty (specifically Black poverty), we effectively planted our moral stakes in the ground as a nation. We have not done enough to move them since.

Our manner of discussing poverty has long smacked of presumptuousness and arrogance. When outraged conservative pundits get up in arms about the fact that food stamps are being used to buy crab legs or organic salmon steaks, they are reinforcing the widespread and wrong-headed notions that a) the poor are living high-on-the-hog off taxpayer dollars, and b) that the taxpayer has a right to determine how the recipients of federal assistance should be allowed to spend their benefits. This second presumption is especially problematic. As Michael Ignatieff notes in *The Needs of Strangers*, "There are

few presumptions in human relations more dangerous than the idea
that one knows what another human being needs better than they
do themselves" (11). This is master/slave or, at the very least, guard/
prisoner thinking. The benefit-collecting poor are not the property
of the tax-paying public; the experience of poverty is humiliating enough without the added indignity of mandatory drug testing
(required in only a small handful of states) or other measures designed
to remind welfare recipients that they are little more than chattel for
as long as they line up for the benefits. Rabble-rousing pundits and
policymakers have grown rather adept at whipping up class resentment—especially when the economy is underperforming. During the
run-up to the 2012 election, an AARP poll found that more than
91 per cent of voters over the age of 50 (the "baby-boomers") cited
the strengthening of social security as a major legislative priority.[46]
Entitlement reform has been a hot-button topic since the early 1970s,
and something that is too often lost in the discussion about the needs
and rightful entitlements of the poor. Again, I turn to Ignatieff: "The
conservative counter-attack on the welfare state is above all an attack
on the idea that these needs make rights; an attack on this idea puts
into question the very notion of a society as a moral community....
Without a language of need, and the language of right that derives
from it, the human world would scarcely be human: between powerful and powerless only the law of hammer and anvil, master and slave
would rule" (13; 27).

Perhaps more so than any other nation in the world, we claim to
be a moral nation—and often in the same breath, a Christian nation.
"Life, Liberty and the pursuit of Happiness": such are the inalienable
rights bestowed upon all who stand on this soil, and if you accept that
providence and the birth of this nation are intertwined, these rights
transcend all others; they are the cornerstone of what we have collectively decided it means to be completely human. Certain material
conditions must be met in order for us to be thus human, and such
are our needs. These needs embody, as Ignatieff reminds us, part and
parcel of our human rights, and the push-back from the conservative
right concerning the rights of the poor to have their basic material
needs met by the state represents an attempt to further marginalize
and dehumanize those who have, for whatever reason, been unable
to meet them satisfactorily. Our semi-mythic Christian roots have

borne strange fruit indeed. Our callousness in the face of poverty and deplorable inequalities, when combined with our holier-than-thou posturing, casts the United States in the role of the hypocrite on the world stage. The divine guidance and providence that we everywhere profess are inconsistent with what we will not do for what Jesus called the least of these.

This hypocrisy has attracted notice from even the Pope. Since the recent change of leadership, the Vatican is increasingly insistent in its calls for reforming the living conditions of the world's poor, but the American response to these claims has been, from some corners, vitriolic. Louis Woodhill of *Forbes*, perhaps unsurprisingly a strong opponent of minimum-wage raises in the U.S., has said that "Pope Francis, unlike his communism-defeating predecessor, John Paul II, is hell-bent on a redistribution of income that is an outright act of class warfare . . . . [He] has lent the prestige of the Catholic Church to leftist/socialist whining."[47] On this side of the Atlantic, Woodhill's is hardly a voice crying in the wilderness: socially conservative Catholic groups in the U.S. have placed significant pressure on the relatively open-handed distribution of charitable funds on the part of Catholic charities; some of the groups that are distributing money, food, or clothing for the poor are not, they say, in lock-step with Catholic values (support for same-sex unions and non-abstinence-based sexual education is a particular thorn in their sides).[48] A pope who has been an outright critic of capitalism's more blatant excesses—namely, the "sacralized workings of the prevailing economic system" and "an impersonal economy lacking a truly human purpose"[49]—is moving institutionalized Christianity at a lusty trot from its much-criticized role as a defender of the status quo. This slide to the left has been met with boos and jeers from the wings (particularly those on stage right), and, again and again, we play the religious hypocrite. Our Christian values, if we do indeed possess them, demand that we assist the poor unconditionally. The Good Book upon which we swear our oaths demands that we recognize another self in the other. This means dropping for good the moralizing and condescending tone when we discuss poverty.

To be clear, I am not suggesting that discussions surrounding personal responsibility and morality are, somehow, less appropriate when talking about life on the economic margins. America's inner cities and rural wastelands are, indeed, the sites of significant moral compromises; likewise, I do not dispute that callousness in the face of the suffering of one's fellows—a callousness that borders on the pathological—attends upon America's most destitute communities at an alarming rate. Concerns about the rapidly expanding federal deficit, which were prevalent during the early Obama years but not as much of a worry as they have been of late, are not necessarily a smoke screen for class-based or racial warfare; sometimes a spade is just a spade. However, America's myopic obsession with success and its tendency to yoke this success to a combination of moral standards and work ethic is a dehumanizing practice that stands between our grossly unequal present and a more equal future.

More than half a century ago, Harrington expressed outrage at America's technological progress, which, while making life easier for many, has left a sizable underclass trailing ever in its wake: "In a nation with a technology that could provide every citizen with a decent life, it is an outrage and a scandal that there be such social misery" (17). Our progress combined with our prosperity means that we can relatively easily provide a life, not of ease or even of comfort, but of dignity for all Americans. For as long as poverty is one of this country's more serious problems, the promise of America has not been met. The right to dignity must be entirely divorced from any notion of the deserving vs. the undeserving poor and instead connected, as Charles A. Reich proposes, to the idea of property: "The traditional view of social welfare deemed aid to the unfortunate to be a form of charity or hand-out. The recipient had no more rights than the street person who begs for spare change from a passerby. By contrast, the more that we advance toward the idea that welfare benefits are property, the more we recognize that every individual life has dignity" (228). Stopgap measures have run their course; it is time to look at new ways to address the issue of poverty and provide dignity for all Americans.

Notes

1   Irving Howe, "Introduction," Harrington, xi.

2   Woolf and Aron 171. See http://www.nap.edu/openbook.php?record_id=13497&page=171.

3   According to a colleague of mine, economist David Wishart, poverty is a relative concept—it is defined as a money income below a certain level. Cross-country comparisons are tricky as a result, since not all countries are working with the same definition. Personal interview, 23 March 2015.

4   Dylan Matthews, "Poverty in the 50 Years since 'The Other America,' in Five Charts," *The Washington Post* 11 July 2012, http://www.washingtonpost.com/ blogs/wonkblog/wp/2012/07/11/poverty-in-the-50-years-since-the-other- america-in-five-charts/.

5   J.B. Wogan, "Poverty Rates Remain Stubbornly High in Big Cities," *Governing the States and Localities*, 24 September 2013, http://www.governing.com/blogs/ view/gov-poverty-rates-remain-stubbornly-high-big-cities.html#data.

6   See Katz, *The Undeserving Poor: America's Enduring Confrontation with Poverty.*

7   Carmen DeNavas-Walt and Bernadette D. Proctor, *Income and Poverty in the United States: 2013. Current Population Reports*, 60-249, United States Census Bureau, http://www.census.gov/content/dam/Census/library/publications/2014/ demo/p60-249.pdf.

8   "How Many Children Are Poor?" Institute for Research on Poverty, University of Wisconsin–Madison, http://www.irp.wisc.edu/faqs/faq6.htm.

9   Pilyoung Kim, et al., "Effects of Childhood Poverty and Chronic Stress on Emotion Regulatory Brain Function in Adulthood," *Proceedings of the National Academy of Sciences of the United States of America* 110.46 (2013): 18442–47, http://www.pnas.org/content/110/46/18442.abstract.

10   Theresa Riley, "Does Income Inequality Cause High Teen Pregnancy Rates?" Moyers & Company, 15 May 2012, http://billmoyers.com/2012/05/15/ does-income-inequality-cause-high-teen-pregnancy-rates/.

11   Table found at http://stateofworkingamerica.org/files/pre-files/family_income_ median_income_growth_productivity_all_years.pdf. See also Doug Short, "U.S. Household Incomes: a 46-Year Perspective," Advisor Perspectives, 17 September 2014. http://www.advisorperspectives.com/dshort/updates/Household-Income- Distribution.php.

12   "Job Openings and Labor Turnover Survey," United States Department of Labor, Bureau of Labor Statistics, http://data.bls.gov/timeseries/JTS00000000JOL.

13   Julie Kliegman, "There Are 3 Unemployed People for Every Job Opening, Obama Adviser Says," *Tampa Bay Times* 7 January 2014, http://www.politifact. com/truth-o-meter/statements/2014/jan/07/gene-sperling/there-are-3-unemployed- people-every-job-opening-ob/.

14   McGeary, 238.

15   Matthew Yglesias, "Smart, Poor Kids Are Applying to the Wrong Colleges," Slate,
     11 March 2013, http://www.slate.com/articles/business/moneybox/2013/03/under
     matching_half_of_the_smartest_kids_from_low_income_households_don_t.html.

16   "The Hidden Supply of High-Achieving, Low-Income Students," National
     Bureau of Economic Research, http://www.nber.org/digest/may13/w18586.html.

17   Associated Press, "Study: Finishing College a Growing Divide between
     Rich, Poor," *The New York Times* 3 February 2015, http://www.nytimes.com/
     aponline/2015/02/03/us/ap-us-college-affordability.html.

18   "The Hidden Supply."

19   Drew Desilver, "Who Makes Minimum Wage?" Pew Research Center, 8
     September 2014, http://www.pewresearch.org/fact-tank/2014/09/08/
     who-makes-minimum-wage/.

20   Elizabeth Warren, "17 Million Reasons to Raise the Minimum Wage," ABC
     News, 25 March 2014, http://abcnews.go.com/Business/17-million-reasons-
     raise-minimum-wage/story?id=23054905.

21   15now.org, "FAQ," http://15now.org/wp-content/uploads/2014/02/Binder1.pdf.

22   Heidi Shierholz, "Fix It and Forget It: Index the Minimum Wage to Growth in
     Average Wages," Economic Policy Institute Briefing Paper #251, 17 December
     2009, http://epi.3cdn.net/91fd33f4e013307415_rum6iydua.pdf, 17.

23   Ibid., 10.

24   Jeffrey Dorfman, "Almost Everything You Have Been Told about the Minimum
     Wage Is False," *Forbes* 30 January 2014, http://www.forbes.com/sites/jeffrey
     dorfman/2014/01/30/almost-everything-you-have-been-told-about-the-
     minimum-wage-is-false/.

25   The same kind of arguments infect discussion about entitlement reform as well,
     with critics arguing that poverty statistics are inflated because they include those
     who are receiving federal aid—as though that aid itself were enough to lift them
     out of poverty rather than merely keeping them from starvation. Tim Worstall
     at *Forbes* is one of the writers most particularly fond of this kind of callous logic,
     which he uses to discredit any arguments for wage increases or poverty relief.

26   Quarterly Capitalism simply refers to American Financial Center's prac-
     tice, regulated by the government, to report earnings and profits every three
     months. Such a practice is believed to hurt workers and to focus more on
     ensuring that profit margins are high for both market and private investors.
     George R. Tyler, "What America Can Learn from Europe about Income
     Inequality," *Salon* 18 March 2014, http://www.salon.com/2014/03/18/
     what_america_can_learn_from_europe_about_income_inequality_partner/.

27   Arthur Delaney and Alissa Scheller, "Who Gets Food Stamps? White People, Mostly," The Huffington Post, 28 February 2015, http://www.huffingtonpost.com/2015/02/28/food-stamp-demographics_n_6771938.html.

28   Jerry Mitchell, "Miss. Third-Grade Gate: Fear of Failure," The Clarion-Ledger 15 February 2015, http://www.clarionledger.com/story/news/2015/02/14/miss-third-grade-gate-fear-failure/23443737/.

29   Ibid. Another way of looking at this is from the human-capital perspective, where this is yet another example of unequal access to a public good—poor communities have inadequate police protection/security, unlike areas where the residents are respected as "upstanding and law-abiding," or in other words "civil." Businesses therefore shy away from investing in these communities. Since such investments (businesses, infrastructure, technology) are equivalent to physical capita, the result is unequal access to the financial by-products of physical capital—property taxes and properly funded schools—which are the precursors to the social and economic mobility and public trust that accompany access to investments in human capital.

30   Gilens, 68.

31   Right-wing representations of Obamaphone recipients leaned heavily upon a bloated mischaracterization of the free cellphone airtime minutes given to the poor to help them secure call-backs for employment, gain access to children's teachers, or for emergencies.

32   Katz, The Undeserving Poor: From the War on Poverty to the War on Welfare, 8.

33   Psalm 101:3

34   Katz, The Undeserving Poor: From the War on Poverty to the War on Welfare.

35   Personal interview, 23 March 2015.

36   Senator Tom Harkin recently published a report on the gouging practices of America's for-profit colleges and universities. See Tamar Lewin, "Senate Committee Report on For-Profit Colleges Condemns Costs and Practices," The New York Times 29 July 2012, http://www.nytimes.com/2012/07/30/education/harkin-report-condemns-for-profit-colleges.html?pagewanted=all&_r=2&.

37   See Gorton, who does a great job of describing the shadow banking system that operates at the highest levels in the world of finance, though one may consider payday loans and subprime mortgages different sides of the same immoral and oppressive coin.

38   The term itself first appeared in the Chicago Tribune of 12 October 1974, but it was Reagan who saw—and exploited—the term's rabble-rousing potential during his 1976 campaign.

39   Josh Levin, "The Welfare Queen," Slate, 19 December 2013, http://www.slate.
     com/articles/news_and_politics/history/2013/12/linda_taylor_welfare_queen_
     ronald_reagan_made_her_a_notorious_american_villain.html.

40   Ibid.

41   Ian Haney-Lopez, "The Racism at the Heart of the Reagan Presidency," Salon,
     11 January 2014, http://www.salon.com/2014/01/11/the_racism_at_the_heart_
     of_the_reagan_presidency/.

42   "Geography of Poverty," United States Department of Agriculture Economic
     Research Service, http://www.ers.usda.gov/topics/rural-economy-population/
     rural-poverty-well-being/geography-of-poverty.aspx#.VACHZ0uZZg0.

43   "Poverty Rate by Race/Ethnicity," Henry J. Kaiser Family Foundation, http://kff.
     org/other/state-indicator/poverty-rate-by-raceethnicity/.

44   Katz, *The Undeserving Poor: From the War on Poverty to the War on Welfare*, 8.

45   Herstein and Murray's *Bell Curve: Intelligence and Class Structure in American Life*
     and Murray's *Coming Apart: The State of White America, 1960-2010* are both
     examples of this kind of victim-blaming, the former blaming low IQs for the
     state of black America, the latter citing the white underclass's moral decline as
     the cause of its own financial and social ills.

46   Erik Wasson, "AARP Poll Highlights Importance of Entitlement Reform in
     Election," The Hill, 8 August 2012, http://thehill.com/policy/finance/
     242755-aarp-poll-highlights-importance-of-entitlement-reform-in-election.

47   Louis Woodhill, "Papal Bull: Why Pope Francis Should be Grateful for
     Capitalism," *Forbes* 4 December 2013, http://www.forbes.com/sites/louiswood
     hill/2013/12/04/papal-bull-why-pope-francis-should-be-grateful-for-capitalism/.

48   Tom Roberts, "Report: Conservatives' Attacks Threaten Bishops' Anti-Poverty
     Organization," *National Catholic Reporter* 12 June 2013, http://ncronline.org/
     news/peace-justice/.
     report-conservatives-attacks-threaten-bishops-anti-poverty-organization.

49   Pope Francis, Apostolic Exhortation, 24 November 2013, http://w2.vatican.va/
     content/francesco/en/apost_exhortations/documents/papa-francesco_esortazione-
     ap_20131124_evangelii-gaudium.html.

Chapter Six

INCOME INEQUALITY: THE UNBRIDGEABLE GAP

UNLIKE THE PRESIDENT'S KENYAN BIRTH OR THE GRADUAL "disprivileging" of the American white male, increasing income inequality in America is a provable fact (see Figure 6.1). Its existence isn't up for debate—the only question is what we are to do about it.

Some—many in fact—would like us to sit on our collective hands and let the free market work its magic. For others, even this is not enough; they bandy about terms like "government overreach" and "regulatory stranglehold," demonizing big government, the tax-man, and pencil-pushing bureaucrats. They claim to stand up for American small business owners by calling for business-friendly tax codes, deregulation, and *laissez faire* economic policy, but a closer look at their math almost always reveals that it is the top earners that will reap the benefits[1] and the medium and lower classes that will, in effect, pay for them (see Figure 6.2).

Figure 6.1: Income Inequality in the United States, 1910-2010

The top decile share in the U.S. national income dropped from 45–60% in the 1910s–1920s to less than 35% in the 1950s (this is the fall documented by Kuznets); it then rose from less than 35% in the 1970s to 45–50% in the 2000s–2010s. Source: Thomas Piketty. Capital in the 21st Century, *translated by Arthur Goldhammer. Page 24. Copyright ©2014 by the President and Fellows of Harvard College.*

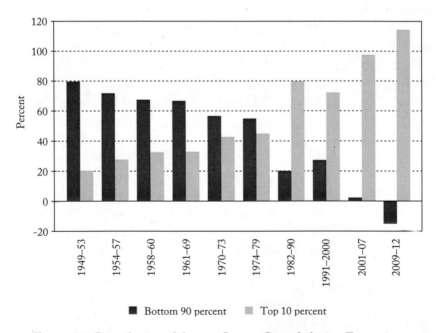

■ Bottom 90 percent   ▨ Top 10 percent

Figure 6.2: Distribution of Average Income Growth during Expansions

"Growth for Whom?" Levy Economics Institute of Bard College, 6 October 2014, http://www. levyinstitute.org/pubs/op_47.pdf. Source: Pavlina R. Tcherneva. "Reorienting Fiscal Policy: A Bottom-up Approach," Journal of Post Keynesian Economics, *Fall 2014, 37 (1): 43–66. Reprinted with permission of Paulina R. Tcherneva.*

In 2005, Paul Ryan—now Chairman of the House Budget Committee—spoke at a gathering of the Atlas Society, a Washington group that pays fealty to Ayn Rand's individualistic ideology. Addressing the assembled acolytes, he said that "the fight we [neo-conservatives] are in here, make no mistake about it, is a fight of individualism versus collectivism."[2] Individualism, according to his Randian formulation, means the success of the individual *at the expense of* the collective. It is dog-eat-dog, women and children last; it is capitalism red in tooth and claw, and, as such, Ryan's proposed Path to Prosperity—which became one of the cornerstones of his and Romney's 2012 presidential bid—was the antithesis of the middle-out (not top-down) economic principles that, in a matter of decades, helped to build the largest, most prosperous economy in the world.

According to the Center on Budget and Policy Priorities (CBPP), Ryan's much-touted budget proposed to cut most deeply in areas that were already feeling the pinch of the financial crisis; 69 per cent of the funding cuts—$2.7 trillion to health-care programs for the less advantaged; $137 billion in Supplemental Nutrition Assistance Program (SNAP) cuts; $150 billion in cuts to unspecified mandatory programs that benefit the poor—would be to programs that help, in small or large ways, Americans who are struggling on the lowest rungs of the country's social and economic ladder,[3] and all of this while treating the top earners to generous tax breaks. The president of the CBPP, Robert Greenstein, went so far as to argue that the Ryan budget would be like "Robin Hood in reverse—on steroids. It would likely produce the largest redistribution of income from the bottom to the top in modern U.S. history."[4] With its included repeal of Obamacare, it may be the case that the Ryan budget (which resurfaces every spring) is more an act of partisan grandstanding than it is a serious proposal, but the message at the heart of it is clear and familiar: fill the cup of the job creators until it overflows onto the lower and middle classes. Talk about middle-class families and prosperity for everyone that peppers the introduction to Ryan's 2015 budget is merely window dressing concealing the establishment-friendly trickle-down ideas that fiscal conservatives have been touting for more than three decades.

The concerted effort on the part of right-wing pundits and politicians to make this doctrine true by repeating its long since disproven claims that a rising tide lifts all boats has been met with significant opposition from the other side of the aisle. The liberal media and public intellectuals concerned about the state of twenty-first-century capitalism have all sounded the alarm as well: growing inequality in the distribution of wealth and income in the United States is incontrovertible, and it is high time that it became an issue important enough to voters that policymakers can no longer ignore it. Public interest in the issue, as gauged by Google Trends, has risen exponentially in the last half-decade—particularly during the Occupy Wall Street protests and the government shutdown over the federal budget in 2013.[5] The appearance of French economist Thomas Piketty's cinderblock-sized tome on income inequality at the top of bestseller lists may have been, as was frequently noted by reviewers, "unlikely," but it seems less of an anomaly when placed in the context of the none-too-gradual movement of social-leveling doctrine out of the fringe and into the mainstream.

Just as the Tea Party, forged in the fires of popular conservative rage, moved conservative politics to the right, so has liberal rage, shaped by similar—though certainly not identical—forces, moved leftist political rhetoric further from the center, bringing new populist darlings onto the national stage. In her bestselling book *A Fighting Chance*, Senator Elizabeth Warren laments the erosion of opportunity in America, laying the majority of the blame at the feet of the "armies of lobbyists" and the corporations that hire them to make sure that "the playing field [remains] tilted in their favor" (2). Thanks to her dogged pursuit of the bankers and Wall Street executives that she (and many others, like Senators David Vitter[6] and Sherrod Brown[7]) feels to be most responsible for both the financial crisis and the middle class's continued struggle for solvency, her popularity grew quickly. Her sensible and articulate critique of the unfair advantage enjoyed by those at the top of the economic food chain is finding more and more sympathetic listeners in every corner of America. Should she choose to vie for the leadership of her party, her reputation as an advocate for the middle class—one who fearlessly speaks truth to power—will carve out for her an important role in the 2016 election, or, at the very least, in the run-up to that election. The qualification I added at the end of the last sentence recognizes that she, at least for the moment, *seems* incorruptible. But, looking at the matter more cynically, in a short time she will give the learned electorate reason to doubt her sincerity, and she too will be bought and sold. Nevertheless, one thing is clear: income inequality is a pillar upon which candidates on the left are leaning in increasing numbers. So long as the economy continues its sluggish recovery (or should it suffer any further setbacks), the disparity between the rich and the poor in this country may just be the issue that decides the next presidential election—provided, of course, that the increasingly apathetic American electorate finds the framing of the issue compelling enough to drive them to the polls.

A Rising Tide Lifts Some Boats Higher than Others

Self-inflating rhetoric that trumpets American exceptionalism, or the land of opportunity enjoyed equally by all, rings hollow when it is addressed to a middle and lower class—especially the latter—that have shared minimally in the economic progress of the last three decades. Profit undoubtedly there has been, and some of that profit has translated into substantial income gains for the middle class, but the cycles of boom and bust have left an increasing gap between the middle and lower classes. One of the great ironies of the current political debate is the extent to which poor, white Americans have ascribed unreflectively to the conservative ethos. On a fundamental level, who can blame them for their disillusionment with the political process as it has played out over the last several decades? I have sat in bingo halls and bowling alleys listening attentively yet incredulously to their us (white) vs. them (black) analysis and the moral condemnation of a race/class hybrid, namely the Black working poor. In their hearts, the working poor in this country must know that the free-market ideological mantra that wealth is the justly deserved reward for industriousness and that poverty is the equally deserved punishment visited upon those who lack a work ethic does not hold.

This becomes increasingly obvious when we are forced to confront the lived reality of America's working poor. Many of them are being forced by their impoverished circumstances to work the kind of hours that even the most industrious executives would find onerous. The August 2014 death of Maria Fernandes, a low-wage worker in New Jersey who died from inhaling gasoline fumes in her car while sleeping, illustrates this particularly well. Fernandes worked four jobs (all of them at Dunkin' Donuts locations), often, her friends said, sleeping in her car in parking lots between long shifts.[8] Stories like this, even if they don't end as tragically as Fernandes's did, are surfacing at alarming frequency.[9] Often employed by large corporations, America's low-wage employees are working their fingers to the bone, but, atop the ivory tower, the upper-echelon executives in these same organizations are pulling down wildly incommensurate salaries that represent a skewed perspective of the economic climate in which their organizations are operating.

According to a recent Economic Policy Institute report CEOs at the top American restaurant chains made, on average, $10.87 million in 2013.[10] That number represents roughly 721 times the average salary of America's full-time minimum-wage workers. To put that in perspective, the CEOs of American fast-food restaurants made as much in their first half day of work as their lowest-paid employees did all year. According to the most recent data from the AFL-CIO, the overall CEO-to-minimum-wage ratio is a whopping 774:1.[11] This, according to the EPI report, represents a 27-per-cent increase since 2006.[12] The overall ratio of CEO-to-worker pay in America is not much better: in 2014 it was 331:1; just one year earlier it was 295:1; in 1980, it was 42:1; during the 1950s and 1960s, it was closer to 20:1 (see Figure 6.3).[13]

If one were to graph these figures, the resulting trend line would be a cause for concern. For whatever reason, though, academic interest in the problem of inequality has been confined mainly to the liberal-minded social sciences. It took a French economist, Thomas Piketty, to turn the gaze of economists (and, indeed, the reading public at large) to both the roots and the severity of the issue. His study, *Capital in the Twenty-First Century*, is the fruit of a decade-long period of research into income inequality in the developed world—research that covered more than 300 years of economic history and resulted in a treasure trove of data from dozens of countries. Piketty's research led him to the following conclusion: "When the rate of return on

Figure 6.3 (facing): This illustrates the staggering CEO-to-worker compensation ratio. (This does not include part-time wage earners, where the ratio differential is even greater.) Source: Lawrence Mishel and Alyssa Davis, "CEO Pay Continues to Rise as Typical Workers Are Paid Less," Economic Policy Institute, 12 June 2014, http://www.epi.org/publication/ceo-pay-continues-to-rise/. Reprinted with the permission of the Economic Policy Institute.

	CEO annual compensation (thousands)*	Worker annual compensation (thousands)		Stock market (adjusted to 2013)		CEO-to-worker compensation ratio***
		Private-sector production/ nonsupervisory workers	Firms' industry**	S&P 500	Dow Jones	
1965	$819	$39.5	n/a			20.0
				570	5,889	
1973	$1,069	$46.4	n/a			22.3
				503	4,330	
1978	$1,463	$47.2	n/a			29.9
				315	2,691	
1989	$2,724	$44.7	n/a			58.7
				586	4,553	
1995	$5,768	$45.6	$51.5			122.6
				822	6,829	
2000	$20,172	$47.9	$53.8			383.4
				1,931	14,506	
2007	$18,541	$50.4	$54.0			351.3
				1,660	14,805	
2009	$10,394	$52.0	$57.3			193.2
				1,030	9,650	
2010	$12,466	$52.7	$58.0			227.9
				1,218	11,398	
2011	$12,667	$52.3	$57.6			231.8
				1,313	12,381	
2012	$14,765	$52.0	$57.1			278.2
				1,400	13,155	
2013	$15,175	$52.1	$55.8			295.9
				1,644	15,010	
	Percent change					Change in ratio
1965–1978	78.7%	19.5%	n/a	-44.8%	-54.3%	9.9
1978–2000	1,279%	1.4%	n/a	513%	439%	353.6
2000–2013	-24.8%	8.7%	3.6%	-14.9%	3.5%	-87.6
1978–2013	937%	10.2%	n/a	422%	458%	237.2

Figure 6.3: CEO compensation, CEO-to-worker compensation ratio, and stock prices, 1965–2013 (2013 dollars)

* CEO annual compensation is computed using the "options realized" compensation series, which includes salary, bonus, restricted stock grants, options exercised, and long-term incentive payouts for CEOs at the top 350 U.S. firms ranked by sales.
** Annual compensation of the workers in the key industry of the firms in the sample
*** Based on averaging specific firm ratios and not the ratio of averages of CEO and worker compensation

capital exceeds the rate of growth of output and income, ... capitalism automatically generates arbitrary and unsustainable inequalities that radically undermine the meritocratic values on which democratic societies are based" (1). Expressed in an accessible and memorable formula, $r > g$,[14] and buttressed by mountains of transparently presented evidence, Piketty's claims confirm what non-expert observers of American economics have long intuited: the economic playing field is not a level one; in fact, the wealthy and the lower classes are, to all intents and purposes, not even playing on the same surface as the rest of society. A large fortune, once established, "grows according to a dynamic of its own" (440), and this growth, untethered from more widespread economic trends, has more often than not over the last 300 years been greater than the growth rate of the economy and the incomes derived therein. Since the early 1980s, the difference between r and g has reached historically unprecedented levels.

Unsurprisingly, Piketty's at times vicious critique of his fellow economists for their decades-long tendency to turn a blind eye to the problem of inequality has produced no small amount of backlash. A number of prominent financial publications, the *Financial Times* chief among them, have published critiques of Piketty's ideas, methods, and policy recommendations.[15] Even so, the core of Piketty's findings has held up under even close and heavily interested scrutiny. Rather than cherry picking his sources, Piketty pulled data from hundreds of technical papers published in professional economics journals over the last decade. The preponderance of evidence supports his conclusions, none more than his rather obvious contention that wealth and income inequality in the United States and the rest of the world have increased at an alarming rate since the 1980s. A more detailed examination of Piketty's findings will bear this out.

First of all, and most glaringly obvious from even a cursory thumbing of *Capital in the Twenty-First Century*, is the fact that income from labor in the U.S. is more unequally distributed than it has been anywhere, at any time (256).

The upper 10 per cent of earners in the U.S. accounted for a little less than 50 per cent of the nation's income in 2010 (see Figure 6.4); if trends continue in this direction, the same 10 per cent will be earning 60 per cent of the national income by 2030 (Piketty 294). When we look at capital rather than income, the distribution is tilted

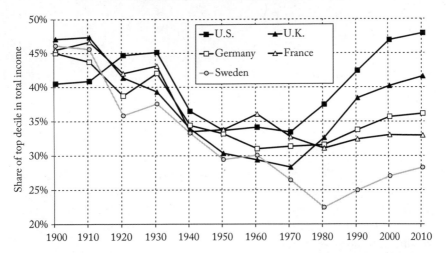

Figure 6.4: The top decile income share: Europe and the U.S. 1900–2010

Democracy Revisited. Economic Wealth is in the hands of a select few. In the 1950s–1970s, the top decile income was about 30–35% of total income in Europe and the U.S. Source: Thomas Piketty. Capital in the 21st Century, *translated by Arthur Goldhammer. Page 323. Copyright ©2014 by the President and Fellows of Harvard College.*

to favor the wealthy even more. According to the Federal Reserve, 72 per cent of America's wealth is controlled by the top decile.[16] If you're not sitting down, now might be a good time to do so: the bottom 50 per cent of American earners control a meager 2 per cent of all American capital (Piketty 258), and, since capital grows faster than their hard-earned wages ever will, the classes above them continue to widen the gap.

While the rate at which pools of inherited capital spread and deepen, seemingly of their own accord, is at the root of much tangible and measurable disparity between the classes, income inequality in terms of earnings is no less troubling. The rise of the supermanager, such as the late Steve Jobs (Apple) or Jamie Dimon (JP Morgan Chase), is further exacerbating the levels of inequality in this country. The figures above lead us to one unavoidable conclusion: left unchecked for more than three decades, late American capitalism has become a system for amassing and protecting extraordinary wealth for the privileged few; for the rest of the country, whose median incomes have been dropping steadily for four years,[17] the American Dream is a receding horizon. The system is broken.

How Did We Get Here?

In the midst of the Great Depression, America was forced to make a choice. During the Roaring Twenties, the briefly imposed and quite steep top tax rate (a product of government debts incurred during World War I) came to a rather abrupt end. Between 1920 and 1929, Secretary of the Treasury Andrew W. Mellon instituted deep, business-friendly tax cuts that saw the top tax rate plummet from 77 per cent to 24 per cent.[18] In the aftermath of the Crash of 1929, America's choice was this: either significantly increase the taxes on those who had been able to weather the figurative and literal storms that had torn through the American heartland, or allow these storms to run their course. America chose the former.

Beginning in 1932 and continuing until 1959, the top income tax was raised to unprecedented levels—between 79 and 94 per cent.[19] While raising taxes in the midst of a widespread depression had undeniably negative short-term effects,[20] the steep rise in tax rates set the table for America's most egalitarian-minded period of taxation. In the midst of World War II, President Roosevelt went so far as to propose that all incomes over $25,000 (about $300,000 today) be taxed at 100%, arguing that in the midst of such "grave national danger, no American citizen ought to have a net income, after he has paid his taxes, of more than $25,000 a year."[21] Roosevelt's proposal wasn't carried forward, but its justification is instructive. While tax revenues were essential (especially after Pearl Harbor), the main purpose of these high tax rates was not only to fill the public coffers, but also to level society—in effect, to discourage the possession of economically useless large fortunes. When the economy slowed in the early 1960s, Kennedy, under considerable pressure, proposed a tax cut aimed at the demand side—namely, middle-class consumers.[22] His plan (which was ratified by Lyndon Johnson after Kennedy's assassination) also lowered the top tax rate to what was felt to be a more reasonable 70%, where it stayed until Reagan began drastically cutting taxes on the wealthy in 1981.[23] All told, between 1932 and 1980, "the top federal income tax rate in the United States averaged 81 percent," and the tax rate for unearned wealth (estates) was within a few percentage points of the same.[24]

Although there were economic ups and downs, the half-century that is characterized by these high tax rates, especially the two decades spanning 1945–65, is the age for which we wax nostalgic—a bygone era of broadly shared economic prosperity. There was, to be sure, a tangible sense of optimism during these years—at least among those whose skin was white—that the American Dream was within the grasp of all. Krugman refers to this period as "the America we love,"[25] and, sentimental though it may be, it's a feeling that is shared by so many who lived through that time. In his 1958 publication *The Affluent Society*, John Kenneth Galbraith, a critic of capitalism and its inequalities, noted that poverty was no longer the "massive affliction" that it was when the New Deal programs were introduced; rather, it had become an "afterthought" (this pronouncement was scrubbed from the revised edition).[26] Even Erich Fromm, a socialist and a harsher critic of capitalist society by far than Galbraith, could not help but be swept up in the optimistic view of America's future, writing the following in 1955: "[T]he economic exploitation of the masses has disappeared to a degree which would have sounded fantastic in Marx's time. The working class, instead of falling behind in the economic development of the whole society, has an increasing share in the national wealth, and it is a perfectly valid assumption that provided no major catastrophe occurs, there will, in about one or two generations, be no more marked poverty in the United States" (98). Though America was clearly not without problems (appalling institutionalized racism springs instantly to mind, alongside the grinding poverty in Appalachia recounted in Michael Harrington's book *The Other America*), there was a widespread feeling that the country's prosperity—present and future—was to be one that would buoy all classes equally.

The Marshall Plan allowed wide swaths of society to benefit from the rebuilding of Europe and Japan after World War II. The G.I. Bill paid for the education and training of millions of veterans and their families, and new banking policies made it possible for millions of families to buy homes, start businesses, take vacations, and send their children to college. The middle class expanded at an unprecedented rate, and American families were treated to a period in which, by and large, a single breadwinner was able to support a nuclear family without too much difficulty. The gap between rich and poor may not have been erased—indeed, distinctions between the working class and the idle rich remained as rigid as ever—but potential abounded in the new America.

Such potential was part and parcel of the project the Greatest Generation signed on for: namely, building and fighting for the world's most promising democracy—a country with an educated people, a strong middle class, and an infrastructure that were to make the United States the envy of the world. It was, of course, a rebuilding as well; America had, it seemed, learned from the mistakes of its adolescence: it had let its success go to its head in the years leading up to the Depression, but, being the land of second chances, it was ready to move forward into new territory armed with new approaches to the process of nation building.

The U.S. economy took a turn for the worse in the 1960s as a result of a deep recession. Inflation, too, reared its ugly head. The 1970s had even a bigger impact. When wage and price controls were lifted after the 1972 re-election of Richard Nixon, OPEC flexed its muscle by imposing an oil embargo. Oil prices skyrocketed and fuel rationing was imposed. In the past, there had never been any reason for interest in being fuel-efficient or energy-efficient, but that all changed in the oil crisis. The impacts were felt everywhere: business profits were squeezed, household incomes adjusted for inflation fell, unemployment increased, and inflation continued to rise. As a result, working-class whites faced numerous challenges in the United States during the 1970s. Declining manufacturing employment opportunities, the necessity of having two income earners in the household, and the decreasing power of unions were all somewhat crippling for whites at this time. For Blacks, too, it seemed as if the rug had been pulled out from under them: breaking into good manufacturing jobs was a trend that had just begun in the 1960s, and the opportunities had all but disappeared by the 1970s. This era is particularly important, as some scholars argue that the current crisis is a direct outcome of what happened in the 1970s.[27] Going even further, one can draw close parallels between the two crises.[28]

WHERE DID WE GO WRONG?

In 1981, President Ronald Reagan took his place in the Oval Office, introducing the American public to supply-side economics, which sought to stimulate a flagging economy by opening pathways to explosive corporate growth through a loosening of regulatory and tax-code pressures. Massive corporate windfalls, according to Reagan and his economic champion David Stockman, would translate to both more and better middle-class jobs. Even with dramatically lowered marginal tax rates, an increase in the amount of taxable income would directly translate to an increase in tax revenues, which, if paired with a substantial reduction in government spending (which it was not), would decrease the ballooning deficit or, at the very least, keep it from spiraling out of control.[29]

I won't go into a great deal of detail here about what, precisely, the problems are with Reagan's fiscal policies—the results, I feel, speak for themselves. Suffice it to say that as deregulation and tax cuts took hold, the relative equality with the upper class that the middle class had come to enjoy in the half-century preceding Reagan's tax cuts began to be replaced with a growing class disparity. The decrease in the top marginal income tax rate precipitated, says Piketty, "an explosion of very high incomes, which then increased the political influence of the beneficiaries of the change in the tax laws, who had an interest in keeping top tax rates low or even decreasing them further and who could use their windfall to finance political parties, pressure groups, and think tanks" (335). I'm not by any means suggesting that money and politics were somehow strange bedfellows before the 1980s, but it is important to recognize that the explosion in private wealth that began during Reagan's terms put new powers in the hands of the financial elite, especially in terms of their relatively newfound (or at least newly empowered) ability to use their increased wealth to ensure that wealth-favoring economic policies became as permanent as possible. They've done so by yoking together low tax rates and capitalism, high tax rates and socialism. Tax raises are, by this logic, un-American. Witness, for example, the outcry surrounding the possible lapse of the Bush tax cuts (which, of course, was not allowed to happen). Rivers of ink were spilled in defense of the cuts, most of which praised the Bush years as a time of almost unmatched prosperity.[30] What many of these supporters of big business forgot to mention is that the lion's share of the gains in, for example, per-capita income and shareholder wealth went to those who already enjoyed the largest share in the national income.[31] Such attempts to justify the tax breaks afforded the wealthy in this country (and there are many such attempts) become transparent when the light of statistical evidence shines through them. "[T]he countries," says Piketty, "with the largest decreases in their top tax rates are also the countries where the top earners' share of national income has increased the most" (509). This is not a coincidence, and neither is the fact that there is no "statistically significant relationship between the decrease in top marginal tax rates and the rate of productivity growth in the developed countries since 1980" (509). A low marginal tax rate assists those least in need of assistance. Any attempts to connect widely enjoyed prosperity with low tax rates for the wealthy should be seen for what it is: empty rhetoric bought and paid for.

The still-accelerating growth of income inequality in the United States and the proliferation of arguments in its defense[32] suggest that we have lost our way, economically, and perhaps morally as well. Thanks to the rhetoric of Reagan and the far right, instead of fiscal governance being a largely benevolent force that helped usher us out of the Depression and through the post-bellum period, government—particularly "big government" and its tax-collecting function—was quite suddenly something that was painted in stark colors as an impediment to our collective success as a nation. The lower and middle classes were thrown under the bus, and the former (thanks to its reliance on the welfare state) was freighted with the blame for rising deficits. Attempts to help the needy and even the sick were unflatteringly portrayed as wasteful and counter-productive crutches. Social-welfare programs and socialism were hastily (and perhaps irrevocably) conflated, food-stamp and welfare recipients were increasingly seen as thieves, and any discussion of expanding health care or government investment constituted steps on the slippery slope toward outright communism.

Conservative politicians and pundits spread the idea that the poor were poor, not due to circumstances or endemic, institutional practices beyond their control, but because they were lazy. Wildly inaccurate though it was, voters swallowed this doctrine hook, line, and sinker; and they continued to do so, even as the evidence of its vacuity spread. There seemed to be waves of collective amnesia as we lost track of the reasons that programs like college financial aid, social security, Medicare, Medicaid, Temporary Assistance for Needy Families (TANF), and SNAP were put in place—namely, to help keep the poor from getting poorer and the middle class stable, healthy, and, if possible, prosperous. We somehow forgot that a large middle class with a relatively high amount of disposable income is the combination of fuel and spark that drives booming economies; it was this combination that turned the wheels of industry during the explosive growth of the American economy during the 1950s and 1960s.

We ought to see the experiment of trickle-down economics as one that has run its course. It has been a good run for the gilded few, but the prosperity they have enjoyed has not overflowed onto the lower or middle classes. I think that Piketty's call for a progressive tax of 80% on all incomes over $1 million is going too far—entrenched interests in Washington would make short work of any proposals that could be so easily labeled as an act of class warfare. However, I do, in the main, concur with Piketty when he says that a steeply progressive tax on extremely large fortunes would represent "an ideal compromise between social justice and individual freedom" (505), one that counters the highly undemocratic concentration of wealth (and the influence it buys) in the hands of the few, one that, though it may not restore an equitable balance between the classes immediately, will at the very least lay the groundwork for a more egalitarian future.

An Unequal Society

It is high time we recognize that the myths we have told ourselves (and, in some circles, continue to tell ourselves) about how big business stimulates the economy are, at best, outdated and, at worst, patently false. Thanks to the fact that those at the top of the income ladder are, by and large, empowered to determine their own salaries[33] (and, of course, corporate board members are roundly approving these raises), record-setting corporate prosperity has, rather than trickling down, flowed upwards. This concentration of income has effectively left the median middle-class wage—and, therefore, the economy at large—to stagnate. Capital needs to change hands frequently—not concentrate—to stimulate widespread economic growth, and the absurdly disproportionate swelling of the net worth of America's top earners seems to be causing the wheels of the economy to lock up. The greed and capital hoarding of supply-side economics have placed unprecedented burdens on the federal government, which is

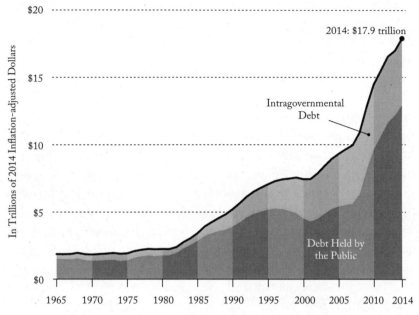

Figure 6.5: U.S. National Debt Approaches $18 Trillion

From "Federal Spending by the Numbers 2014: Government Spending Trends in Graphics, Tables and Key Points," The Heritage Foundation, 8 December 2014, http://www.heritage.org/research/ reports/2014/12/federal-spending-by-the-numbers-2014. Source: Romina Boccia. Reprinted with the permission of the Heritage Foundation.

expected to provide succor to the working poor, the infirm, and the unemployed with social security, disability, medical, unemployment, and SNAP benefits.

The poor, they say, can make do with less; opening the federal purse to the poor discourages them from entering the workforce and creates a nation of entitlement addicts.[34] This makes it sound as though there are a plethora of viable options for the disadvantaged (both the unemployed and the working poor) in this country, but such alternatives are fewer and farther between than they are presumed to be. Taking the place of middle-class jobs are the soul-crushing minimum-wage jobs that are helping corporations build twenty-first-century empires on the backs of a workforce positively desperate for work of any kind.

Take Walmart as a single instance. As the largest employer in America, the company provides work for roughly 1.4 million people within the U.S., but many of these employees scrape by on less than $9 per hour. Not only does Walmart pay some of the lowest across-the-board wages in the country, but it is fiercely determined to keep it that way. It has been accused of threatening (and, in some cases, sacking) employees who announce plans to unionize;[35] it set up in-store food banks for *its own employees* who were unable to afford a Thanksgiving dinner;[36] it canceled plans to build three new stores in D.C. after a council bill was passed prohibiting big-box retailers from paying their employees less than $12.50 per hour[37]—and all of this within a six-month period in 2013, a year in which Walmart's annual profits rose to nearly $120 billion,[38] which personally netted the Walton family $33 billion to add to their already considerable personal fortunes.[39]

To put the Waltons' wealth into perspective, their combined $154.8 billion represents enough to buy every single home in Seattle outright, with more than $40 billion left over.[40] In 2012, Bernie Sanders raised eyebrows by claiming that the Walton family owned more than the bottom 40% of America combined—a claim that turned out to be perfectly accurate.[41]

This story of inequitable socioeconomic disparity is appalling and all too familiar. The last time income inequality was at the level we are witnessing today was in the months leading up to the Great Depression. In 1928, the top one per cent of American families controlled 23.9 per cent of all pre-tax income, while the bottom 90 per cent controlled 50.7 per cent of the same. One year later, the stock market crashed, sending the country into an economic tailspin that left millions upon millions of able-bodied Americans out of work. The effects of the crash rippled outwards from Wall Street, spreading to touch every corner of the U.S. and crossing the Atlantic in a stride. In the developed countries, production and employment both dropped a full 25 per cent. It would take a world war and the manufacturing boom that came with and after it to re-establish the United States as a global economic powerhouse; it would be a full quarter-century before the stock market would again cross its 1929 high-water mark.[42]

World War II leveled everything in its path—including incomes. By 1944, the economic gap between the rich and the poor had closed considerably; the top one per cent now controlled a commensurate 11.3 per cent of all pre-tax income, while the bottom 90 per cent controlled a little more than two thirds of the same.[43] Nearly identical levels of income distribution would remain in place until 1980, but since then, despite dips in the top decile's share of the nation's wealth, coinciding with adverse stock market events in 1987, 2001, and 2008, income inequality has, within a matter of decades, exploded to unprecedented levels, well beyond even those witnessed in the pre-Depression era.[44] In 2012, America's top earners, the 1 per cent, controlled 22.5 per cent of pre-tax income, while the bottom 90 per cent controlled, for the first time in history, less than 50 per cent.[45]

Put simply, over the past three and a half decades, only a sliver of the population has been getting rich, while the share enjoyed by the majority of the country has become—to put it mildly—less worthy of enjoyment. The middle class, once the engine of economic prosperity in this country, is everywhere feeling the pinch and, at the same time, is being asked to tighten its belt. Even the famously patient middle class has its limits. Listen carefully, and you can hear the rolling thunder of discontent building across the land.

The Ailing and the Failing

As resilient as the middle class may be, with incomes lagging behind inflation[46] and the costs for health care rising exponentially in the last three decades, it is groaning beneath the weight of its burdens. When sickness or injury visits the uninsured, many of whom barely surpass the federal threshold under which they would receive federal health-care assistance, they are all too often presented with a dilemma: either complete financial insolvency or untreated illness. The cost of care or even medication for the uninsured is so high as to be prohibitive, so high that health-care costs are the most commonly cited cause for family bankruptcy petitions.[47] Many of the middle-class families that are able to afford insurance are able to afford little else[48]—this is especially true in families with ill children or ailing seniors. Between 2003 and 2013, average premiums skyrocketed by 80 per cent; during the same period, employee contributions rose by almost 90 per cent.[49] There is already evidence that the *Affordable Care Act* (Obamacare) is easing this burden,[50] but the sad truth of the matter is that, for many, this help is coming too late. The middle class in this country has already racked up medical bills it can't pay, and this has ballooned the personal debt crisis—private household debt reached $13 trillion in the first quarter of 2014, slightly more than that of the federal government.[51]

Because of their ability to pay high insurance premiums that guarantee them exclusive levels of care or the services of private physicians who charge a premium to keep the number of patients they treat as low as possible, the American upper class is proving (and celebrating the fact) that the American health-care system dramatically favors the affluent. Leslie Michelson, chairman and CEO of Private Health Management, an L.A.-based high-end health-care provider, says, "There's an enormous difference between the very best the health-care system has to offer and the very worst. We help our patients get the very best."[52] We seem to have swallowed this pill, accepting that premium care is no different from fine wine or luxury automobiles and allowing that, in the free market for health care, it is only natural (not to say just) for those who can afford it to expect and receive better health-care outcomes.

The distinct branching of American health care into two separate levels of care—one for the rich, the other for everybody else—has made us appear ridiculous to the world outside our borders. We have the most expensive health care in the world, but year after year we continue to underperform when compared to the other developed nations, ranking, according to the Commonwealth Fund, "last or near last on dimensions of access, efficiency, and equity."[53] This is not, to be sure, a reflection of the American health-care system as it is experienced by those who can afford the top tier of care; it *is*, however, a reflection of how the vast majority of Americans experience it.

The same kind of tiering that we are witnessing in the health-care system is becoming increasingly evident in America's postsecondary education system as well. There are undoubtedly inequalities in the primary and secondary systems too, but, since these problems reach epic proportions in the postsecondary system, I will confine my brief analysis in what follows to America's public and private colleges. According to Labor Board data, the cost of an American college education increased twelve-fold between 1978 and 2012—doubling even the six-fold increase in health-care costs over the same period.[54] As has been extremely well documented, this exorbitant increase in the cost of a college degree is shackling students from lower-middle- and lower-class families with unprecedented debt loads. In 2012, the average student-loan debt for graduates was $29,400, which was up from $18,750 for graduates in 2004,[55] a 57-per-cent increase within a pair of election cycles. At the same time, the jobs waiting for this year's graduates, when adjusted for inflation, compensate recent graduates at about the same level as the entry positions waiting for the Boomers and the Gen-Xers when they graduated.[56]

Why the increase in tuition and its concomitant student debt? Is this merely a matter of the free market testing consumers to see how much they can bear? It seems they can bear quite a lot, but those with the broadest financial shoulders can take the weight a great deal more easily than those with parents in the bottom quartile of earners. It is a twenty-first-century truism that a college degree is the new high-school diploma, and there is mounting evidence that more and more Americans are choosing to educate themselves before entering the workforce,[57] but the majority of that increase has been the result of a doubling in the percentage of children with parents in the top quartile of earners who are pursuing or have pursued a college degree. For those with little access to resources, it has become increasingly difficult to achieve the "new high-school diploma." In the last 40 years, the percentage of students whose families are in the lowest quartile of earners has changed very little; in fact, while 80 per cent of the children with top-quartile parents pursue higher education, the lowest quartile's percentage of the same has never broken the 20-per-cent mark.[58] This is in large part thanks to increasing uneasiness about the debt loads that students from lower-income brackets face when they pursue a four-year degree. It can also be attributed to geography, since major metropolitan areas tend to promote college "in order to make it!", while in some rural towns the same push is not made.[59]

In America's top schools, this problem is magnified. The gates have been all but barred to those without deep pockets. Though higher educational institutions may claim to select only the best and the brightest, such self-congratulation seems not to be merited. A pair of researchers, Jonathan Meer and Henry Rosen—one from Princeton, the other from Stanford—recently explored the relatedness of alumni donations and the child cycle; they found a strong correlation between the average size of donations from alumni and the proximity of the donors' children to university entrance age (2). Though they found that, due to a lack of transparency in the selection process at Ivy League universities, the children of alumni were three times more likely to be accepted to their parents' alma mater than were non-legacy students, Meer and Rosen were unwilling to go so far as to connect alumni donations and the acceptance of their offspring in concrete ways (3). However, when one examines the student body as a whole, the persuasive power of wealth comes into sharp focus. As Piketty notes, "[T]he average income of the parents of Harvard students is currently about $450,000, which corresponds to the average income of the top 2 percent of the U.S. income hierarchy. Such a finding does not seem entirely compatible with the idea of selection based solely on merit. The contrast between the official meritocratic discourse and the reality seems particularly extreme in this case. The total absence of transparency regarding selection procedures should also be noted" (485). Whether students who aren't of a certain financial pedigree are being priced out of the best education that America has to offer or they are being passed over by administrators who are kowtowing to alumni and donors (often the same), the results are identical: income inequality perpetuates itself seemingly interminably by reserving the highest levels of education and the high-paying jobs that follow in their wake for the few that can afford them.

The Myth of American Meritocracy

The massive and still-growing gulf separating the poor from the rich in this country[60] has grown so disproportionately large that even dyed-in-the-wool capitalists are unable to provide a reasonable or even plausible defense for its existence. A certain degree of inequality, it is true, is socially useful. However, as Paine pointed out in his 1791 *Declaration of the Rights of Man and the Citizen*, "[C]ivil distinctions [...] can only be founded on public utility" (87). Thus, even at the moment of its birth, America doggedly held onto the belief that success and its concomitant wealth are (or ought to be) picture-perfect reflections of the individual's contribution to society or the economy taken as a whole. This is a highly egalitarian principle, provided that there is a high degree of social mobility in the society in which it operates. Harper Lee's level-headed and imminently fair Atticus Finch, though his calm plea to his auditors is for equality under the law, nevertheless recognizes that "all men are *not* created equal ... some men are smarter than others, some have more opportunity because they're born with it, some men make more money, some ladies make better cakes, some people are born gifted beyond the normal scope of most men."[61]

Combine Lee's mid-twentieth-century recognition of a certain necessary degree of inequality between men with Paine's late-eighteenth-century pronouncement that any degree of social inequality must be founded upon a pragmatic foundation, and you have a rough picture of American meritocracy: through a steady application of his talents and intelligence (whether bestowed naturally—presumably by his creator—or the result of training or practice), man raises his position—or lowers it—each according to his deserts and each according to his utility.[62] Built upon a bedrock of relative equality (at the very least equality of opportunity), meritocratic capitalism is, as it were, the sorting tool that assures that class divisions are, in essence, meaningful, patriarchical, and not arbitrary.

For such a meritocratic system to function justly and effectively, a balance must be struck between the rewards at the opposite ends of the merit spectrum—let's call it an inequality ceiling. Such a ceiling was in place when the top tax rate was high enough to serve as both a revenue generator and a deterrent to possessing fortunes too large to be economically useful. Not everybody saw the social utility in this steeply progressive tax rate, though. While it was in place, ideologies equating free-market capitalism and freedom took root (they would bear fruit in the age of Reagan, and they have done so once again in the reactionary calls for the shrinking of government during Obama's presidency). Popular texts like Friedrich von Hayek's *The Road to Serfdom* and Milton Friedman's *Capitalism and Freedom* yoked together the ideas of political and economic freedom, arguing that competitive capitalism, according to Friedman, "promotes political freedom because it separates economic power from political power and in this way enables the one to offset the other" (9). Leaving aside, for the moment at least, the long-since disproven notion that political and economic power run in discrete channels, it is clear that Friedman is striving for a balance of sorts between centralized authority (i.e., the state) and self-determination (the individual). Within the non-political class, however, an unhindered free market leads inevitably to a fracturing of the balance, not between political and economic power, but between the free citizens themselves.

When we began cutting the top tax rate dramatically in the 1980s, starting what Piketty aptly calls the "endless race to the bottom" (496), we took the power to regulate the free market from the state and gave it—with the flimsiest of excuses for doing so, such as government regulation causing an inefficient allocation of resources, or market being best at deciding when and how to produce—to the market itself. Is it any surprise that, almost immediately, the rules under which American meritocracy operated for nearly a half-century were lifted, and, without a steeply progressive tax to rein in excessive wealth, the top decile quickly began to pull away from the rest of the country? Not wealth but *extreme* wealth became the measure of true success, and, though its rules had changed, though its checks and balances had been all but removed entirely, the system of reward based on merit was claimed to be at the heart of this success. Indeed, the rise of super-managers and their super-salaries meant that the *nouveaux riches* and the rentier class were competing in a class of their own. "Meritocratic extremism," says Piketty, "can thus lead to a race between super-managers and rentier, to the detriment of those who are neither" (417). Such has undoubtedly been the case in these United States.

Perhaps most troubling about extreme meritocracy is the ways in which free-market defenders turn the notion of merit on its head and use meritocratic principles to justify the self-same inequalities it produces. Thanks to the insidious and coercive machinery that operates in the defense of late American capitalism, Americans seem willing— eager even—to accept that historically high levels of inequality are the price of our freedom and that there is a direct correlation between positive traits like industriousness, intelligence, and even moral fiber, and success.

This logic is especially seductive for those who have been able to put some distance between themselves and the lower classes. In 1994, Richard J. Hernstein and Charles Murray published *Bell Curve: Intelligence and Class Structure in American Life*, which argued that both success and IQs follow a similar bell-shaped arc, and that "the twenty-first century will open on a world in which cognitive ability is the decisive dividing force" (25). While such ideas played nicely into the long-enduring culture of victim blaming, scholars were apoplectic, citing the book's repugnant conclusion, that the lower classes are, by and large, characterized by a genetically inherited intellectual inferiority, as a racist ideology that flirts with eugenic principles.[63] A respected trio of inequality researchers, Samuel Bowles, Herbert Gintis, and Melissa Osborne Groves, found that, with all things being equal, it was not IQ but, rather, wealth, race, and schooling that were "important to the inheritance of economic status."[64] Undeterred, Murray built upon his controversial ideas in his 2012 study of America's class structure, *Coming Apart: The State of White America, 1960-2010*, in which he recognizes that there is a growing divide between rich and poor; but, as you might expect, he finds the root of this split to be—just as he and Hernstein predicted—intelligence: it is the growing demand for the intelligence-based skills possessed by the "cognitive elite" that has shaped what he calls "the new upper class" (16). Like his previous work, *Coming Apart* represents the view from the top; wherever there is wealth, there must also be merit, and, of course, the inverse is true as well.

This book, and the countless others that make similarly broad generalizations about the personality traits that are inevitably present in the wealthy and lacking in the poor, rely largely on self-reporting to draw their personality profiles of the successful. To nobody's surprise, respondents cite their industriousness and their moral fiber as direct contributors to their success. This is what makes a meritocracy (especially American meritocracy) so hard on those who, for whatever reason, have been unable to scale the economic or the social ladder. As Piketty says, "[I]t seeks to justify domination on the grounds of justice, virtue, and merit, to say nothing of the insufficient productivity of those at the bottom" (416). Its propensity for hero-worship is troubling, but perhaps more troubling is its willingness to denigrate those living hand to mouth.

Hackneyed sports metaphors abound in the business world: one hits a home run, scores a touchdown, performs an effortless slam dunk. Such metaphors assume the kind of equality that allows superstars to rightly claim their exorbitant salaries. Although it is probably safe to assume that sports like downhill skiing, polo, and golf, due to their high associated costs, are played mostly by those in the top income brackets, the top spectator sports in the United States (excluding NASCAR) are those played by children in nearly every neighborhood—rich and poor alike. Thus, those who exceed in basketball, baseball, or football are those who can justifiably claim to be the nation's best players. The same cannot be said of the world of business. The rags-to-riches narrative is salivated over by business writers, but anecdotal evidence inconsistent with the broader experience of late American capitalism weakly supports the belief that the meritocratic system is indeed functioning as it should in America. These Horatio Alger–inflected myths are keeping the American middle class largely complacent, dreaming (fantasizing might be a better word) about the success that is surely to come their way if they only work harder. What we don't want to admit to ourselves—we show as much by relying on sports metaphors and trumpeting our egalitarian values despite widespread proof that they are no longer operating—is that inequalities have resulted in a class apart from the rest of the country, one in which the only appropriate sports metaphor is one where the player begins the game perched atop the basket, with one foot in the end-zone, or with a corked bat in hand. We need to accept that when we describe late American capitalism as a meritocratic system similar or identical to the one the founders envisaged, we are, in fact, deluding ourselves. While some in this system are succeeding immensely, this is but a tiny sliver of the impact—and perhaps the only positive one at all—that is being felt across the country.

At the End of Their Rope

While the wealthiest 1 per cent are seeing their fortunes rise, the rest of the country is sliding further and further down the income ladder. The middle-class dollar is being forced to stretch more and more, and the personal debt that many American families are accruing is proving to be more onerous than many of them can bear. Just when they need it the most, the middle class is watching as the social safety net erodes beneath them. Massive cuts to programs designed to help the poorest families, like the welfare reforms of the 1990s, and recent cuts to SNAP, have cut large holes in the safety net through which countless working-class families are falling. Hunger is a growing problem in both rural areas and inner cities. One in four children is a recipient of SNAP, and the program is unable to keep up with rising demand for the assistance it offers.[65] Food banks and soup kitchens are overwhelmed as they attempt to feed the working poor.

Not since the dismal years preceding FDR's New Deal has the need for a re-imagining of the role that government plays in securing the afflicted been so apparent. The values that held sway during the New Deal years, values woven into Truman's Fair Deal (as it was proposed) and Johnson's Great Society, put aside—even if only for a moment—self-interest in the name of the collective good. America could, without irony, claim to be a model to the rest of the world. We once boasted the best public education system and the most productive middle class in the world. Once upon a time, we invested in ourselves and our children, and this investment paid off in spades. Not since the dismal years preceding FDR's New Deal has the need to re-imagine the role that government plays in succoring the afflicted been so apparent. Now, our connective technologies have reached new heights while our tangible connections to each other have fallen to new depths. We are digitally bonded to each other but physically isolated. The selfishness and even callousness that this retreat from our physical communities has brought on has rent the social fabric. At least in terms of our commitment to each other, our sails have drooped; we seem to be adrift, rudderless, and dangerously close to foundering. Looking over the gunwales, there are millions of bodies in the water frantically trying to resist the water's downward pull, and, rather than pulling them onboard to help man the rigging, we are doing the opposite: pulling the lifeboats out of the water.

In the 1950s and 1960s, one could feel the moral arc of the American nation bending in palpable ways toward economic prosperity for many (although admittedly not all); today, it is not the arc's bend but its length that is in question. The palpable liberty and justice promised for all in equal share is a more distant prospect than we would like to admit in our professed "Shining City on a Hill," pontificated by Ronald Reagan during his farewell address from the Oval Office in 1989 and nostalgically envisioned by Conservatives ever since.

Inequality has long been a pet topic of the left, but there was an explosion of media coverage of the topic beginning on September 17, 2011, when the Occupy Wall Street protests began. A group of protesters camped out in Zuccotti Park, in the heart of New York's financial district, to protest widespread greed and corruption on Wall Street. The protests represented the cresting of the wave of the public discontent with income inequality and the apparent immunity from prosecution enjoyed by America's super wealthy, or, as they were styled

Occupy Wall Street Marchers on Day 14 of the protest in New York City. https://commons.wikimedia. org/wiki/File:Day_14_Occupy_Wall_Street_September_30_2011_Shankbone_44.JPG. Credit: David Shankbone, 30 September 2011.

by the protesters, the 1 per cent. Though the lack of a powerful and articulate unifying figure at the head of the protests meant that the demands of the protesters were frequently muddied by their largely unfocused anger, the widespread coverage of the protests—even when that coverage unflatteringly misrepresented the protests as an act of class warfare—brought the 99 per cent, and income inequality with them, onto the national stage.

Occupy protests quickly spread around the United States and, indeed, around the world as well. In part thanks to these protests and the media's coverage of them, income inequality played a larger role in the 2012 presidential election than Republican strategists had perhaps planned for. Near the end of Mitt Romney's campaign, a video surfaced of the candidate speaking to a group of wealthy contributors at a private fundraiser. In no uncertain terms, Romney spoke of nearly half of the country as entitled dependents. These "47%" comments, widely circulated and widely derided, all but sealed the

The voices from America's demos. https://commons.wikimedia.org/wiki/Occupy_Wall_Street#/media/File:Day_20_Occupy_Wall_Street_October_5_2011_Shankbone_8.JPG. Credit: David Shankbone, 5 October 2011.

election in Obama's favor. In a 2013 interview with Chris Wallace, Romney admitted that those comments, in particular, "hurt and did real damage to [his] campaign."[66] Wildly insensitive and inaccurate though they were, Romney's comments might have played less of a role in determining the election's outcome if they had not dovetailed so neatly with ongoing conversation in the media, in the nation's parks, and on its street corners about income inequality. No matter how frequently the protests themselves were described as ineffectual or unfocused, they influenced in a significant way the scrutiny of wealth demographics in the United States.

And this is where we find ourselves today: faced with increasingly pressing questions about the way in which wealth and its concomitants, power and influence, are distributed in society. We have, for far too long, turned away from the difficult questions—especially if an honest answer does little to flatter us as a nation of exceptional values and opportunity. Poverty, as I explored in depth in the previous chapter, is a growing issue and a direct outcome of the dramatic increase in the income inequality gap. As a consequence, the tide is turning, and we need to recognize that the discontent being widely expressed in America is not—as we are being told it is—the product of a misguided or selfish generation. Quite the contrary: the misguided and selfish generation is the one trying to shout down those who would see America become a far more egalitarian country. America may not need a revolution, but it does need an intervention. It needs to be saved from its self-indulgence.

Notes

1 See Reich, *Supercapitalism.*

2 Jane Mayer, "Ayn Rand Joins the Ticket," *The New Yorker* 11 August 2012, http://www.newyorker.com/news/news-desk/ayn-rand-joins-the-ticket.

3 Richard Kogan and Joel Friedman, "Ryan Plan Gets 69 Percent of Its Budget Cuts from Programs for People with Low or Moderate Incomes," Center on Budget and Policy Priorities, 8 April 2014, http://www.cbpp.org/research/ryan-plan-gets-69-percent-of-its-budget-cuts-from-programs-for-people-with-low-or-moderate.

4 Robert Greenstein, "Statement of Robert Greenstein, President, on Chairman Ryan's Budget Plan," Center on Budget and Policy Priorities, 21 March 2012, http://www.cbpp.org/cms/index.cfm?fa=view&id=3712.

5 Peter W. Atwater, "Interest in Income Inequality: U.S. Case Study," World Policy Blog, 26 May 2014, http://www.worldpolicy.org/blog/2014/05/26/interest-income-inequality-us-case-study.

6 Peter Schroeder, "GOP Senator Joins Foes of Wall Street Provision in Spending Bill," The Hill, 11 December 2014, http://thehill.com/policy/finance/226816-gop-senator-criticizes-dodd-frank-rollback-in-cromnibus.

7 Zachary Warmbrodt and Dave Clarke, "Wall Street Critic Sherrod Brown to Be Top Democrat on Banking," *Politico* 12 December 2014, http://www.politico.com/story/2014/12/sherrod-brown-senate-banking-committee-113535.html.

8 Jillian Berman, "Dunkin' Donuts Worker's Death Reveals the True Cost of Our Low-Wage, Part-Time Economy," The Huffington Post, 29 August 2014, http://www.huffingtonpost.com/2014/08/29/maria-fernandes-low-wage-work_n_5736790.html.

9 See, for example, the "All Work, No Pay; The False Promise of the American Economy" article compilation of the Huffington Post: http://www.huffingtonpost.com/news/@working_poor/.

10   Alyssa Davis, Lawrence Mishel, and Ross Eisenbrey, "Top Restaurant
       Industry CEOs Made 721 Times More than Minimum-Wage Workers in
       2013," Economic Policy Institute, 2 July 2014, http://www.epi.org/publication/
       top-restaurant-industry-ceos-721-times-minimum/.

11   "Executive Paywatch," AFL-CIO, 2014, http://www.aflcio.org/Corporate-Watch/
       Paywatch-2014.

12   Davis, Mishel, and Eisenbrey, "Top Restaurant Industry CEOs."

13   Elliot Smith and Phil Kuntz, "CEO Pay 1,795-to-1 Multiple of Wages Skirts
       U.S. Law," Bloomberg Business, 30 April 2013, http://www.bloomberg.com/
       news/2013-04-30/ceo-pay-1-795-to-1-multiple-of-workers-skirts-law-as-sec-
       delays.html.

14   In Piketty's formula, r stands for the average rate of return on capital, g for the
       annual increase in income or output.

15   Chris Giles, "Thomas Piketty's Exhaustive Inequality Data Turn Out to Be
       Flawed," *Financial Times* 23 May 2014, http://www.ft.com/intl/cms/s/0/c9ce1a54-
       e281-11e3-89fd-00144feabdc0.html.

16   The Federal Reserve relies on self-reported income, so the share of the top decile
       is almost certainly higher than this. Conservative estimate though it is, it is still a
       shockingly high figure.

17   AP/HuffPost, "Median Household Income Dropped 4 Percent since the End of
       the Great Recession: Report," The Huffington Post, 22 August 2014, http://www.
       huffingtonpost.com/2013/08/22/median-household-income-dropped_n_3794191.
       html.

18   "The Income Tax Arrives," Tax Analysts, http://taxhistory.tax.org/www/website.
       nsf/Web/THM1901?OpenDocument#1920.

19   "Table: History of Federal Individual Income Tax Bottom and Top Brackets,"
       National Taxpayers Union, http://www.ntu.org/tax-basics/history-of-federal-
       individual-1.html.

20   Arthur B. Laffer, "Taxes, Depression, and Our Current Troubles," *The Wall Street
       Journal* 22 September 2009, http://www.wsj.com/articles/SB1000142405297020
       3440104574402822202944230.

21   Qtd. in Jeff Haden, "How Would You Feel about a 94% Tax Rate?" CBS Money
       Watch, 7 December 2011, http://www.cbsnews.com/news/how-would-you-feel-
       about-a-94-tax-rate/.

22   David Greenberg, "Tax Cuts in Camelot?" Slate, 16 January 2004, http://www.
       slate.com/articles/news_and_politics/history_lesson/2004/01/tax_cuts_in_
       camelot.html.

23   "Table: History of Federal Individual Income Tax Bottom and Top Brackets."

24   Piketty 507.

25   Qtd. in Piketty, 294.

26   Qtd. in Dwight MacDonald, "Our Invisible Poor," *The New Yorker* 19 January
     1963, http://www.newyorker.com/magazine/1963/01/19/our-invisible-poor.

27   Peter Wagner, "The Democratic Crisis of Capitalism: Reflections on Political
     and Economic Modernity in Europe," LEQS Paper No. 44, http://ssrn.com/
     abstract=1969031.

28   Iana Dreyer, "Crisis Today and the 1970s. Some Musings on Hayekian vs
     Keynesian Thinking," Splendid Exchanges, 13 September 2011, https://
     splendidexchanges.wordpress.com/2011/09/13/crisis-today-and-the-1970s-
     some-musings-on-hayekian-vs-keynesian-thinking/.

29   Nouriel Roubini, "Supply Side Economics: Do Tax Rate Cuts Increase Growth
     and Revenues and Reduce Budget Deficits? Or Is It Voodoo Economics All
     Over Again?", 1997, http://people.stern.nyu.edu/nroubini/SUPPLY.HTM.

30   See, for example, Peter Ferrara, "Why America Is Going to Miss the Bush Tax
     Cuts," *Forbes* 6 December 2012, http://www.forbes.com/sites/peterferrara/2012/
     12/06/why-america-is-going-to-miss-the-bush-tax-cuts/.

31   Piketty, 323–24.

32   See, for example, Scott Winship, "Income Inequality Is Good for the Poor,"
     The Federalist, 5 November 2014, http://thefederalist.com/2014/11/05/income-
     inequality-is-good-for-the-poor/.

33   Marianne Bertrand and Sendhil Mullainathan, "Do CEOs Set Their Own Pay?
     The Ones Without Principals Do," National Bureau of Economic Research,
     Working Paper 7604, March 2000, http://www.nber.org/papers/w7604.pdf.

34   Todd Beamon, "Dick Morris: Obama's Policies Create 'Nation of Dependents,'"
     Newsmax, 5 February 2014, http://www.newsmax.com/Newsmax-Tv/
     dick-morris-obama-employment/2014/02/05/id/551121/.

35   Dave Jamieson, "Walmart Broke Labor Law and Retaliated against Workers,
     NLRB Charges," The Huffington Post, 18 November 2013, http://www.
     huffingtonpost.com/2013/11/18/walmart-nlrb_n_4298387.html.

36   Rick Ungar, "Walmart Store Holding Thanksgiving Charity Food Drive—For
     Its Own Employees!" *Forbes* 18 November 2013, http://www.forbes.com/sites/
     rickungar/2013/11/18/walmart-store-holding-thanksgiving-charity-food-drive
     -for-its-own-employees/.

37   Caroline Fairchild, "$12 Wage for Walmart Workers Would Cost the Average
     Shopper Just 46 Cents per Trip," The Huffington Post, 18 July 2013, http://www.
     huffingtonpost.com/2013/07/18/walmart-worker-wages_n_3611531.html.

38   Wal-Mart Stores, Inc. (WMT) Income Statement, Yahoo! Finance, https://
     finance.yahoo.com/q/is?s=WMT+Income+Statement&annual.

39   Mark Perry, "Another Year, Another $33 Billion for the Waltons," The Walmart 1%, 5 March 2014, http://walmart1percent.org/2014/03/05/another-year-another-33-billion-for-the-waltons/.

40   Tommy Unger, "Which Billionaire Could Buy Your City?" Redfin Research Center, 5 June 2014, http://www.redfin.com/research/reports/special-reports/2014/us-cities-that-billionaires-could-buy.html#.VA8lBEuZZg0.

41   Molly Moorhead, "Bernie Sanders Says Walmart Heirs Own More Wealth than Bottom 40 Percent of Americans," *Tampa Bay Times* Politifact, 31 July 2012, http://www.politifact.com/truth-o-meter/statements/2012/jul/31/bernie-s/sanders-says-walmart-heirs-own-more-wealth-bottom-/.

42   Piketty, 472.

43   Drew DeSilver, "U.S. Income Inequality, on Rise for Decades, Is Now Highest since 1928," Pew Research Center, 5 December 2013, http://www.pewresearch.org/fact-tank/2013/12/05/u-s-income-inequality-on-rise-for-decades-is-now-highest-since-1928/.

44   Piketty, 24.

45   DeSilver, "U.S. Income Inequality."

46   Drew DeSilver, "For Most Workers, Real Wages Have Barely Budged for Decades," Pew Research Centre, 9 October 2014, http://www.pewresearch.org/fact-tank/2014/10/09/for-most-workers-real-wages-have-barely-budged-for-decades/.

47   Dan Mangan, "Medical Bills Are the Biggest Cause of US Bankruptcies," CNBC.com, 25 June 2013, http://www.cnbc.com/id/100840148#.

48   Ryan Knutso and Theo Francis, "Basic Costs Squeeze Families," *The Wall Street Journal* 1 December 2014, http://www.wsj.com/articles/americans-reallocate-their-dollars-1417476499.

49   Kaiser Family Foundation and Health Research & Educational Trust, "Employer Health Benefits, Summary of Findings 2013," http://kaiserfamilyfoundation.files.wordpress.com/2013/08/8466-employer-health-benefits-2013_summary-of-findings2.pdf.

50   Phil Schiliro, "The Affordable Care Act Is Working," *Politico* 24 March 2014, http://www.politico.com/magazine/story/2014/03/affordable-care-act-is-working-104942.html#.VBBVpEuZZg0.

51   Board of Governors of the Federal Reserve System, "Financial Accounts of The United States," Federal Reserve Statistical Release Z.1, 11 June 2015, http://www.federalreserve.gov/releases/z1/Current/z1.pdf.

52   Qtd. in Elizabeth Ody, "Wealthy Families Skip Waiting Rooms with Concierge Medical Plans," Bloomberg Business, 16 March 2012, http://www.bloomberg.

com/news/2012-03-16/wealthy-families-skip-waiting-rooms-with-concierge-medical-plans.html.

53   Karen Davis, et al., "Mirror, Mirror on the Wall, 2014 Update: How the U.S. Health Care System Compares Internationally," The Commonwealth Fund, June 2014, http://www.commonwealthfund.org/publications/fund-reports/2014/jun/mirror-mirror.

54   Michelle Jamrisko and Ilan Kolet, "Cost of College Degree in U.S. Soars 12 Fold," Bloomberg Business, 15 August 2012, http://www.bloomberg.com/news/2012-08-15/cost-of-college-degree-in-u-s-soars-12-fold-chart-of-the-day.html.

55   Susannah Snider, "10 Colleges That Leave Graduates with the Most Student Loan Debt," U.S. News & World Report, 17 February 2015, http://www.usnews.com/education/best-colleges/the-short-list-college/articles/2013/12/17/10-colleges-where-grads-have-the-most-student-loan-debt.

56   "The Rising Cost of Not Going to College," Pew Research Center Social & Demographic Trends Project, 11 February 2014, http://www.pewsocialtrends.org/2014/02/11/the-rising-cost-of-not-going-to-college/.

57   Ibid.

58   Piketty, 485.

59   In an interview, Mrs. Gina Taylor, an administrator at Archer Daniels Midland company in Decatur, Illinois, admitted that "being from a big city, in my case Oklahoma City, you are encouraged from birth to go to college but in the agricultural town of Decatur, kids are encouraged to get a job at Cat [Caterpillar] or ADM, or with the State in Springfield, or on your grandfather's farm. I do not see the same push for college here as in the bigger cities." Personal interview, 28 April 2015.

60   Ben Lubsdorf, "Fed: Gap between Rich, Poor Americans Widened during Recovery," The Wall Street Journal 4 September 2014, http://www.wsj.com/articles/fed-gap-between-rich-poor-americans-widened-during-recovery 1409853628.

61   Harper Lee, To Kill a Mockingbird (London: Arrow, 2010), 226; emphasis mine.

62   I am intentionally using the historically accurate non–gender-neutral pronouns, in keeping with Paine's era.

63   See, for instance, Stephen Jay Gould's The Mismeasure of Man, which the author revised and republished in 1996 as a direct refutation of Bell Curve.

64   Qtd. in McNamee and Miller, 27.

65   Caroline May, "New Data Show 1 in 4 Children on Food Stamps in FY 2011,"
     The Daily Caller 9 January 2013, http://dailycaller.com/2013/01/09/new-data-
     show-1-in-4-children-on-food-stamps-in-fy-2011/.

66   "Romney Relays Disappointment over Loss, Admits Mistakes, in First Sitdown
     since 2012 Election," Fox News, 3 March 2013, http://www.foxnews.com/
     politics/2013/03/03/romney-still-disappointed-over-loss-admits-mistakes-
     critical-obama-second-term/.

Chapter Seven

REPOSITIONING
THE MORAL ARC

"It is not biology that dictates relationship, but it is spirit."
—Dr. Melina Abdullah, 20th Anniversary of the Million Man
March, October 10, 2015

WE THE PEOPLE OF THE UNITED STATES OF AMERICA—ALL HER people: whites, people of color, and immigrants of all hues who came here in search of a new home—face a challenge. We must be honest with each other and with ourselves. We must examine unflinchingly our place in history, asking how we want to be remembered. We must ask whether or not our goals are the same as they once were. Do we truly want to form Reverend Jackson's much-vaunted rainbow coalition? Do we want to say, with Jesse, that, though our flag is red, white, and blue, our nation is a rainbow? Do we want to forgive each other and redeem each other? Do we want to move on or hold on? Do we want to continue to erect and maintain the boundaries that separate us from each other, separating black from white, brown from black, Christian from Muslim, north from south, and liberal from conservative? These boundaries exist both within and without each of us; they make it as difficult to speak honestly with each other as it is to speak honestly with ourselves, taking a true reckoning of our own interior selves.

We stand faced with a challenge, but it is an opportunity we face as well. We can either continue to gaze upon an unchanging and idealized image of ourselves and our nation, or we can take this moment to gaze into a mirror that reflects us and our nation as we are and as it is. Love, they say, is blind, but surely a sightless, romantic love that can see only the object of its desire's perfections is not a respectable model for patriotism. We may love this country in spite of its flaws, but this shouldn't mean that these flaws are pushed out of our consciousness, for ignoring those things about this country that deserve not our love but our outrage is doing her (and all of us) a tremendous injustice. If we love this country as much as we are so fond of saying we do, we must demand more of her. We must demand of her that she give us (all of us) her very best. Do we love her this much? Do we love America enough to speak straight with her about her shortcomings? Do we love her enough to demand that she live up to the promises she made so long ago?

America needs a spiritual revolution—albeit one that isn't religiously based. Our nation was born of a largely secular and humanist philosophy that represented the dawn of a new age of democracy. Though there were problems then with how some of the founding fathers interpreted the first of their self-evident truths—namely that "all men are created equal"—with some men, to paraphrase Orwell, apparently being created more equal than others, the fact that, even as it cleared its throat, the American experiment was declared to be one in which equality was paramount shows a powerful and spiritual ethic at work. Much of our work as a community and, indeed, as a nation has been dedicated to making our institutions and people act in way that adheres to the spirit that animates our great founding documents. But there is, to be sure, a long way to go and many mountains to climb before we can truly claim to be realizing our potential (even as that potential was imagined so long ago).

Can we rise above contemporary negativity and fully embrace the words that my daughter recites at the beginning of every school day: "One nation, under God, indivisible, with liberty and justice for all"? Do we get the chills, the goosebumps, and the starburst of pride and recognition many experienced when we first learned how revolutionary our Constitution was (and still is). It's more than a sheet of paper with words written on it; it's the beating heart of our country. Can we embrace our role as caretaker of this document and its promises and recognize that our Constitution needs our care and protection. We the people of the United States of America were granted power by that document (a power guaranteed by its amendments), but we've forgotten what it means to exercise that power and to exercise it responsibly yet boldly, just as David Walker or Maria Stewart of the nineteenth century did. We haven't stepped into adulthood; like children we whine and complain that our democracy isn't serving our needs or treating us equally (and, indeed, it isn't), we complain that our politicians are bought and paid for (and, indeed, they are), but we've allowed this to happen. We've forgotten that we are not children—even if the political system treats us as if we were. We the people share in owning this country; it's time we started acting like co-owners and stewards. It's time we spoke up, raising our voices so that what is heard is unmistakable. It's time that we threw open our windows and shouted for all to hear so that the powers that be know that we're mad as hell and that we're not going to take this anymore.

America's moral arc is undeniably long, and though it might seem as if it has flattened out in recent years, it hasn't. Though our list of grievances might seem to be endless, it isn't. I have endeavored throughout this book to highlight the social ills that are keeping us from being as good as we claim to be, as good as our founders promised we would be. I have tried to rekindle the discussion about the moral purpose that animates the American democratic experiment, hoping that this conversation might—as it has in the past—lead us to bend the moral arc to our will, to make this land live up to its promises, to demand that we finally see the best of America. This discussion is similar to the one that led to the birth and outlining of our nation and its first contract with the people; it's the same discussion that history's great reformers have forced us to resume or to approach from new angles. That conversation has become increasingly democratic with time, including voices that had long been forced to the margins of the national consciousness. In the last few decades, race has become an increasingly prominent topic in this conversation. At its best, this conversation is about honest assessment, about a desire to move, not backward, but forward. It is about the moral arc of the nation, about using our collective weight to bend it so that it dips more tangibly toward the justice we seek.

A Superpower Has Super Responsibilities

While the vast majority of my focus in these pages has been on the United States and its problematic relationship with the minorities within its borders, it is important to note that America is also falling significantly short of the mark in terms of its role on the international stage. Any examination of the moral arc and its trajectory demands that we come to grips with our actions abroad, particularly with the ways in which America uses its military and economic power to shape the destiny of the world at large. We seem to be convinced that America's superpower status is premised on our military might. We have far and away the most powerful military in the history of the world. Our defense spending exceeds the total military budgets of the next ten largest military spenders combined. Our hawkish spending tells the world that it is not moral or intellectual leadership that we offer—it is leadership based on strength and strength alone.

What is more, our ludicrous military expenditure comes at a greater cost here than we realize. We've spent money on our military as though we were still running in a global arms race, even though that race has been over for more than twenty years. All of this investment has meant that America's infrastructure has been left to blow in the wind or, in some parts of the country, crumble to dust. Our highways and byways are pockmarked and crumbling, our bridges sag and groan beneath their burdens, and our public education system is failing this generation of children. Kicking the can down the road to the next generation is a risky gambit. Especially in terms of education, the impacts of such a long period of neglect have been showing up for decades now in our plunging test scores. We've never had to deal with a generational learning gap like the one we're facing now, and it's entirely uncertain what the long-term impacts of our misguided priorities will be. If we don't take this present moment to re-evaluate these priorities, the United States will fall further behind in the indicators that, unlike military spending, measure the well-being (actual and potential) of a country and its citizens. We still boast some of the brightest individuals and the finest educational institutions in the world, but the skyrocketing price of tuition is a barrier to the kind of broadly educated population that this country needs in order to turn the corner. We haven't truly re-evaluated our priorities, and our refusal to do so has meant that we are losing our competitive edge. To regain that edge, we need to start investing, not in the machinery of production, but in the machinery of progress (namely, education). In order to be even remotely effective, this investment has to start in the schools that have been hit the hardest by the pronounced lack of investment in education: those in poorer districts. If it's intellectual leadership we're after, we have to start with an acknowledgement that all students (no matter what color and no matter what neighborhood they live in) deserve to be treated equally. Education spending per pupil should be reasonably close, if not the same, for all schools regardless of racial mix, yet such is far from the case. The average spending per pupil varies depending on the percentage of white or non-white students at the schools. In 2012, the Center for American Progress found that a 10-per-cent drop in the number of white students in a school corresponded with a $75/pupil drop in spending. At schools that were 90-per-cent or more non-white versus 90-per-cent or more white, the gap in spending per pupil was $733. Nationwide, the average expenditure per student was $11,153 per student, which means that $773 represents a difference of almost 7%.[1] This kind of spending gap is unconscionable.

Schools in poorer districts (also those that tend to have higher numbers of minority students) receive less tax money—a structural flaw in our education system, which relies too much on local property taxes. New evidence uncovered in the same study cited above demonstrates that there are other, less reputable, factors in play. Within a single school district, different schools receive funding allowances for a slew of reasons, including the skills and experience of teachers and other school personnel. The study notes that, by assigning "the least-experienced teachers in high-minority, high-poverty schools, the total spending at these high-needs schools is likely to be lower than spending at schools in wealthier neighborhoods that employ veteran teachers." In such instances, the resulting funding inequality is purposefully discriminatory.

If it's moral leadership we're after, we need to start with the decriminalization of the Black body. The Black body (and especially the young, male, Black body) is subject to incarceration and state-sponsored violence based on the assumption that the state has something to fear in Blackness. The Black body is presented and acted upon as though it were an irredeemably hyperviolent and hypersexual object, and this is introducing an alarmingly high number of young, Black males and females to handcuffs and jail cells at an early age. Repositioning the moral arc means demanding that the justice system treat and sentence non-white bodies no differently than it does white ones.

This, too, starts in the education system. A 2014 Department of Education study found that teachers and administrators punish Black children far more often than they do white children. Though Black children comprised only 18 per cent of the preschool children studied, they made up 48 per cent of the number of suspended students.[2] Either Black children are being treated and disciplined differently, or Black children really are worse behaved than their white counterparts (there are no data to support the latter claim, however).

And yet there are plenty of people (many of whom last stepped foot in a classroom when they were students themselves) who claim that, as in the justice system, only the guilty are punished. They perpetuate the myth of the Black body as menace, as an ever-present threat to peace and order. This myth blankets all Black bodies—not only adults but children as well. It is an extension of the belief—one that I have returned to quite frequently in these pages—that America is a post-racial nation, one in which the racial injustices of the past have been fully atoned for and transcended. Lower test scores in Black schools are, according to post-racialists, the result, not of an unequal system of education, but of intelligence deficits. More disciplinary measures taken against Black students reflect, not a flaw in the putatively even-handed system, but a failure on the part of Black parents to teach their children to respect authority. In the same way, disproportionately high numbers of Black inmates are the inevitable consequence of the Black compulsion to act in violent and criminal ways. Racial profiling, according to this line of thinking, is not an injustice; it's an effective police tactic.

This is not to suggest that those being disciplined in school, detained and searched by the authorities, or incarcerated by the state are entirely blameless (though we have reason to believe that some of them are). Definitively answering the question of culpability is a slippery endeavor, but one thing we do know, and know with some certainty, is that poverty is an incubator for crime. We also know that discrimination is at the root of racial economic inequality and that class mobility is at arm's length for many of those at the bottom of the social and economic ladder. Our search for easy answers leads, inevitably, to scapegoats, and the easiest answer of all is that it is America that is at fault—and the country's shoulders are certainly wide enough to bear the blame—but blaming the system or country *in toto* is about as satisfying as pinning the blame on a single individual for the faults of many. Albert Camus once said in reference to the crimes of Nazi Germany, "A trial cannot be conducted by announcing the culpability of an entire civilization" (179). Modern America seems willing to indict, if not itself, at least its history, especially those parts of its history replete with unjust treatment of Black bodies. What it seems less willing to recognize is the fact that America's history of racial injustice substantially informs the present. Its ramifications, though invisible to some, are, in urban America, as ubiquitous as asphalt. Those who cling to the delusional notion that the Civil Rights Movement effectively ended racism dismiss evidence of the legacies of slavery and legal racism in this country, but technology is coming to our aid. While claims of police brutality and racial injustice were once dismissed with a wave of the hand as "your word against mine," there is now a growing body of evidence that proves what we have long contended: that black and brown Americans are afforded quite different treatment than that afforded to white Americans. With each new incident captured in living color, the number of Americans who seek to speak out against these injustices grows in strength and in number. The images of Walter Scott, the unarmed Black man shot in the back by a South Carolina officer while running away, give our claims a face and a body (in terms of both the victim and the villain). Technology, and its ability to turn bystanders into citizen journalists, has become a powerful ally, the kind that is able to help spread the news (good and bad). And there is good news: the tide is turning; all hope is not lost.

Ferguson, Baltimore, and the Fire Inside

On a social media post on July 4, 2015, I wrote, "another Black church burned. Another unarmed Black man killed by police. Another officer of the state cleared of all charges. Meanwhile the fireworks of America are being launched.... Maybe it is best to be silent. Maybe it is best to disappear." In *The Rebel*, Albert Camus, speaking of the rebel and his rebellious act, says:

> In every act of rebellion, the rebel simultaneously experiences a feeling
> of revulsion at the infringement of his rights and a complete and spon-
> taneous loyalty to certain aspects of himself. Thus he implicitly brings
> into play a standard of values so far from being gratuitous that he is
> prepared to support it no matter what the risks. Up to this point he
> has at least remained silent and has abandoned himself to the form
> of despair in which a condition is accepted even though it is consid-
> ered unjust. To remain silent is to give the impression that one has no
> opinions, that one wants nothing, and in certain cases it really amounts
> to wanting nothing. (14)

Camus speaks of a tipping point, a point at which the weight of injustice becomes too much to bear. The abiding ennui that precedes that tipping point is thrown off in a moment in favor of an all-encompassing spirit of resistance that will brook no opposition. Reaching this point can take decades, but, if the conditions are right, hundreds, thousands, even millions can reach this point in an instant. It's as though the despair of helplessness is a wet blanket that keeps the dry tinder beneath—e.g., the African-American soul relegated to its concrete reservations—from catching fire. The dry tinder smolders beneath the dampness, waiting, building, spreading its heat through the substrates of consciousness until it reaches critical mass. Mike-Mike is murdered in the street—a spark ignites the tinder. Eric Garner is choked to death—the tinder finds kindling. Freddie Gray's neck is snapped—the kindling catches fire. Sandra Bland and Kindra Chapman's lynchings are called by their killers a suicide, or there is no indictment in 12-year-old Tamir Rice's murder—the flames leap high and the conflagration rages out of control. A bonfire of repressed emotion erupts. Our black youth take to the streets in open riot and rebellion; the fire inside, which began as self-loathing, now has a target and fuel: the oppressor and his machinery. The internal frustration, first mistaken for ennui, turns outward: windows are broken, police are attacked, Molotov cocktails are thrown. The flaming heart of the African-American experience is externalized, and there can be no mistake: we the people have reached the tipping point. We will take it no longer.

Whether it is lines of officers in riot gear or elected officials who dehumanize and criminalize their brown and black constituents, or predominantly white university officials who ignore the macro and micro aggressions imposed upon students of color, the manifest contempt and latent disregard that many in positions of authority have for minorities is utterly transparent. Without a show of respect, without an allowance for human dignity, why should we be obliged to respect or defer to the authorities that oppress us? Should we acquiesce simply because not doing so would make the system break down, a system that benefits those with a majority stake in complacency? Perhaps the system needs to be broken down, torn down to its foundations, so that a new one can be constructed in its place, one that serves all those within its purview as equal, one that makes good on America's promises of liberty and justice for all.

The racially oppressed see very little in terms of authority that we are obliged to respect. Bound by what esteemed philosopher Charles Mills calls a "racial contract," those with black and brown skin are treated as second-class citizens; the poor, too, are treated as sub-human, as social parasites that have no right to share in America's bounty; immigrants of all colors are somehow threats to the American way of life; immigrant-vilifying politicians clamber over each other trying to say the most inflammatory things possible about those who dare to come to this land in search of the freedom we explicitly promise; Native Americans, the first sons of this land, after a long period of extermination and appropriation, have been swept under the rug, utterly powerless and entirely forgotten; this country of ours treats abysmally even the veterans who have served our country in its wars abroad. We are surrounded by these reminders, each of which tells us that we have a long way to go before we can say that America is giving us (all of us) her best. And yet we are asked to bow our heads and show our love and respect for this country and those institutions that facilitate the ugliness of our democratic spirit.

But, so often, those who cause the most hurt are those who are meant to represent love, caring, and respect for the wholeness of persons. Churches and schools are beacons of light in communities, yet our churches denounce gay, transgendered, and queer parishioners in favor of pedantic adherence to an old exegesis of scripture, while our inner-city schools arrest students before counseling them, remove them before reviving them. Even our centers of higher education, which made great strides of inclusion through the protests of the late 1960s and the wave of progressive post-Vietnam War sentiments, have had their progressivism stifled by a business model of education that puts profit before progress.

These are truly trying times for the souls who dare to test their voices in spaces that purport to support them in the name of diversity but instead drown them in a babble of condescending platitudes that fail to cultivate and protect diversity. The distance between a university administration and its young students of color can be as long and cold as the distance between the stars. The caretakers silently consent as our brave youth are emotionally beaten, psychologically alienated, and physically overrun. But at what cost? The cost of making those who comfortably operate upon the ideal of diversity feel much less comfortable?

For campuses it is the cost of feeling out of touch with the movement that they themselves started fifty years ago. It is the cost of giving the racial quota a quorum, the token Negro a dime, the Native a nickel, and the intellectual stakeholders (upon whose labor borders are smashed) a corner of dust to call their own—or a corner to cry in—as they attempt to be fully fledged tenants of the institution and not merely asterisks of diversity. At Yale the cost was a splash of black ink on the pure white tower of ivory. At Mizzou (The University of Missouri), in the heartland, where the corn and hogs and soy line the stomach of America and soak up the distilled spirit of overt racism, the cost was a cool million: the fine for canceling a D-1 football game. But just as students of color responded to the call of hunger striker Jonathan Butler, culminating in months of student activism and public dissent, November 2015 marked a turning point for students at Mizzou: the public pressure forced its president to resign. Similarly, heightened protests by students at Claremont McKenna College in Los Angeles led to the resignation of its dean of students.

Univ. of Missouri graduate student Jonathan Butler, whose eight day hunger strike prompted football players to join the protest that led to the resignation of System President Tom Wolfe. https://www.flickr.com/photos/komunews/21379191934/in/photolist-a5FMNo-yzcJ8f-zeBgxb-zwezrK-zeB2ch-yzcWVu-5ATP5z-4dGuUX/ Credit: Mikala Compton, 6 October 2015.

Administrators at Yale, under the pressure to maintain the international reputation of its brand, are quickly circling the inclusive wagons and denouncing racial insensitivity.

We are, it seems, starting to see glimmers of hope. Take the recent fracas surrounding the confederate flag in South Carolina, for instance. After flying for more than fifty years above the South Carolina State House, the flag, a symbol that united all of those who thought that the right to own slaves was a cause worth dying for, was finally lowered (with undue ceremony) on July 10, 2015. As the flag was lowered, chants of "USA, USA, USA" rang out through the crowd. The moment was celebrated, even described as a beautiful day for South Carolina. Many of those who watched the ceremony, however, myself included, were not as quick to reach for the nearest patriotic or otherwise celebratory platitude at hand. The flag was removed, not because those who inhabit the South Carolina State House finally came to see that the divisive and racist symbol had no business flying over a government building, but because the public clamored so loudly and insistently for it to be taken down that not doing so would have represented an abrogation of the state representatives' responsibility to speak on behalf of those who elected them. And even still, there were twenty votes against the motion—twenty adult lawmakers who took a stand on the wrong side of history, representing those who may even wish the South had won the Civil War and continue to hold to the ridiculous notion that the confederate flag is not a racist symbol but, rather, an extricable banner for Southern pride and heritage. Even in mourning the deaths of nine Christians killed under this banner of Southern (white) pride and heritage—the type of Christians who go to weeknight bible study, one of whom was a state senator himself in South Carolina—there still are those who spurn this movement to take the flag down. All I can do is shake my head.

And yet it was a victory—that much can't be denied. It was one of those rare moments when common sense prevailed and we chose, together, to do the right thing, to stand for the right thing. Like the popular #BlackLivesMatter movement that sprang up and spread like wildfire in the wake of a string of young Black people killed by those charged with protecting them, the lowering of the confederate flag shows that there are millions upon millions of us (white, black, and brown) who have reached our tipping point, that point at which exasperation and despair turn to palpable outrage. In 2015, when hundreds of campuses, from state universities and local community colleges to Ivy League and Historically Black Universities joined in solidarity on November 12th and 13th to support the plight of Black lives (not) mattering on campuses across America and beyond. The walls separating our anger from the world have fallen; we burn openly, for all the world to see. If our nation continues to take the side of the strong and use its might against the weak, if it refuses to discuss race and its manifold effects in a frank and meaningful way, if it does not lend its weight to the repositioning of the moral arc, these conflagrations will occur more and more frequently. More uprisings will break out and more cities will burn, more campuses will be disrupted, more sporting events boycotted, more highways diverted and maybe more properties burned, because inside the heart of every oppressed individual, there is a spirit waiting to catch fire.

Notes

1   Ary Spatig-Amerikaner, *Unequal Education: Federal Loophole Enables Lower Spending on Students of Color*, Center for American Progress, https://www. americanprogress.org/wp-content/uploads/2012/08/UnequalEduation.pdf.

2   U.S. Department of Education, Office of Civil Rights, "Data Snapshot: School Discipline," March 2014, http://www2.ed.gov/about/offices/list/ocr/docs/crdc-discipline-snapshot.pdf.

Works Cited

Abramsky, Sasha. *The American Way of Poverty: How the Other Half Still Lives*. New York: Nation Books, 2013.

Alexander, Michelle. *The New Jim Crow: Mass Incarceration in the Age of Colorblindness*. New York: The New Press, 2010.

Allen, Danielle. *Our Declaration: A Reading of the Declaration of Independence in Defense of Equality*. New York: Liveright, 2014.

Anderson, Victor. *Pragmatic Theology*. Albany: State University of New York Press, 1998.

Andreas, Peter. *Border Games: Policing the US–Mexico Divide*. Ithaca, NY: Cornell University Press, 2009.

Banfield, Edward C. *The Unheavenly City Revisited*. Boston: Little, Brown & Co., 1974.

Barreto, Matt A., Betsy L. Cooper, Benjamin Gonzalez, Christopher S. Parker, and Christopher Towler. "The Tea Party in the Age of Obama: Mainstream Conservatism or Out-Group Anxiety?" *Political Power and Social Theory* 22.1 (2011): 105–37.

Bonilla-Silva, Eduardo. *Racism without Racists: Color-Blind Racism and the Persistence of Racial Inequality in the United States*. 2nd ed. New York: Rowman and Littlefield, 2006.

Buchanan, Pat. *The Death of the West*. New York: St. Martin's Press, 2002.

Camus, Albert. *The Rebel: An Essay on Revolt*. New York: Vintage, 1991.

Chomsky, Noam, and Praful Bidwai. "The Tyranny of Global Systems." *India International Centre Quarterly* 31.2/3 (2004): 221–30.

Cobb, William Jelani. *The Substance of Hope*. New York: Walker & Co., 2010.

Crenshaw, Kimberle Williams. "Foreword: Toward a Race-Conscious Pedagogy in Legal Education." *National Black Law Journal* 11.1 (1989): 1–14.

Davidson, Chandler. "The Voting Rights Act: A Brief History." *Controversies in Minority Voting: The Voting Rights Act in Perspective*. Ed. Bernard Grofman and Chandler Davidson. Washington, DC: The Brookings Institution, 1992. 7–51.

Dzidzienyo, Anani, and Suzanne Oboler, eds. *Neither Enemies nor Friends: Latinos, Blacks, Afro-Latinos*. New York: Palgrave Macmillan, 2005.

Enck-Wanzer, Darrel. "Barack Obama, the Tea Party, and the Threat of Race: On Racial Neoliberalism and Born Again Racism." *Communication, Culture & Critique* 4.1 (2011): 23–30.

Esposito, John L., and Ibrahim Kalin. *Islamophobia: The Challenge of Pluralism in the 21st Century*. New York: Oxford University Press, 2011.

Fields, Karen E., and Barbara J. Fields. *Racecraft: The Soul of Inequality in American Life*. New York: Verso, 2012.

Flower, Harriet. *The Art of Forgetting: Disgrace and Oblivion in Roman Political Culture*. Chapel Hill: University of North Carolina Press, 2006.

Friedman, Milton. *Capitalism and Freedom*. 40th Anniversary ed. Chicago: University of Chicago Press, 2002.

Fromm, Erich. *The Sane Society*. London: Routledge, 2002.

Gans, Herbert J. *People, Plans, and Policies*. New York: Columbia University Press, 1991.

Gilens, Martin. *Why Americans Hate Welfare: Race, Media, and the Politics of Antipoverty Policy*. Chicago: University of Chicago Press, 1999.

Goffman, Erving. *Frame Analysis: An Essay on the Organization of Experience*. New York: Harper and Row, 1974.

Gorton, Gary B. *Slapped by the Invisible Hand: The Panic of 2007*. Oxford: Oxford University Press, 2010.

Gould, Stephen Jay. *The Mismeasure of Man*. 2nd ed. New York: Norton, 2006.

Haney-López, Ian F. "Post-racial Racism: Racial Stratification and Mass Incarceration in the Age of Obama." *California Law Review* 98.3 (2010): 1023–74.

Harrington, Michael. *The Other America: Poverty in America*. New York: Touchstone, 1997.

Herstein, Richard J., and Charles Murray. *Bell Curve: Intelligence and Class Structure in American Life*. New York: Free Press Paperbacks, 1994.

Hout, Michael, and Joshua R. Goldstein. "How 4.5 Million Irish Immigrants Became 40 Million Irish Americans: Demographic and Subjective Aspects of the Ethnic Composition of White Americans." *American Sociological Review* 59.1 (1994): 64–82.

Hughey, Matthew W., and Gregory S. Parks. *The Wrongs of the Right: Language, Race, and the Republican Party in the Age of Obama*. New York: NYU Press, 2014.

Ignatieff, Michael. *The Needs of Strangers*. New York: Picador, 2001.

Ikard, David, and Martell L. Teasley. *Nation of Cowards*. Bloomington: Indiana University Press, 2012.

Jaffe, A.J., R.M. Cullen, and T.D. Boswell. *The Changing Demography of Spanish Americans*. New York: Academic Press, 1980.

Jurca, Catherine. *The White Diaspora: The Suburb and the Twentieth Century Novel*. Princeton, NJ: Princeton University Press.

Katz, Michael. *The Undeserving Poor: America's Enduring Confrontation with Poverty.* 2nd ed. New York: Oxford University Press, 2013.

——. *The Undeserving Poor: From the War on Poverty to the War on Welfare.* New York: Pantheon, 1989.

Keyssar, Alexander. *The Right to Vote.* New York: Basic Books, 2000.

Kohler-Hausmann, Julilly. "'The Crime of Survival': Fraud Prosecutions, Community Surveillance, and the Original 'Welfare Queen.'" *Journal of Social History* 41.2 (2007): 329–54.

Kot, Greg. *I'll Take You There: Mavis Staples, the Staple Singers, and the March Up Freedom's Highway.* Toronto: Simon and Schuster, 2014.

Lawrence, C.R., III. "The Epidemiology of Color-Blindness: Learning to Think and Talk about Race, Again." *Boston College Third World Law Journal* 15.1 (1995): 1–18.

Lee, Harper. *To Kill a Mockingbird.* London: Arrow, 2010.

Lewis, Oscar. *The Children of Sanchez: Autobiography of a Mexican Family.* New York: Vintage Books, 2001.

Massey, Douglas S. "Racial Formation in Theory and Practice: The Case of Mexicans in the United States." *Race and Social Problems* 1.1 (2009): 12–26.

McGeary, Michael G.H. "Ghetto Poverty and Federal Policies and Programs." *Inner City Poverty in the United States.* Ed. Laurence E. Lynn and Michael G.H. McGeary. Washington, DC: National Academy Press, 1990. 223–52.

McNamee, Stephen J., and Robert K. Miller Jr. *The Meritocracy Myth.* Lanham, MD: Rowman and Littlefield, 2009.

Meer, Jonathan, and Henry S. Rosen. "Altruism and the Child-Cycle of Alumni Donations." Princeton, NJ: Princeton University, 2007.

Mills, Charles. *The Racial Contract.* Ithaca, NY: Cornell University Press, 1999.

Mooney, Chris. *The Republican Brain: The Science of Why They Deny Science—and Reality.* Hoboken, NJ: John Wiley & Sons, 2002.

Moynihan, Daniel P. *The Negro Family: The Case for National Action.* Washington, DC: Office of Planning and Research, U.S. Department of Labor, 1965.

Murray, Charles A. *Coming Apart: The State of White America, 1960–2010.* New York: Crown Forum, 2012.

Nunn, Kenneth B. "Race, Crime, and the Pool of Surplus Criminality: or Why the 'War on Drugs' Was a 'War on Blacks.'" *Journal of Gender, Race & Justice* 6 (2002): 381–445.

Obama, Barack. *Dreams from My Father.* New York: Three Rivers Press, 2004.

——. "A More Perfect Union." *The Black Scholar* 38.1 (2008): 17–23.

Paine, Thomas. *Rights of Man.* New York: Cosimo, 2008.

Patterson, Orlando. *Slavery and Social Death*. Cambridge, MA: Harvard University Press, 1982.

Perry, Imani. *More Beautiful and More Terrible*. New York: New York University Press, 2011.

Piketty, Thomas. *Capital in the Twenty-First Century*. Trans. Arthur Goldhammer. Cambridge, MA: Belknap, 2014.

Plouffe, David. *The Audacity to Win: How Obama Won and How We Can Beat the Party of Limbaugh, Beck and Palin*. New York: Penguin, 2010.

Portes, Alejandro, and Ruben G. Rumbaut. *Immigrant America: A Portrait*. Berkeley: University of California Press, 2006.

Prashad, V., J.H. Blackman, and R.D. Kelley. "Genteel Racism." *Amerasia Journal* 26.3 (2000): 21–33.

Reich, Charles A. "The New Property after 25 Years." *University of San Francisco Law Review* 24 (1990): 223–41.

Reich, Robert. *Supercapitalism*. New York: Vintage Books, 2007.

Ross, L. "The Intuitive Psychologist and His Shortcomings: Distortions in the Attribution Process." *Advances in Experimental Social Psychology 10*. Ed. L. Berkowitz. New York: Academic Press, 1977. 173–220.

Sabato, Larry, ed. *The Year of Obama: How Barack Obama Won the White House*. New York: Longman, 2010.

Said, Edward. *Covering Islam: How the Media and Experts Determine How We See the Rest of the World*. New York: Vintage Books, 1998.

Shapiro, Ben. *The People vs. Barack Obama: The Criminal Case against the Obama Administration*. New York: Threshold Editions, 2014.

Sharpley-Whiting, T. Denean, ed. *The Speech: Race and Barack Obama's "A More Perfect Union."* New York: Bloomsbury, 2009.

Spivak, Gayatri. "Can the Subaltern Speak?" *The Spivak Reader: Selected Works of Gayatri Spivak*. New York: Routledge, 1996.

Street, Paul Lewis. *Barack Obama and the Future of American Politics*. Boulder, CO: Paradigm Publishers, 2009.

Warren, Elizabeth. *A Fighting Chance*. New York: Metropolitan Books, 2014.

West, Cornel. *Democracy Matters*. New York: Penguin Press, 2004.

———. *Race Matters*. Boston: Beacon Press, 1993; rev. ed. 2001.

———. "Race Matters." YouTube, 13 January 2014, https://www.youtube.com/watch?v=cRZcfEToN-A

Williamson, Vanessa, Theda Skocpol, and John Coggin. "The Tea Party and the Remaking of Republican Conservatism." *Perspectives on Politics* 9.1 (2011): 25–43.

Wise, Tim. *Between Barack and a Hard Place: Racism and White Denial in the Age of Obama*. San Francisco: City Lights Publishing, 2009.

Woolf, Steven H., and Laudan Aron, eds. *U.S. Health in International Perspective: Shorter Lives, Poorer Health*. Washington, DC: National Academies Press, 2013.

Yancey, George A. *Who Is White?* Boulder, CO: Lynne Rienner, 2003.

From the Publisher

A name never says it all, but the word "Broadview" expresses a good deal of the philosophy behind our company. We are open to a broad range of academic approaches and political viewpoints. We pay attention to the broad impact book publishing and book printing has in the wider world; we began using recycled stock more than a decade ago, and for some years now we have used 100% recycled paper for most titles. Our publishing program is internationally oriented and broad-ranging. Our individual titles often appeal to a broad readership too; many are of interest as much to general readers as to academics and students.

Founded in 1985, Broadview remains a fully independent company owned by its shareholders—not an imprint or subsidiary of a larger multinational.

For the most accurate information on our books (including information on pricing, editions, and formats) please visit our website at www.broadviewpress.com. Our print books and ebooks are also available for sale on our site.

On the Broadview website we also offer several goods that are not books—among them the Broadview coffee mug, the Broadview beer stein (inscribed with a line from Geoffrey Chaucer's *Canterbury Tales*), the Broadview fridge magnets (your choice of philosophical or literary), and a range of T-shirts (made from combinations of hemp, bamboo, and/or high-quality pima cotton, with no child labor, sweatshop labor, or environmental degradation involved in their manufacture).

All these goods are available through the "merchandise" section of the Broadview website. When you buy Broadview goods you can support other goods too.

broadview press
www.broadviewpress.com

The interior of this book is printed on 100% recycled paper.